THE WORKS OF
ROBERT LOUIS STEVENSON

———

SOUTH SEAS EDITION

VOLUME XIII

MEMORIES AND PORTRAITS
RANDOM MEMORIES
MEMOIRS OF HIMSELF

BY

ROBERT LOUIS STEVENSON

NEW YORK

CHARLES SCRIBNER'S SONS

1925

Printed in the United States of America

CONTENTS

MEMORIES AND PORTRAITS

RANDOM MEMORIES

MEMORIES AND PORTRAITS

NOTE

THIS volume of papers, unconnected as they are, it will be better to read through from the beginning, rather than dip into at random. A certain thread of meaning binds them. Memories of childhood and youth, portraits of those who have gone before us in the battle—taken together, they build up a face that " I have loved long since and lost awhile," the face of what was once myself. This has come by accident; I had no design at first to be auto-biographical; I was but led away by the charm of beloved memories and by regret for the irrevocable dead; and when my own young face (which is a face of the dead also) began to appear in the well as by a kind of magic, I was the first to be surprised at the occurrence.

My grandfather the pious child, my father the idle eager sentimental youth, I have thus uncon-sciously exposed. Of their descendant, the person of to-day, I wish to keep the secret: not because I love him better, but because, with him, I am still in a business partnership, and cannot divide inter-ests.

Of the papers which make up the volume, some have appeared already in *The Cornhill, Longman's, Scribner's, The English Illustrated, The Magazine of Art, The Contemporary Review;* three are here in print for the first time; and two others have enjoyed only what may be regarded as a private circulation.

R. L. S.

TO

MY MOTHER

IN THE

NAME OF PAST JOY AND PRESENT SORROW

I DEDICATE

THESE MEMORIES AND PORTRAITS

S.S. " Ludgate Hill"
within sight of Cape Race

THE first collected edition of *Memories and Portraits* appeared in 1887.

The individual essays, which had previously appeared, were first printed in the following periodicals:—

MEMORIES AND PORTRAITS

I

THE FOREIGNER AT HOME

*"This is no' my ain house;
I ken by the biggin' o't."*

TWO recent books, one by Mr. Grant White on England, one on France by the diabolically clever Mr. Hillebrand, may well have set people thinking on the divisions of races and nations. Such thoughts should arise with particular congruity and force to inhabitants of that United Kingdom, peopled from so many different stocks, babbling so many different dialects, and offering in its extent such singular contrasts, from the busiest over-population to the unkindliest desert, from the Black Country to the Moor of Rannoch. It is not only when we cross the seas that we go abroad; there are foreign parts of England; and the race that has conquered so wide an empire has not yet managed to assimilate the islands whence she sprang. Ireland, Wales, and the Scottish mountains still cling, in part, to their old Gaelic speech. It was but the other day that English triumphed in Cornwall, and they still show in Mousehole, on St. Michael's Bay, the house of the last Cornish-speaking woman. English itself, which will now frank the traveller through the most of North America, through the greater South Sea Islands, in India, along much of the coast of Africa, and in the ports of China and

Japan, is still to be heard, in its home country, in half a hundred varying stages of transition. You may go all over the States, and—setting aside the actual intrusion and influence of foreigners, negro, French, or Chinese—you shall scarce meet with so marked a difference of accent as in the forty miles between Edinburgh and Glasgow, or of dialect as in the hundred miles between Edinburgh and Aberdeen. Book English has gone round the world, but at home we still preserve the racy idioms of our fathers, and every county, in some parts every dale, has its own quality of speech, vocal or verbal. In like manner, local custom and prejudice, even local religion and local law, linger on into the latter end of the nineteenth century—*imperia in imperio*, foreign things at home.

In spite of these promptings to reflection, ignorance of his neighbours is the character of the typical John Bull. His is a domineering nature, steady in fight, imperious to command, but neither curious nor quick about the life of others. In French colonies, and still more in the Dutch, I have read that there is an immediate and lively contact between the dominant and the dominated race, that a certain sympathy is begotten, or at the least a transfusion of prejudices, making life easier for both. But the Englishman sits apart, bursting with pride and ignorance. He figures among his vassals in the hour of peace with the same disdainful air that led him on to victory. A passing enthusiasm for some foreign art or fashion may deceive the world, it cannot impose upon his intimates. He may be amused by a foreigner as by a monkey, but he will never condescend to study him with any patience. Miss Bird, an authoress with whom I profess myself in love, declares all the viands of Japan to be uneatable—a staggering pretension. So, when the Prince of Wales's marriage was celebrated at Mentone by a dinner to the Mentonese, it was proposed to give them solid English fare—roast beef and plum pudding, and no tomfoolery. Here we have either pole of the Britannic folly. We will not eat the food of any foreigner; nor, when we have the chance, will we suffer him to eat of it himself. The same spirit inspired Miss Bird's American missionaries, who had come thousands of miles to change the faith of Japan, and openly professed their ignorance of the religions they were trying to supplant.

I quote an American in this connection without scruple. Uncle Sam is better than John Bull, but he is tarred with the English stick. For Mr. Grant White the States are the New England States and nothing more. He wonders at the amount of drinking in London; let him try San Francisco. He wittily reproves English ignorance as to the status of women in America; but has he not himself forgotten Wyoming? The name Yankee, of which he is so tenacious, is used over the most of the great Union as a term of reproach. The Yankee States, of which he is so staunch a subject, are but a drop in the bucket. And we find in his book a vast virgin ignorance of the life and prospects of America; every view partial, parochial, not raised to the horizon; the moral feeling proper, at the largest, to a clique of States; and the whole scope and atmosphere not American, but merely Yankee. I will go far beyond him in reprobating the assumption and the incivility of my countryfolk to their cousins from beyond the sea; I grill in my blood over the silly rudeness of our newspaper articles; and I do not know where to look when I find myself in company with an American and see my countrymen unbending to him as to a performing dog. But in the case of Mr. Grant White example were better than precept. Wyoming is, after all, more readily accessible to Mr. White than Boston to the English, and the New England self-sufficiency no better justified than the Britannic.

It is so, perhaps, in all countries; perhaps in all, men are most ignorant of the foreigners at home. John Bull is ignorant of the States; he is probably ignorant of India; but considering his opportunities, he is far more ignorant of countries nearer his own door. There is one country, for instance—its frontier not so far from London, its people closely akin, its language the same in all essentials with the English—of which I will go bail he knows nothing. His ignorance of the sister kingdom cannot be described; it can only be illustrated by anecdote. I once travelled with a man of plausible manners and good intelligence—a University man, as the phrase goes—a man, besides, who had taken his degree in life and knew a thing or two about the age we live in. We were deep in talk, whirling between Peterborough and London; among other things, he began to describe some piece of legal injustice he had recently encountered, and I observed in my innocence that things were not so in Scotland. " I beg your pardon," said he, " this is a matter of law." He had never heard of the Scots law; nor did he choose to be informed. The law was the same for the whole country, he told me roundly; every child knew that. At last, to settle matters, I explained to him that I was a member of a Scottish legal body, and had stood the brunt of an examination in the very law in question. Thereupon he looked me for a moment full in the face and dropped the conversation. This is a monstrous instance, if you like, but it does not stand alone in the experience of Scots.

England and Scotland differ, indeed, in law, in history, in religion, in education, and in the very look of nature and men's faces, not always widely, but always trenchantly. Many particulars that struck Mr. Grant White, a Yankee, struck me, a Scot, no less forcibly; he and I felt ourselves foreigners on many common provocations. A Scotsman may tramp the better part of Europe and the United States, and never again receive so vivid an impression of foreign travel and strange lands and manners as on his first excursion into England. The change from a hilly to a level country strikes him with delighted wonder. Along the flat horizon there arise the frequent venerable towers of churches. He sees at the end of airy vistas the revolution of the windmill sails. He may go where he pleases in the future; he may see Alps, and pyramids, and lions; but it will be hard to beat the pleasure of that moment. There are, indeed, few merrier spectacles than that of many windmills bickering together in a fresh breeze over a woody country; their halting alacrity of movement, their pleasant business, making bread all day with uncouth gesticulations, their air, gigantically human, as of a creature half alive, put a spirit of romance into the tamest landscape. When the Scottish child sees them first he falls immediately in love; and from that time forward windmills keep turning in his dreams. And so, in their degree, with every feature of the life and landscape. The warm, habitable age of towns and hamlets, the green, settled, ancient look of the country; the lush hedgerows, stiles, and privy pathways in the fields; the sluggish, brimming rivers; chalk and smock-frocks; chimes of bells and the rapid, pertly-sounding English speech—they are all new to the curiosity; they are all set to English airs in the child's story that he tells himself at night. The sharp edge of novelty wears off; the feeling is scotched, but I doubt whether it is ever killed. Rather it keeps returning, ever the more rarely and strangely, and even in scenes to which you have been long accustomed suddenly awakes and gives a relish to enjoyment or heightens the sense of isolation.

One thing especially continues unfamiliar to the Scotsman's eye—the domestic architecture, the look of streets and buildings; the quaint, venerable age of many, and the thin walls and warm colouring of all. We have, in Scotland, far fewer ancient buildings, above all in country places; and those that we have are all of hewn or harled masonry. Wood has been sparingly used in their construction; the window-frames are sunken in the wall, not flat to the front, as in England; the roofs are steeper-pitched; even a hill farm will have a massy, square, cold, and permanent appearance. English houses, in comparison, have the look of cardboard toys, such as a puff might shatter. And to this the Scotsman never becomes used. His eye can never rest consciously on one of these brick houses—rickles of brick, as he might call them—or on one of these flat-chested streets, but he is instantly reminded where he is, and instantly travels back in fancy to his home. "This is no' my ain house; I ken by the biggin' o't." And yet perhaps it is his own, bought with his own money, the key of it long polished in his pocket; but it has not yet, and never will be, thoroughly adopted by his imagination; nor does he cease to remember that, in the whole length and breadth of his native country, there was no building even distantly resembling it.

But it is not alone in scenery and architecture that we count England foreign. The constitution of society, the very pillars of the empire, surprise and even pain us. The dull, neglected peasant, sunk in matter, insolent, gross, and servile, makes a startling contrast with our own long-legged, long-headed, thoughtful, Bible-quoting ploughman. A week or two in such a place as Suffolk leaves the Scotsman gasping. It seems incredible that within the boundaries of his own island a class should have been thus forgotten. Even the educated and intelligent, who hold our own opinions and speak in our own words, yet seem to hold them with a difference or from another reason, and to speak on all things with less interest and conviction. The first shock of English society is like a cold plunge. It is possible that the Scot comes looking for too much, and to be sure his first experiment will be in the wrong direction. Yet surely his complaint is grounded; surely the speech of Englishmen is too often lacking in generous ardour, the better part of the man too often withheld from the social commerce, and the contact of mind with mind evaded as with terror. A Scottish peasant will talk more liberally out of his own experience. He will not put you by with conversational counters and small jests; he will give you the best of himself, like one interested in life and man's chief end. A Scotsman is vain, interested in himself and others, eager for sympathy, setting forth his thoughts and experience in the best light. The egoism of the Englishman is self-contained. He does not seek to proselytise. He takes no interest in Scotland or the Scots, and, what is the unkindest cut of all, he does not care to justify his indifference. Give him the wages of going on and being an Englishman, that is all he asks; and in the meantime, while you continue to associate, he would rather not be reminded of your baser origin. Compared with the grand, tree-like self-sufficiency of his demeanour, the vanity and curiosity of the Scot seem uneasy, vulgar, and immodest. That you should continually try to establish human and serious relations, that you should actually feel an interest in John Bull, and desire and invite a return of interest from him, may argue something more awake and lively in your mind, but it stills puts you in the attitude of a suitor and a poor relation. Thus even the lowest class of the educated English towers over a Scotsman by the head and shoulders.

Different indeed is the atmosphere in which Scottish and English youth begin to look about them, come to themselves in life, and gather up those first apprehensions which are the material of future thought and, to a great extent, the rule of future conduct. I have been to school in both countries, and I found, in the boys of the North, something at once rougher and more tender, at once more reserve and more expansion, a greater habitual distance chequered by glimpses of a nearer intimacy, and on the whole wider extremes of temperament and sensibility. The boy of the South seems more wholesome, but less thoughtful; he gives himself to games as to a business, striving to excel, but is not readily transported by imagination; the type remains with me as cleaner in mind and body, more active, fonder of eating, endowed with a lesser and a less romantic sense of life and of the future, and more

immersed in present circumstances. And certainly, for
one thing, English boys are younger for their age. Sabbath observance makes a series of grim, and perhaps
serviceable, pauses in the tenor of Scottish boyhood—
days of great stillness and solitude for the rebellious
mind, when in the dearth of books and play, and in the
intervals of studying the Shorter Catechism, the intellect and senses prey upon and test each other. The
typical English Sunday, with the huge midday dinner
and the plethoric afternoon, leads perhaps to different
results. About the very cradle of the Scot there goes a
hum of metaphysical divinity; and the whole of two
divergent systems is summed up, not merely speciously,
in the two first questions of the rival catechisms, the
English tritely inquiring, " What is your name? " the
Scottish striking at the very roots of life with, " What
is the chief end of man? " and answering nobly, if obscurely, " To glorify God and to enjoy Him for ever."
I do not wish to make an idol of the Shorter Catechism;
but the fact of such a question being asked opens to us
Scots a great field of speculation; and the fact that it is
asked of all of us, from the peer to the ploughboy, binds
us more nearly together. No Englishman of Byron's
age, character, and history, would have had patience for
long theological discussions on the way to fight for
Greece; but the daft Gordon blood and the Aberdonian
schooldays kept their influence to the end. We have
spoken of the material conditions; nor need much more
be said of these: of the land lying everywhere more
exposed, of the wind always louder and bleaker, of the
black, roaring winters, of the gloom of high-lying, old
stone cities, imminent on the windy seaboard; compared
with the level streets, the warm colouring of the brick,
the domestic quaintness of the architecture, among
which English children begin to grow up and come to
themselves in life. As the stage of the University approaches, the contrast becomes more express. The
English lad goes to Oxford or Cambridge; there, in an
ideal world of gardens, to lead a semi-scenic life,

costumed, disciplined, and drilled by proctors. Nor is this to be regarded merely as a stage of education; it is a piece of privilege besides, and a step that separates him further from the bulk of his compatriots. At an earlier age the Scottish lad begins his greatly different experience of crowded class-rooms, of a gaunt quadrangle, of a bell hourly booming over the traffic of the city to recall him from the public-house where he has been lunching, or the streets where he has been wandering fancy-free. His college life has little of restraint, and nothing of necessary gentility. He will find no quiet clique of the exclusive, studious, and cultured; no rotten borough of the arts. All classes rub shoulders on the greasy benches. The raffish young gentleman in gloves must measure his scholarship with the plain, clownish laddie from the parish school. They separate, at the session's end, one to smoke cigars about a watering-place, the other to resume the labours of the field beside his peasant family. The first muster of a college class in Scotland is a scene of curious and painful interest; so many lads, fresh from the heather, hang round the stove in cloddish embarrassment, ruffled by the presence of their smarter comrades, and afraid of the sound of their own rustic voices. It was in these early days, I think, that Professor Blackie won the affection of his pupils, putting these uncouth, umbrageous students at their ease with ready human geniality. Thus, at least, we have a healthy democratic atmosphere to breathe in while at work; even when there is no cordiality there is always a juxtaposition of the different classes, and in the competition of study the intellectual power of each is plainly demonstrated to the other. Our tasks ended, we of the North go forth as freemen into the humming, lamplit city. At five o'clock you may see the last of us hiving from the college gates, in the glare of the shop windows, under the green glimmer of the winter sunset. The frost tingles in our blood, no proctor lies in wait to intercept us; till the bell sounds again, we are the masters of the world; and some portion of our lives is always Saturday, *la trêve de Dieu*.

Nor must we omit the sense of the nature of his country and his country's history gradually growing in the child's mind from story and from observation. A Scottish child hears much of shipwreck, outlying iron skerries, pitiless breakers, and great sea-lights; much of heathery mountains, wild clans, and hunted Covenanters. Breaths come to him in song of the distant Cheviots and the ring of foraying hoofs. He glories in his hard-fisted forefathers, of the iron girdle and the handful of oatmeal, who rode so swiftly and lived so sparely on their raids. Poverty, ill-luck, enterprise, and constant resolution are the fibres of the legend of his country's history. The heroes and kings of Scotland have been tragically fated; the most marking incidents in Scottish history—Flodden, Darien, or the Forty-five—were still either failures or defeats; and the fall of Wallace and the repeated reverses of the Bruce combine with the very smallness of the country to teach rather a moral than a material criterion for life. Britain is altogether small, the mere taproot of her extended empire; Scotland, again, which alone the Scottish boy adopts in his imagination, is but a little part of that, and avowedly cold, sterile, and unpopulous. It is not so for nothing. I once seemed to have perceived in an American boy a greater readiness of sympathy for lands that are great, and rich, and growing, like his own. It proved to be quite otherwise: a mere dumb piece of boyish romance, that I had lacked penetration to divine. But the error serves the purpose of my argument; for I am sure, at least, that the heart of young Scotland will be always touched more nearly by paucity of number and Spartan poverty of life.

So we may argue, and yet the difference is not explained. That Shorter Catechism which I took as being so typical of Scotland, was yet composed in the city of Westminster. The division of races is more sharply marked within the borders of Scotland itself than between the countries. Galloway and Buchan, Lothian and Lochaber, are like foreign parts; yet you may choose a man from any of them, and, ten to one, he shall prove to have the headmark of a Scot. A century and a half ago the Highlander wore a different costume, spoke a different language, worshipped in another church, held different morals, and obeyed a different social constitution from his fellow-countrymen either of the south or north. Even the English, it is recorded, did not loathe the Highlander and the Highland costume as they were loathed by the remainder of the Scots. Yet the Highlander felt himself a Scot. He would willingly raid into the Scottish lowlands; but his courage failed him at the border, and he regarded England as a perilous, unhomely land. When the Black Watch, after years of foreign service, returned to Scotland, veterans leaped out and kissed the earth at Port Patrick. They had been in Ireland, stationed among men of their own race and language, where they were well liked and treated with affection; but it was the soil of Galloway that they kissed at the extreme end of the hostile lowlands, among a people who did not understand their speech, and who had hated, harried, and hanged them since the dawn of history. Last, and perhaps most curious, the sons of chieftains were often educated on the continent of Europe. They went abroad speaking Gaelic; they returned speaking, not English, but the broad dialect of Scotland. Now, what idea had they in their minds when they thus, in thought, identified themselves with their ancestral enemies? What was the sense in which they were Scottish and not English, or Scottish and not Irish? Can a bare name be thus influential on the minds and affections of men, and a political aggregation blind them to the nature of facts? The story of the Austrian Empire would seem to answer, No; the far more galling business of Ireland clenches the negative from nearer home. Is it common education, common morals, a common language, or a common faith, that join men into nations? There were practically none of these in the case we are considering.

The fact remains: in spite of the difference of blood and language, the Lowlander feels himself the sentimental countryman of the Highlander. When they meet abroad, they fall upon each other's necks in spirit; even at home there is a kind of clannish intimacy in their talk. But from his compatriot in the south the Lowlander stands consciously apart. He has had a different training; he obeys different laws; he makes his will in other terms, is otherwise divorced and married; his eyes are not at home in an English landscape or with English houses; his ear continues to remark the English speech; and even though his tongue acquire the Southern knack, he will still have a strong Scots accent of the mind.

SOME COLLEGE MEMORIES *

I AM asked to write something (it is not specifically
stated what) to the profit and glory of my *Alma
Mater;* and the fact is I seem to be in very nearly the
same case with those who addressed me, for while I am
willing enough to write something, I know not what to
write. Only one point I see, that if I am to write at all,
it should be of the University itself and my own days
under its shadow; of the things that are still the same
and of those that are already changed: such talk, in
short, as would pass naturally between a student of
to-day and one of yesterday, supposing them to meet
and grow confidential.

The generations pass away swiftly enough on the
high seas of life; more swiftly still in the little bubbling
backwater of the quadrangle; so that we see there, on a
scale startlingly diminished, the flight of time and the
succession of men. I looked for my name the other
day in last year's case-book of the Speculative.
Naturally enough I looked for it near the end; it was
not there, nor yet in the next column, so that I began
to think it had been dropped at press; and when at last
I found it, mounted on the shoulders of so many successors, and looking in that posture like the name of a
man of ninety, I was conscious of some of the dignity
of years. This kind of dignity of temporal precession is
likely, with prolonged life, to become more familiar,
possibly less welcome; but I felt it strongly then, it is
strongly on me now, and I am the more emboldened to

* Written for the "Book" of the Edinburgh University Union
Fancy Fair.

speak with my successors in the tone of a parent and a praiser of things past.

For, indeed, that which they attend is but a fallen University; it has doubtless some remains of good, for human institutions decline by gradual stages; but decline, in spite of all seeming embellishments, it does; and what is perhaps more singular, began to do so when I ceased to be a student. Thus, by an odd chance, I had the very last of the very best of *Alma Mater;* the same thing, I hear (which makes it the more strange), had previously happened to my father; and if they are good and do not die, something not at all unsimilar will be found in time to have befallen my successors of to-day. Of the specific points of change, of advantage in the past, of shortcoming in the present, I must own that, on a near examination, they look wondrous cloudy. The chief and far the most lamentable change is the absence of a certain lean, ugly, idle, unpopular student, whose presence was for me the gist and heart of the whole matter; whose changing humours, fine occasional purposes of good, flinching acceptance of evil, shiverings on wet, east-windy, morning journeys up to class, infinite yawnings during lecture and unquenchable gusto in the delights of truantry, made up the sunshine and shadow of my college life. You cannot fancy what you missed in missing him; his virtues, I make sure, are inconceivable to his successors, just as they were apparently concealed from his contemporaries, for I was practically alone in the pleasure I had in his society. Poor soul, I remember how much he was cast down at times, and how life (which had not yet begun) seemed to be already at an end, and hope quite dead, and misfortune and dishonour, like physical presences, dogging him as he went. And it may be worth while to add that these clouds rolled away in their season, and that all clouds roll away at last, and the troubles of youth in particular are things but of a moment. So this student, whom I have in my eye, took his full share of these concerns, and that very largely by his own fault; but he still clung to his fortune, and in the midst of much misconduct, kept on in his own way learning how to work; and at last, to his wonder, escaped out of the stage of studentship not openly shamed; leaving behind him the University of Edinburgh shorn of a good deal of its interest for myself.

But while he is (in more senses than one) the first person, he is by no means the only one whom I regret, or whom the students of to-day, if they knew what they had lost, would regret also. They have still Tait, to be sure—long may they have him!—and they have still Tait's class-room, cupola and all; but think of what a different place it was when this youth of mine (at least on roll days) would be present on the benches, and, at the near end of the platform, Lindsay senior * was airing his robust old age. It is possible my successors may have never even heard of Old Lindsay; but when he went, a link snapped with the last century. He had something of a rustic air, sturdy and fresh and plain; he spoke with a ripe east-country accent, which I used to admire; his reminiscences were all of journeys on foot or highways busy with post-chaises—a Scotland before steam; he had seen the coal fire on the Isle of May, and he regaled me with tales of my own grandfather. Thus he was for me a mirror of things perished; it was only in his memory that I could see the huge shock of flames of the May beacon stream to leeward, and the watchers, as they fed the fire, lay hold unscorched of the windward bars of the furnace; it was only thus that I could see my grandfather driving swiftly in a gig along the seaboard road from Pittenweem to Crail, and for all his business hurry, drawing up to speak good-humouredly with those he met. And now, in his turn, Lindsay is gone also; inhabits only the memories of other men, till these shall follow him; and figures in my reminiscences as my grandfather figured in his.

To-day, again, they have Professor Butcher, and I

* Professor Tait's laboratory assistant.

hear he has a prodigious deal of Greek; and they have
Professor Chrystal, who is a man filled with the mathe-
matics. And doubtless these are set-offs. But they
cannot change the fact that Professor Blackie has retired, and that Professor Kelland is dead. No man's
education is complete or truly liberal who knew not
Kelland. There were unutterable lessons in the mere
sight of that frail old clerical gentleman, lively as a boy,
kind like a fairy godfather, and keeping perfect order in
his class by the spell of that very kindness. I have
heard him drift into reminiscences in class time, though
not for long, and give us glimpses of old-world life in
out-of-the-way English parishes when he was young;
thus playing the same part as Lindsay—the part of the
surviving memory, signalling out of the dark backward
and abysm of time the images of perished things. But
it was a part that scarce became him; he somehow
lacked the means: for all his silver hair and worn face,
he was not truly old; and he had too much of the unrest
and petulant fire of youth, and too much invincible innocence of mind, to play the veteran well. The time
to measure him best, to taste (in the old phrase) his
gracious nature, was when he received his class at home.
What a pretty simplicity would he then show, trying to
amuse us like children with toys; and what an engaging
nervousness of manner, as fearing that his efforts might
not succeed! Truly he made us all feel like children,
and like children embarrassed, but at the same time
filled with sympathy for the conscientious, troubled
elder-boy who was working so hard to entertain us. A
theorist has held the view that there is no feature in
man so tell-tale as his spectacles; that the mouth may
be compressed and the brow smoothed artificially, but
the sheen of the barnacles is diagnostic. And truly it
must have been thus with Kelland; for as I still fancy
I behold him frisking actively about the platform,
pointer in hand, that which I seem to see most clearly
is the way his glasses glittered with affection. I never
knew but one other man who had (if you will permit

the phrase) so kind a spectacle; and that was Dr. Appleton.* But the light in his case was tempered and passive; in Kelland's it danced, and changed, and flashed vivaciously among the students, like a perpetual challenge to goodwill.

I cannot say so much about Professor Blackie, for a good reason. Kelland's class I attended, once even gained there a certificate of merit, the only distinction of my University career. But although I am the holder of a certificate of attendance in the professor's own hand, I cannot remember to have been present in the Greek class above a dozen times. Professor Blackie was even kind enough to remark (more than once) while in the very act of writing the document above referred to, that he did not know my face. Indeed, I denied myself many opportunties; acting upon an extensive and highly rational system of truantry, which cost me a great deal of trouble to put in exercise—perhaps as much as would have taught me Greek—and sent me forth into the world and the profession of letters with the merest shadow of an education. But they say it is always a good thing to have taken pains, and that success is its own reward, whatever be its nature; so that, perhaps, even upon this I should plume myself, that no one ever played the truant with more deliberate care, and none ever had more certificates for less education. One consequence, however, of my system is that I have much less to say of Professor Blackie than I had of Professor Kelland; and as he is still alive, and will long, I hope, continue to be so, it will not surprise you very much that I have no intention of saying it.

Meanwhile, how many others have gone—Jenkin, Hodgson, and I know not who besides; and of that tide of students that used to throng the arch and blacken the quadrangle, how many are scattered into the remotest parts of the earth, and how many more have lain down beside their fathers in their " resting-graves "! And again, how many of these last have not

* Founder and first editor of *The Academy*.

found their way there, all too early, through the stress
of education! That was one thing, at least, from which
my truantry protected me. I am sorry indeed that I
have no Greek, but I should be sorrier still if I were
dead; nor do I know the name of that branch of knowledge which is worth acquiring at the price of a brain
fever. There are many sordid tragedies in the life of
the student, above all if he be poor, or drunken, or both;
but nothing more moves a wise man's pity than the case
of the lad who is in too much hurry to be learned. And
so, for the sake of a moral at the end, I will call up one
more figure, and have done. A student, ambitious of
success by that hot, intemperate manner of study that
now grows so common, read night and day for an
examination. As he went on, the task became more
easy to him, sleep was more easily banished, his brain
grew hot and clear and more capacious, the necessary
knowledge daily fuller and more orderly. It came to
the eve of the trial and he watched all night in his high
chamber, reviewing what he knew, and already secure of
success. His window looked eastward, and being (as I
said) high up, and the house itself standing on a hill,
commanded a view over dwindling suburbs to a country
horizon. At last my student drew up his blind, and still
in quite a jocund humour, looked abroad. Day was
breaking, the east was tinging with strange fires, the
clouds breaking up for the coming of the sun; and at
the sight, nameless terror seized upon his mind. He was
sane, his senses were undisturbed; he saw clearly, and
knew what he was seeing, and knew that it was normal;
but he could neither bear to see it nor find the strength
to look away, and fled in panic from his chamber into
the enclosure of the street. In the cool air and silence,
and among the sleeping houses, his strength was renewed. Nothing troubled him but the memory of what
had passed, and an abject fear of its return.

" Gallo canente, spes redit,
    Aegris salus refunditur,
    Lapsis fides revertitur,"

as they sang of old in Portugal in the Morning Office. But to him that good hour of cockcrow, and the changes of the dawn, had brought panic, and lasting doubt, and such terror as he still shook to think of. He dared not return to his lodging; he could not eat; he sat down, he rose up, he wandered; the city woke about him with its cheerful bustle, the sun climbed overhead; and still he grew but the more absorbed in the distress of his recollection and the fear of his past fear. At the appointed hour, he came to the door of the place of examination; but when he was asked, he had forgotten his name. Seeing him so disordered, they had not the heart to send him away, but gave him a paper and admitted him, still nameless, to the Hall. Vain kindness, vain efforts. He could only sit in a still growing horror, writing nothing, ignorant of all, his mind filled with a single memory of the breaking day and his own intolerable fear. And that same night he was tossing in a brain fever.

People are afraid of war and wounds and dentists, all with excellent reason; but these are not to be compared with such chaotic terrors of the mind as fell on this young man, and made him cover his eyes from the innocent morning. We all have by our bedsides the box of the Merchant Abudah, thank God, securely enough shut; but when a young man sacrifices sleep to labour, let him have a care, for he is playing with the lock.

III

OLD MORTALITY

I

THERE is a certain graveyard, looked upon on the one side by a prison, on the other by the windows of a quiet hotel; below, under a steep cliff, it beholds the traffic of many lines of rail, and the scream of the engine and the shock of meeting buffers mount to it all day long. The aisles are lined with the inclosed sepulchres of families, door beyond door, like houses in a street; and in the morning the shadow of the prison turrets, and of many tall memorials, fall upon the graves. There, in the hot fits of youth, I came to be unhappy. Pleasant incidents are woven with my memory of the place. I here made friends with a certain plain old gentleman, a visitor on sunny mornings, gravely cheerful, who, with one eye upon the place that awaited him, chirped about his youth like winter sparrows; a beautiful housemaid of the hotel once, for some days together, dumbly flirted with me from a window and kept my wild heart flying; and once—she possibly remembers—the wise Eugenia followed me to that austere inclosure. Her hair came down, and in the shelter of the tomb my trembling fingers helped her to repair the braid. But for the most part I went there solitary and, with irrevocable emotion, pored on the names of the forgotten. Name after name, and to each the conventional attributions and the idle dates: a regiment of the unknown that had been the joy of mothers, and had thrilled with the illusions of youth, and at last, in the dim sick-room, wrestled with the pangs of old mortality. In that whole crew of the silenced there was but one of whom my fancy had received a picture; and he, with his comely, florid countenance, bewigged and habited in scarlet, and in his day combining fame and popularity, stood forth, like a taunt, among that company of phantom appellations. It was then possible to leave behind us something more explicit than these severe, monotonous, and lying epitaphs; and the thing left, the memory of a painted picture and what we call the immortality of a name, was hardly more desirable than mere oblivion. Even David Hume, as he lay composed beneath that " circular idea," was fainter than a dream; and when the housemaid, broom in hand, smiled and beckoned from the open window, the fame of that bewigged philosopher melted like a raindrop in the sea.

And yet in soberness I cared as little for the housemaid as for David Hume. The interests of youth are rarely frank; his passions, like Noah's dove, come home to roost. The fire, sensibility, and volume of his own nature, that is all that he has learned to recognise. The tumultuary and gray tide of life, the empire of routine, the unrejoicing faces of his elders, fill him with contemptuous surprise; there also he seems to walk among the tombs of spirits; and it is only in the course of years, and after much rubbing with his fellow-men, that he begins by glimpses to see himself from without and his fellows from within: to know his own for one among the thousand undenoted countenances of the city street, and to divine in others the throb of human agony and hope. In the meantime he will avoid the hospital doors, the pale faces, the cripple, the sweet whiff of chloroform— for there, on the most thoughtless, the pains of others are burned home; but he will continue to walk, in a divine self-pity, the aisles of the forgotten graveyard. The length of man's life, which is endless to the brave and busy, is scorned by his ambitious thought. He cannot bear to have come for so little, and to go again so wholly. He cannot bear, above all, in that brief scene, to be still idle, and by way of cure, neglects the little that he has to do. The parable of the talent is the brief epitome of youth. To believe in immortality is one thing, but it is first needful to believe in life. Denunciatory preachers seem not to suspect that they may be taken gravely and in evil part; that young men may come to think of time as of a moment, and with the pride of Satan wave back the inadequate gift. Yet here is a true peril; this it is that sets them to pace the graveyard alleys and to read, with strange extremes of pity and derision, the memorials of the dead.

Books were the proper remedy: books of vivid human import, forcing upon their minds the issues, pleasures, busyness, importance, and immediacy of that life in which they stand; books of smiling or heroic temper, to excite or to console; books of a large design, shadowing the complexity of that game of consequences to which we all sit down, the hanger-back not least. But the average sermon flees the point, disporting itself in that eternity of which we know, and need to know, so little; avoiding the bright, crowded, and momentous fields of life where destiny awaits us. Upon the average book a writer may be silent; he may set it down to his ill-hap that when his own youth was in the acrid fermentation, he should have fallen and fed upon the cheerless fields of Obermann. Yet to Mr. Arnold, who led him to these pastures, he still bears a grudge. The day is perhaps not far off when people will begin to count *Moll Flanders*, ay, or *The Country Wife*, more wholesome and more pious diet than these guide-books to consistent egoism.

But the most inhuman of boys soon wearies of the inhumanity of Obermann. And even while I still continued to be a haunter of the graveyard, I began insensibly to turn my attention to the grave-diggers, and was weaned out of myself to observe the conduct of visitors. This was dayspring, indeed, to a lad in such great darkness. Not that I began to see men, or to try to see them, from within, nor to learn charity and modesty and justice from the sight; but still stared at them externally from the prison windows of my affectation. Once I remember to have observed two working-women with a baby halting by a grave; there was something monumental in the grouping, one upright carrying the child, the other with bowed face crouching by her side. A wreath of immortelles under a glass dome had thus attracted them; and, drawing near, I overheard their judgment on that wonder. " Eh! what extravagance! " To a youth afflicted with the callosity of sentiment, this quaint and pregnant saying appeared merely base.

My acquaintance with grave-diggers, considering its length, was unremarkable. One indeed, whom I found plying his spade in the red evening, high above Allan Water and in the shadow of Dunblane Cathedral, told me of his acquaintance with the birds that still attended on his labours; how some would even perch about him, waiting for their prey; and in a true Sexton's Calendar, how the species varied with the season of the year. But this was the very poetry of the profession. The others whom I knew were somewhat dry. A faint flavour of the gardener hung about them, but sophisticated and disbloomed. They had engagements to keep, not alone with the deliberate series of the seasons, but with mankind's clocks and hour-long measurement of time. And thus there was no leisure for the relishing pinch, or the hour-long gossip, foot on spade. They were men wrapped up in their grim business; they liked well to open long-closed family vaults, blowing in the key and throwing wide the grating; and they carried in their minds a calendar of names and dates. It would be " in fifty-twa " that such a tomb was last opened for " Miss Jemimy." It was thus they spoke of their past patients—familiarly but not without respect, like old family servants. Here is indeed a servant, whom we forget that we possess; who does not wait at the bright table, or run at the bell's summons, but patiently smokes his pipe beside the mortuary fire, and in his

faithful memory notches the burials of our race. To
suspect Shakespeare in his maturity of a superficial
touch savours of paradox; yet he was surely in error
when he attributed insensibility to the digger of the
grave. But perhaps it is on Hamlet that the charge
should lie; or perhaps the English sexton differs from
the Scottish. The " goodman delver," reckoning up his
years of office, might have at least suggested other
thoughts. It is a pride common among sextons. A
cabinet-maker does not count his cabinets, nor even an
author his volumes, save when they stare upon him
from the shelves; but the grave-digger numbers his
graves. He would indeed be something different from
human if his solitary open-air and tragic labours left
not a broad mark upon his mind. There, in his tranquil
aisle, apart from city clamour, among the cats and
robins and the ancient effigies and legends of the tomb,
he waits the continual passage of his contemporaries,
falling like minute drops into eternity. As they fall,
he counts them; and this enumeration, which was at
first perhaps appalling to his soul, in the process of
years and by the kindly influence of habit grows to be
his pride and pleasure. There are many common stories
telling how he piques himself on crowded cemeteries.
But I will rather tell of the old grave-digger of Monk-
ton, to whose unsuffering bedside the minister was sum-
moned. He dwelt in a cottage built into the wall of the
churchyard; and through a bull's-eye pane above his
bed he could see, as he lay dying, the rank grasses and
the upright and recumbent stones. Dr. Laurie was, I
think, a Moderate: 'tis certain, at least, that he took a
very Roman view of death-bed dispositions; for he told
the old man that he had lived beyond man's natural
years, that his life had been easy and reputable, that his
family had all grown up and been a credit to his care,
and that it now behoved him unregretfully to gird his
loins and follow the majority. The grave-digger heard
him out; then he raised himself upon one elbow, and
with the other hand pointed through the window to the

scene of his life-long labours. " Doctor," he said, " I
ha'e laid three hunner and fower-score in that kirk-
yaird; an it had been His wull," indicating Heaven, " I
would ha'e likit weel to ha'e made out the fower
hunner." But it was not to be; this tragedian of the
fifth act had now another part to play; and the time
had come when others were to gird and carry him.

II

I would fain strike a note that should be more
heroical; but the ground of all youth's suffering, solitude,
hysteria, and haunting of the grave, is nothing else than
naked, ignorant selfishness. It is himself that he sees
dead; those are his virtues that are forgotten; his is
the vague epitaph. Pity him but the more, if pity be
your cue; for where a man is all pride, vanity, and
personal aspiration, he goes through fire unshielded. In
every part and corner of our life, to lose oneself is to
be gainer; to forget oneself is to be happy; and this
poor, laughable, and tragic fool has not yet learned the
rudiments; himself, giant Prometheus, is still ironed
on the peaks of Caucasus. But by and by his truant
interests will leave that tortured body, slip abroad
and gather flowers. Then shall death appear before him
in an altered guise; no longer as a doom peculiar to
himself, whether fate's crowning injustice or his own
last vengeance upon those who fail to value him; but
now as a power that wounds him far more tenderly, not
without solemn compensations, taking and giving, be-
reaving and yet storing up.

The first step for all is to learn to the dregs our own
ignoble fallibility. When we have fallen through storey
after storey of our vanity and aspiration, and sit rueful
among the ruins, then it is that we begin to measure the
stature of our friends: how they stand between us and
our own contempt, believing in our best; how, linking
us with others, and still spreading wide the influential

circle, they weave us in and in with the fabric of contemporary life; and to what petty size they dwarf the virtues and the vices that appeared gigantic in our youth. So that at the last, when such a pin falls out— when there vanishes in the least breath of time one of those rich magazines of life on which we drew for our supply—when he who had first dawned upon us as a face among the faces of the city, and, still growing, came to bulk on our regard with those clear features of the loved and living man, falls in a breath to memory and shadow, there falls along with him a whole wing of the palace of our life.

III

One such face I now remember; one such blank some half a dozen of us labour to dissemble. In his youth he was most beautiful in person, most serene and genial by disposition; full of racy words and quaint thoughts. Laughter attended on his coming. He had the air of a great gentleman, jovial and royal with his equals, and to the poorest student gentle and attentive. Power seemed to reside in him exhaustless; we saw him stoop to play with us, but held him marked for higher destinies; we loved his notice; and I have rarely had my pride more gratified than when he sat at my father's table, my acknowledged friend. So he walked among us, both hands full of gifts, carrying with nonchalance the seeds of a most influential life.

The powers and the ground of friendship is a mystery; but, looking back, I can discern that, in part, we loved the thing he was, for some shadow of what he was to be. For with all his beauty, power, breeding, urbanity, and mirth, there was in those days something soulless in our friend. He would astonish us by sallies, witty, innocent, and inhumane; and by a misapplied Johnsonian pleasantry, demolish honest sentiment. I can still see and hear him, as he went his way along the lamplit streets, *Là ci darem la mano* on his lips, a noble figure of a youth, but following vanity and incredulous of good; and sure enough, somewhere on the high seas of life, with his health, his hopes, his patrimony, and his self-respect, miserably went down.

From this disaster, like a spent swimmer, he came desperately ashore, bankrupt of money and consideration; creeping to the family he had deserted; with broken wing, never more to rise. But in his face there was a light of knowledge that was new to it. Of the wounds of his body he was never healed; died of them gradually, with clear-eyed resignation; of his wounded pride, we knew only from his silence. He returned to that city where he had lorded it in his ambitious youth; lived there alone, seeing few; striving to retrieve the irretrievable; at times still grappling with that mortal frailty that had brought him down; still joying in his friend's successes; his laugh still ready but with kindlier music; and over all his thoughts the shadow of that unalterable law which he had disavowed and which had brought him low. Lastly, when his bodily evils had quite disabled him, he lay a great while dying, still without complaint, still finding interests; to his last step gentle, urbane, and with the will to smile.

The tale of this great failure is, to those who remained true to him, the tale of a success. In his youth he took thought for no one but himself; when he came ashore again, his whole armada lost, he seemed to think of none but others. Such was his tenderness for others, such his instinct of fine courtesy and pride, that of that impure passion of remorse he never breathed a syllable; even regret was rare with him, and pointed with a jest. You would not have dreamed, if you had known him then, that this was that great failure, that beacon to young men, over whose fall a whole society had hissed and pointed fingers. Often have we gone to him, red-hot with our own hopeful sorrows, railing on the rose-leaves in our princely bed of life, and he would patiently give ear and wisely counsel; and it was only upon some

return of our own thoughts that we were reminded what
manner of man this was to whom we disembosomed: a
man, by his own fault, ruined; shut out of the garden
of his gifts; his whole city of hope both ploughed and
salted; silently awaiting the deliverer. Then something
took us by the throat; and to see him there, so gentle,
patient, brave, and pious, oppressed but not cast down,
sorrow was so swallowed up in admiration that we could
not dare to pity him. Even if the old fault flashed out
again, it but awoke our wonder that, in that lost battle,
he should have still the energy to fight. He had gone
to ruin with a kind of kingly *abandon*, like one who
condescended; but once ruined, with the lights all out,
he fought as for a kingdom. Most men, finding themselves the authors of their own disgrace, rail the louder
against God or destiny. Most men, when they repent,
oblige their friends to share the bitterness of that re-
pentance. But he had held an inquest and passed sentence: *mene, mene;* and condemned himself to smiling
silence. He had given trouble enough; had earned
misfortune amply, and foregone the right to murmur.

Thus was our old comrade, like Samson, careless in
his days of strength; but on the coming of adversity,
and when that strength was gone that had betrayed him
—" for our strength is weakness "—he began to blossom
and bring forth. Well, now, he is out of the fight: the
burden that he bore thrown down before the great
deliverer. We

> " in the vast cathedral leave him;
>   God accept him,
>   Christ receive him! "

IV

If we go now and look on these innumerable epitaphs,
the pathos and the irony are strangely fled. They do
not stand merely to the dead, these foolish monuments;
they are pillars and legends set up to glorify the difficult

but not desperate life of man. This ground is hallowed
by the heroes of defeat.

I see the indifferent pass before my friend's last
resting-place; pause, with a shrug of pity, marvelling
that so rich an argosy had sunk. A pity, now that he is
done with suffering, a pity most uncalled for, and an
ignorant wonder. Before those who loved him, his
memory shines like a reproach; they honour him for
silent lessons; they cherish his example; and in what
remains before them of their toil, fear to be unworthy
of the dead. For this proud man was one of those who
prospered in the valley of humiliation—of whom
Bunyan wrote that, " Though Christian had the hard
hap to meet in the valley with Apollyon, yet I must tell
you, that in former times men have met with angels
here; have found pearls here; and have in this place
found the words of life."

A COLLEGE MAGAZINE

I

ALL through my boyhood and youth, I was known and pointed out for the pattern of an idler; and yet I was always busy on my own private end, which was to learn to write. I kept always two books in my pocket, one to read, one to write in. As I walked, my mind was busy fitting what I saw with appropriate words; when I sat by the roadside, I would either read, or a pencil and a penny version-book would be in my hand, to note down the features of the scene or commemorate some halting stanzas. Thus I lived with words. And what I thus wrote was for no ulterior use, it was written consciously for practice. It was not so much that I wished to be an author (though I wished that too) as that I had vowed that I would learn to write. That was a proficiency that tempted me; and I practised to acquire it, as men learn to whittle, in a wager with myself. Description was the principal field of my exercise; for to any one with senses there is always something worth describing, and town and country are but one continuous subject. But I worked in other ways also; often accompanied my walks with dramatic dialogues, in which I played many parts; and often exercised myself in writing down conversations from memory.

This was all excellent, no doubt; so were the diaries I sometimes tried to keep, but always and very speedily discarded, finding them a school of posturing and melancholy self-deception. And yet this was not the

most efficient part of my training. Good though it was,
it only taught me (so far as I have learned them at all)
the lower and less intellectual elements of the art, the
choice of the essential note and the right word: things
that to a happier constitution had perhaps come by
nature. And regarded as training, it had one grave
defect; for it set me no standard of achievement. So
that there was perhaps more profit, as there was certainly more effort, in my secret labours at home.
Whenever I read a book or a passage that particularly
pleased me, in which a thing was said or an effect
rendered with propriety, in which there was either some
conspicuous force or some happy distinction in the style,
I must sit down at once and set myself to ape that
quality. I was unsuccessful, and I knew it; and tried
again, and was again unsuccessful and always unsuccessful; but at least in these vain bouts, I got some
practice in rhythm, in harmony, in construction and the
co-ordination of parts. I have thus played the sedulous
ape to Hazlitt, to Lamb, to Wordsworth, to Sir Thomas
Browne, to Defoe, to Hawthorne, to Montaigne, to
Baudelaire, and to Obermann. I remember one of these
monkey tricks, which was called *The Vanity of Morals:*
it was to have had a second part, *The Vanity of Knowledge;* and as I had neither morality nor scholarship,
the names were apt; but the second part was never attempted, and the first part was written (which is my
reason for recalling it, ghostlike, from its ashes) no less
than three times: first in the manner of Hazlitt, second
in the manner of Ruskin, who had cast on me a passing
spell, and third, in a laborious pasticcio of Sir Thomas
Browne. So with my other works: *Cain,* an epic, was
(save the mark!) an imitation of *Sordello: Robin Hood,*
a tale in verse, took an eclectic middle course among
the fields of Keats, Chaucer, and Morris: in *Mon-
mouth,* a tragedy, I reclined on the bosom of Mr. Swinburne; in my innumerable gouty-footed lyrics, I
followed many masters; in the first draft of *The King's
Pardon,* a tragedy, I was on the trail of no lesser man

than John Webster; in the second draft of the same piece, with staggering versatility, I had shifted my allegiance to Congreve, and of course conceived my fable in a less serious vein—for it was not Congreve's verse, it was his exquisite prose, that I admired and sought to copy. Even at the age of thirteen I had tried to do justice to the inhabitants of the famous city of Peebles in the style of the *Book of Snobs*. So I might go on for ever, through all my abortive novels, and down to my later plays, of which I think more tenderly, for they were not only conceived at first under the bracing influence of old Dumas, but have met with resurrections: one, strangely bettered by another hand, came on the stage itself and was played by bodily actors; the other, originally known as *Semiramis: a Tragedy*, I have observed on book-stalls under the *alias* of *Prince Otto*. But enough has been said to show by what arts of impersonation, and in what purely ventriloquial efforts I first saw my words on paper.

That, like it or not, is the way to learn to write; whether I have profited or not, that is the way. It was so Keats learned, and there was never a finer temperament for literature than Keats's; it was so, if we could trace it out, that all men have learned; and that is why a revival of letters is always accompanied or heralded by a cast back to earlier and fresher models. Perhaps I hear some one cry out: But this is not the way to be original! It is not; nor is there any way but to be born so. Nor yet, if you are born original, is there anything in this training that shall clip the wings of your originality. There can be none more original than Montaigne, neither could any be more unlike Cicero; yet no craftsman can fail to see how much the one must have tried in his time to imitate the other. Burns is the very type of a prime force in letters: he was of all men the most imitative. Shakespeare himself, the imperial, proceeds directly from a school. It is only from a school that we can expect to have good writers; it is almost invariably from a school that great writers, these lawless exceptions, issue. Nor is there anything here that should astonish the considerate. Before he can tell what cadences he truly prefers, the student should have tried all that are possible; before he can choose and preserve a fitting key of words, he should long have practised the literary scales; and it is only after years of such gymnastic that he can sit down at last, legions of words swarming to his call, dozens of turns of phrase simultaneously bidding for his choice, and he himself knowing what he wants to do and (within the narrow limit of a man's ability) able to do it.

And it is the great point of these imitations that there still shines beyond the student's reach his inimitable model. Let him try as he please, he is still sure of failure; and it is a very old and a very true saying that failure is the only highroad to success. I must have had some disposition to learn; for I clear-sightedly condemned my own performances. I liked doing them indeed; but when they were done, I could see they were rubbish. In consequence, I very rarely showed them even to my friends; and such friends as I chose to be my confidants I must have chosen well, for they had the friendliness to be quite plain with me. "Padding," said one. Another wrote: "I cannot understand why you do lyrics so badly." No more could I! Thrice I put myself in the way of a more authoritative rebuff, by sending a paper to a magazine. These were returned; and I was not surprised nor even pained. If they had not been looked at, as (like all amateurs) I suspected was the case, there was no good in repeating the experiment; if they had been looked at—well, then I had not yet learned to write, and I must keep on learning and living. Lastly, I had a piece of good fortune which is the occasion of this paper, and by which I was able to see my literature in print, and to measure experimentally how far I stood from the favour of the public.

II

The Speculative Society is a body of some antiquity,
and has counted among its members Scott, Brougham,
Jeffrey, Horner, Benjamin Constant, Robert Emmet,
and many a legal and local celebrity besides. By an
accident, variously explained, it has its rooms in the
very buildings of the University of Edinburgh: a hall,
Turkey-carpeted, hung with pictures, looking, when
lighted up at night with fire and candle, like some
goodly dining-room; a passage-like library, walled with
books in their wire cages; and a corridor with a fire-
place, benches, a table, many prints of famous members, and a mural tablet to the virtues of a former
secretary. Here a member can warm himself and loaf
and read; here, in defiance of Senatus-consults, he can
smoke. The Senatus looks askance at these privileges;
looks even with a somewhat vinegar aspect on the whole
society; which argues a lack of proportion in the learned
mind, for the world, we may be sure, will prize far
higher this haunt of dead lions than all the living dogs
of the professorate.

I sat one December morning in the library of the
Speculative; a very humble-minded youth, though it
was a virtue I never had much credit for; yet proud of
my privileges as a member of the Spec.; proud of the
pipe I was smoking in the teeth of the Senatus; and in
particular, proud of being in the next room to three
very distinguished students, who were then conversing
beside the corridor fire. One of these has now his name
on the back of several volumes, and his voice, I learn,
is influential in the law courts. Of the death of the
second, you have just been reading what I had to say.
And the third also has escaped out of that battle of life
in which he fought so hard, it may be so unwisely.
They were all three, as I have said, notable students;
but this was the most conspicuous. Wealthy, handsome, ambitious, adventurous, diplomatic, a reader of

Balzac, and of all men that I have known, the most like
to one of Balzac's characters, he led a life, and was
attended by an ill fortune, that could be properly set
forth only in the *Comédie Humaine*. He had then his
eye on Parliament; and soon after the time of which I
write, he made a showy speech at a political dinner, was
cried up to heaven next day in the *Courant,* and the day
after was dashed lower than earth with a charge of
plagiarism in the *Scotsman.* Report would have it (I
daresay, very wrongly) that he was betrayed by one in
whom he particularly trusted, and that the author of
the charge had learned its truth from his own lips.
Thus, at least, he was up one day on a pinnacle, admired and envied by all; and the next, though still but
a boy, he was publicly disgraced. The blow would have
broken a less finely tempered spirit; and even him I
suppose it rendered reckless; for he took flight to London, and there, in a fast club, disposed of the bulk of
his considerable patrimony in the space of one winter.
For years thereafter he lived I know not how; always
well dressed, always in good hotels and good society,
always with empty pockets. The charm of his manner
may have stood him in good stead; but though my own
manners are very agreeable, I have never found in them
a source of livelihood; and to explain the miracle of his
continued existence, I must fall back upon the theory of
the philosopher, that in his case, as in all of the same
kind, " there was a suffering relative in the background."
From this genteel eclipse he reappeared upon the scene,
and presently sought me out in the character of a
generous editor. It is in this part that I best remember
him; tall, slender, with a not ungraceful stoop; looking
quite like a refined gentleman, and quite like an urbane
adventurer; smiling with an engaging ambiguity; cock-
ing at you one peaked eyebrow with a great appearance
of finesse; speaking low and sweet and thick, with a
touch of burr; telling strange tales with singular de-
liberation and, to a patient listener, excellent effect.
After all these ups and downs, he seemed still, like the

rich student that he was of yore, to breathe of money;
seemed still perfectly sure of himself and certain of his
end. Yet he was then upon the brink of his last over-
throw. He had set himself to found the strangest thing
in our society: one of those periodical sheets from which
men suppose themselves to learn opinions; in which
young gentlemen from the universities are encouraged,
at so much a line, to garble facts, insult foreign nations,
and calumniate private individuals; and which are now
the source of glory, so that if a man's name be often
enough printed there, he becomes a kind of demigod;
and people will pardon him when he talks back and
forth, as they do for Mr. Gladstone; and crowd him to
suffocation on railway platforms, as they did the other
day to General Boulanger; and buy his literary works,
as I hope you have just done for me. Our fathers, when
they were upon some great enterprise, would sacrifice
a life; building, it may be, a favourite slave into the
foundations of their palace. It was with his own life
that my companion disarmed the envy of the gods.
He fought his paper single-handed; trusting no one, for
he was something of a cynic; up early and down late,
for he was nothing of a sluggard; daily ear-wigging
influential men, for he was a master of ingratiation. In
that slender and silken fellow there must have been a
rare vein of courage, that he should thus have died at
his employment; and doubtless ambition spoke loudly
in his ear, and doubtless love also, for it seems there
was a marriage in his view had he succeeded. But he
died, and his paper died after him; and of all this grace,
and tact, and courage, it must seem to our blind eyes
as if there had come literally nothing.

These three students sat, as I was saying, in the
corridor, under the mural tablet that records the virtues
of Macbean, the former secretary. We would often
smile at that ineloquent memorial, and thought it a poor
thing to come into the world at all and have no more
behind one than Macbean. And yet of these three, two
are gone and have left less; and this book, perhaps,

when it is old and foxy, and some one picks it up in a corner of a book-shop, and glances through it, smiling at the old, graceless turns of speech, and perhaps for the love of *Alma Mater* (which may be still extant and flourishing) buys it, not without haggling, for some pence—this book may alone preserve a memory of James Walter Ferrier and Robert Glasgow Brown.

Their thoughts ran very differently on that December morning; they were all on fire with ambition; and when they had called me in to them, and made me a sharer in their design, I too, became drunken with pride and hope. We were to found a University magazine. A pair of little, active brothers—Livingstone by name, great skippers on the foot, great rubbers of the hands, who kept a book-shop over against the University building—had been debauched to play the part of publishers. We four were to be conjunct editors and, what was the main point of the concern, to print our own works; while, by every rule of arithmetic—that flatterer of credulity—the adventure must succeed and bring great profit. Well, well: it was a bright vision. I went home that morning walking upon air. To have been chosen by these three distinguished students was to me the most unspeakable advance; it was my first draught of consideration; it reconciled me to myself and to my fellowmen; and as I steered round the railings at the Tron, I could not withhold my lips from smiling publicly. Yet, in the bottom of my heart, I knew that magazine would be a grim fiasco; I knew it would not be worth reading; I knew, even if it were, that nobody would read it; and I kept wondering how I should be able, upon my compact income of twelve pounds per annum, payable monthly, to meet my share in the expense. It was a comfortable thought to me that I had a father.

The magazine appeared, in a yellow cover which was the best part of it, for at least it was unassuming; it ran four months in undisturbed obscurity, and died without a gasp. The first number was edited by all four of us with prodigious bustle; the second fell principally into the hands of Ferrier and me; the third I edited alone; and it has long been a solemn question who it was that edited the fourth. It would perhaps be still more difficult to say who read it. Poor yellow sheet, that looked so hopefully in the Livingstones' window! Poor, harmless paper, that might have gone to print a *Shakespeare* on, and was instead so clumsily defaced with nonsense! And, shall I say, Poor Editors? I cannot pity myself, to whom it was all pure gain. It was no news to me, but only the wholesome confirmation of my judgment, when the magazine struggled into half-birth, and instantly sickened and subsided into night. I had sent a copy to the lady with whom my heart was at that time somewhat engaged, and who did all that in her lay to break it; and she, with some tact, passed over the gift and my cherished contributions in silence. I will not say that I was pleased at this; but I will tell her now, if by any chance she takes up the work of her former servant, that I thought the better of her taste. I cleared the decks after this lost engagement; had the necessary interview with my father, which passed off not amiss; paid over my share of the expense to the two little, active brothers, who rubbed their hands as much, but methought skipped rather less than formerly, having perhaps, these two also, embarked upon the enterprise with some graceful illusions; and then, reviewing the whole episode, I told myself that the time was not yet ripe, nor the man ready; and to work I went again with my penny version-books, having fallen back in one day from the printed author to the manuscript student.

III

From this defunct periodical I am going to reprint one of my own papers. The poor little piece is all tail-foremost. I have done my best to straighten its array, I have pruned it fearlessly, and it remains invertebrate and wordy. No self-respecting magazine would print the thing; and here you behold it in a bound volume, not for any worth of its own, but for the sake of the man whom it purports dimly to represent and some of whose sayings it preserves; so that in this volume of Memories and Portraits, Robert Young, the Swanston gardener, may stand alongside of John Todd, the Swanston shepherd. Not that John and Robert drew very close together in their lives; for John was rough, he smelt of the windy brae; and Robert was gentle, and smacked of the garden in the hollow. Perhaps it is to my shame that I liked John the better of the two; he had grit and dash, and that salt of the Old Adam that pleases men with any savage inheritance of blood; and he was a wayfarer besides, and took my gipsy fancy. But however that may be, and however Robert's profile may be blurred in the boyish sketch that follows, he was a man of a most quaint and beautiful nature, whom, if it were possible to recast a piece of work so old, I should like well to draw again with a maturer touch. And as I think of him and of John, I wonder in what other country two such men would be found dwelling together, in a hamlet of some twenty cottages, in the woody fold of a green hill.

V

AN OLD SCOTS GARDENER

I THINK I might almost have said the last: somewhere, indeed, in the uttermost glens of the Lam-
mermuir or among the south-western hills there may
yet linger a decrepit representative of this bygone good
fellowship; but as far as actual experience goes, I have
only met one man in my life who might fitly be quoted
in the same breath with Andrew Fairservice—though
without his vices. He was a man whose very presence
could impart a savour of quaint antiquity to the baldest
and most modern flower-plots. There was a dignity
about his tall stooping form, and an earnestness in his
wrinkled face that recalled Don Quixote; but a Don
Quixote who had come through the training of the
Covenant, and been nourished in his youth on *Walker's
Lives* and *The Hind let Loose*.

Now, as I could not bear to let such a man pass away
with no sketch preserved of his old-fashioned virtues, I
hope the reader will take this as an excuse for the
present paper, and judge as kindly as he can the infirmities of my description. To me, who find it so
difficult to tell the little that I know, he stands essentially as a *genius loci*. It is impossible to separate his
spare form and old straw hat from the garden in the
lap of the hill, with its rocks overgrown with clematis,
its shadowy walks, and the splendid breadth of cham-
paign that one saw from the north-west corner. The
garden and gardener seem part and parcel of each other.
When I take him from his right surroundings and try
to make him appear for me on paper, he looks unreal
and phantasmal: the best that I can say may convey

some notion to those that never saw him, but to me it will be ever impotent.

The first time that I saw him, I fancy Robert was pretty old already: he had certainly begun to use his years as a stalking-horse. Latterly he was beyond all the impudences of logic, considering a reference to the parish register worth all the reasons in the world. "*I am old and well stricken in years*," he was wont to say; and I never found any one bold enough to answer the argument. Apart from this vantage that he kept over all who were not yet octogenarian, he had some other drawbacks as a gardener. He shrank the very place he cultivated. The dignity and reduced gentility of his appearance made the small garden cut a sorry figure. He was full of tales of greater situations in his younger days. He spoke of castles and parks with a humbling familiarity. He told of places where under-gardeners had trembled at his looks, where there were meres and swanneries, labyrinths of walk and wildernesses of sad shrubbery in his control, till you could not help feeling that it was condescension on his part to dress your humbler garden plots. You were thrown at once into an invidious position. You felt that you were profiting by the needs of dignity, and that his poverty and not his will consented to your vulgar rule. Involuntarily you compared yourself with the swineherd that made Alfred watch his cakes, or some bloated citizen who may have given his sons and his condescension to the fallen Dionysius. Nor were the disagreeables purely fanciful and metaphysical, for the sway that he exercised over your feelings he extended to your garden, and, through the garden, to your diet. He would trim a hedge, throw away a favourite plant, or fill the most favoured and fertile section of the garden with a vegetable that none of us could eat, in supreme contempt for our opinion. If you asked him to send you in one of your own artichokes, "*That I wull, mem*," he would say, "*with pleasure, for it is mair blessed to give than to receive.*" Ay, and even when, by extra twisting of

the screw, we prevailed on him to prefer our commands
to his own inclination, and he went away, stately and
sad, professing that "*our wull was his pleasure*," but
yet reminding us that he would do it "*with feelin's*"—
even then, I say, the triumphant master felt humbled
in his triumph, felt that he ruled on sufferance only,
that he was taking a mean advantage of the other's low
estate, and that the whole scene had been one of those
"slights that patient merit of the unworthy takes."

In flowers his taste was old-fashioned and catholic;
affecting sunflowers and dahlias, wallflowers and roses,
and holding in supreme aversion whatsoever was fantastic, new-fashioned or wild. There was one exception
to this sweeping ban. Foxgloves, though undoubtedly
guilty on the last count, he not only spared, but loved;
and when the shrubbery was being thinned, he stayed
his hand and dexterously manipulated his bill in order
to save every stately stem. In boyhood, as he told me
once, speaking in that tone that only actors and the
old-fashioned common folk can use nowadays, his heart
grew "*proud*" within him when he came on a burn-
course among the braes of Manor that shone purple
with their graceful trophies; and not all his apprenticeship and practice for so many years of precise
gardening had banished these boyish recollections from
his heart. Indeed, he was a man keenly alive to the
beauty of all that was bygone. He abounded in old
stories of his boyhood, and kept pious account of all his
former pleasures; and when he went (on a holiday) to
visit one of the fabled great places of the earth where
he had served before, he came back full of little pre-
Raphaelite reminiscences that showed real passion for
the past, such as might have shaken hands with Hazlitt
or Jean-Jacques.

But however his sympathy with his old feelings might
affect his liking for the foxgloves, the very truth was
that he scorned all flowers together. They were but
garnishings, childish toys, trifling ornaments for ladies'
chimney-shelves. It was towards his cauliflowers and

peas and cabbage that his heart grew warm. His preference for the more useful growths was such that cabbages were found invading the flower-plots, and an outpost of savoys was once discovered in the centre of the lawn. He would prelect over some thriving plant with wonderful enthusiasm, piling reminiscence on reminiscence of former and perhaps yet finer specimens. Yet even then he did not let the credit leave himself. He had, indeed, raised *" finer o' them "*; but it seemed that no one else had been favoured with a like success. All other gardeners, in fact, were mere foils to his own superior attainments; and he would recount, with perfect soberness of voice and visage, how so and so had wondered, and such another could scarcely give credit to his eyes. Nor was it with his rivals only that he parted praise and blame. If you remarked how well a plant was looking, he would gravely touch his hat and thank you with solemn unction; all credit in the matter falling to him. If, on the other hand, you called his attention to some back-going vegetable, he would quote Scripture: *" Paul may plant and Apollos may water;"* all blame being left to Providence, on the score of deficient rain or untimely frosts.

There was one thing in the garden that shared his preference with his favourite cabbages and rhubarb, and that other was the bee-hive. Their sound, their industry, perhaps their sweet product also, had taken hold of his imagination and heart, whether by way of memory or no I cannot say, although perhaps the bees too were linked to him by some recollection of Manor braes and his country childhood. Nevertheless, he was too chary of his personal safety or (let me rather say) his personal dignity to mingle in any active office towards them, But he could stand by while one of the contemned rivals did the work for him, and protest that it was quite safe in spite of his own considerate distance and the cries of the distressed assistant. In regard to bees, he was rather a man of word than deed, and some of his most striking sentences had the bees for text. *" They*

are indeed wonderfu' creatures, mem," he said once.
*" They just mind me o' what the Queen of Sheba said
to Solomon—and I think she said it wi' a sigh—' The
half of it hath not been told unto me.' "*

As far as the Bible goes, he was deeply read. Like
the old Covenanters, of whom he was the worthy representative, his mouth was full of sacred quotations; it
was the book that he had studied most and thought
upon most deeply. To many people in his station the
Bible, and perhaps Burns, are the only books of any
vital literary merit that they read, feeding themselves,
for the rest, on the draff of country newspapers, and
the very instructive but not very palatable pabulum
of some cheap educational series. This was Robert's
position. All day long he had dreamed of the Hebrew
stories, and his head had been full of Hebrew poetry
and Gospel ethics; until they had struck deep root into
his heart, and the very expressions had become a part
of him; so that he rarely spoke without some antique
idiom or Scripture mannerism that gave a raciness to
the merest trivialities of talk. But the influence of the
Bible did not stop here. There was more in Robert than
quaint phrase and ready store of reference. He was
imbued with a spirit of peace and love: he interposed
between man and wife: he threw himself between the
angry, touching his hat the while with all the ceremony
of an usher: he protected the birds from everybody but
himself, seeing, I suppose, a great difference between
official execution and wanton sport. His mistress telling
him one day to put some ferns into his master's particular corner, and adding, " Though, indeed, Robert,
he doesn't deserve them, for he wouldn't help me to
gather them," " *Eh, mem,*" replies Robert, " *but I
wouldnae say that, for I think he's just a most deservin'
gentleman.*" Again, two of our friends, who were on
intimate terms, and accustomed to use language to each
other, somewhat without the bounds of the parliamentary, happened to differ about the position of a seat in
the garden. The discussion, as was usual when these

two were at it, soon waxed tolerably insulting on both
sides. Every one accustomed to such controversies
several times a day was quietly enjoying this prize-
fight of somewhat abusive wit—every one but Robert,
to whom the perfect good faith of the whole quarrel
seemed unquestionable, and who, after having waited
till his conscience would suffer him to wait no more,
and till he expected every moment that the disputants
would fall to blows, cut suddenly in with tones of
almost tearful entreaty: *"Eh, but, gentlemen, I wad
hae nae mair words about it!"* One thing was notice
able about Robert's religion: it was neither dogmatic
nor sectarian. He never expatiated (at least, in my
hearing) on the doctrines of his creed, and he never
condemned anybody else. I have no doubt that he held
all Roman Catholics, Atheists, and Mahometans as
considerably out of it; I don't believe he had any
sympathy for Prelacy; and the natural feelings of man
must have made him a little sore about Free-
Churchism; but at least, he never talked about these
views, never grew controversially noisy, and never
openly aspersed the belief or practice of anybody. Now
all this is not generally characteristic of Scots piety;
Scots sects being churches militant with a vengeance,
and Scots believers perpetual crusaders the one against
the other, and missionaries the one to the other. Perhaps Robert's originally tender heart was what made
the difference; or, perhaps, his solitary and pleasant
labour among fruits and flowers had taught him a more
sunshiny creed than those whose work is among the
tares of fallen humanity; and the soft influences of the
garden had entered deep into his spirit,

> "Annihilating all that's made
> To a green thought in a green shade."

But I could go on for ever chronicling his golden
sayings or telling of his innocent and living piety. I
had meant to tell of his cottage, with the German pipe
hung reverently above the fire, and the shell box that

he had made for his son, and of which he would say pathetically: " *He was real pleased wi' it at first, but I think he's got a kind o' tired o' it now* "—the son being then a man of about forty. But I will let all these pass. " 'Tis more significant: he's dead." The earth, that he had digged so much in his life, was dug out by another for himself; and the flowers that he had tended drew their life still from him, but in a new and nearer way. A bird flew about the open grave, as if it too wished to honour the obsequies of one who had so often quoted Scripture in favour of its kind: " Are not two sparrows sold for the farthing? and yet not one of them falleth to the ground."

Yes, he is dead. But the kings did not rise in the place of death to greet him " with taunting proverbs " as they rose to greet the haughty Babylonian; for in his life he was lowly, and a peacemaker and a servant of God.

VI

PASTORAL

TO leave home in early life is to be stunned and
quickened with novelties; but when years have
come, it only casts a more endearing light upon the
past. As in those composite photographs of Mr. Gal-
ton's, the image of each new sitter brings out but the
more clearly the central features of the race; when once
youth has flown, each new impression only deepens the
sense of nationality and the desire of native places.
So may some cadet of Royal Écossais or the Albany
Regiment, as he mounted guard about French citadels,
so may some officer marching his company of the
Scots-Dutch among the polders, have felt the soft rains
of the Hebrides upon his brow, or started in the ranks
at the remembered aroma of peat-smoke. And the
rivers of home are dear in particular to all men. This
is as old as Naaman, who was jealous for Abana
and Pharpar; it is confined to no race nor country, for
I know one of Scottish blood but a child of Suffolk,
whose fancy still lingers about the lilied lowland waters
of that shire. But the streams of Scotland are incomparable in themselves—or I am only the more Scottish
to suppose so—and their sound and colour dwell for
ever in the memory. How often and willingly do I not
look again in fancy on Tummel, or Manor, or the talking Airdle, or Dee swirling in its Lynn; on the bright
burn of Kinnaird, or the golden burn that pours and
sulks in the den behind Kingussie! I think shame to
leave out one of these enchantresses, but the list would
grow too long if I remembered all; only I may not forget Allan Water, nor birch-wetting Rogie, nor yet

Almond; nor, for all its pollutions, that Water of Leith
of the many and well-named mills—Bell's Mills, and
Canon Mills, and Silver Mills; nor Redford Burn of
pleasant memories; nor yet, for all its smallness, that
nameless trickle that springs in the green bosom of
Allermuir, and is fed from Halkerside with a perennial
teacupful, and threads the moss under the Shearer's
Knowe, and makes one pool there, overhung by a rock,
where I loved to sit and make bad verses, and is then
kidnapped in its infancy by subterranean pipes for the
service of the sea-beholding city in the plain. From
many points in the moss you may see at one glance its
whole course and that of all its tributaries; the geog-
rapher of this Lilliput may visit all its corners without sitting down, and not yet begin to be breathed;
Shearer's Knowe and Halkerside are but names of adjacent cantons on a single shoulder of a hill, as names
are squandered (it would seem to the inexpert, in superfluity) upon these upland sheepwalks; a bucket would
receive the whole discharge of the toy river; it would
take it an appreciable time to fill your morning bath;
for the most part, besides, it soaks unseen through the
moss; and yet for the sake of auld lang syne, and the
figure of a certain *genius loci,* I am condemned to linger
awhile in fancy by its shores; and if the nymph (who
cannot be above a span in stature) will but inspire my
pen, I would gladly carry the reader along with me.

John Todd, when I knew him, was already "the
oldest herd on the Pentlands," and had been all his days
faithful to that curlew-scattering, sheep-collecting life.
He remembered the droving days, when the drove
roads, that now lie green and solitary through the
heather, were thronged thoroughfares. He had himself often marched flocks into England, sleeping on the
hillsides with his caravan; and by his account it was
a rough business not without danger. The drove roads
lay apart from habitation; the drovers met in the
wilderness, as to-day the deep-sea fishers meet off the
banks in the solitude of the Atlantic; and in the one as

in the other case rough habits and fist-law were the
rule. Crimes were committed, sheep filched, and
drovers robbed and beaten; most of which offences had
a moorland burial and were never heard of in the
courts of justice. John, in those days, was at least once
attacked—by two men after his watch—and at least
once, betrayed by his habitual anger, fell under the
danger of the law and was clapped into some rustic
prison-house, the doors of which he burst in the night
and was no more heard of in that quarter. When I
knew him, his life had fallen in quieter places, and he
had no cares beyond the dulness of his dogs and the inroads of pedestrians from town. But for a man of his
propensity to wrath these were enough; he knew neither
rest nor peace, except by snatches; in the gray of the
summer morning, and already from far up the hill, he
would wake the " toun " with the sound of his shout-
ings; and in the lambing time, his cries were not yet
silenced late at night. This wrathful voice of a man
unseen might be said to haunt that quarter of the Pentlands, an audible bogie; and no doubt it added to the
fear in which men stood of John a touch of something
legendary. For my own part, he was at first my
enemy, and I, in my character of a rambling boy, his
natural abhorrence. It was long before I saw him near
at hand, knowing him only by some sudden blast of
bellowing from far above, bidding me " c'way oot
amang the sheep." The quietest recesses of the hill
harboured this ogre; I skulked in my favourite wilderness like a Cameronian of the Killing Time, and John
Todd was my Claverhouse, and his dogs my questing
dragoons. Little by little we dropped into civilities;
his hail at sight of me began to have less of the ring
of a war-slogan; soon, we never met but he produced
his snuff-box, which was with him, like the calumet
with the Red Indian, a part of the heraldry of peace;
and at length, in the ripeness of time, we grew to be a
pair of friends, and when I lived alone in these parts
in the winter, it was a settled thing for John to " give

me a cry " over the garden wall as he set forth upon his
evening round, and for me to overtake and bear him
company.

That dread voice of his that shook the hills when he
was angry, fell in ordinary talk very pleasantly upon
the ear, with a kind of honied, friendly whine, not far
off singing, that was eminently Scottish. He laughed
not very often, and when he did, with a sudden, loud
haw-haw, hearty but somehow joyless, like an echo
from a rock. His face was permanently set and coloured; ruddy and stiff with weathering; more like a
picture than a face; yet with a certain strain and a
threat of latent anger in the expression, like that of a
man trained too fine and harassed with perpetual vigi-
lance He spoke in the richest dialect of Scots I ever
heard; the words in themselves were a pleasure and
often a surprise to me, so that I often came back from
one of our patrols with new acquisitions; and this vocabulary he would handle like a master, stalking a little before me, " beard on shoulder," the plaid hanging
loosely about him, the yellow staff clapped under his
arm, and guiding me uphill by that devious, tactical
ascent which seems peculiar to men of his trade. I
might count him with the best talkers; only that talking Scots and talking English seem incomparable acts.
He touched on nothing at least, but he adorned it;
when he narrated, the scene was before you; when he
spoke (as he did mostly) of his own antique business,
the thing took on a colour of romance and curiosity
that was surprising. The clans of sheep with their
particular territories on the hill, and how, in the yearly
killings and purchases, each must be proportionately
thinned and strengthened; the midnight busyness of
animals, the signs of the weather, the cares of the
snowy season, the exquisite stupidity of sheep, the exquisite cunning of dogs: all these he could present so
humanly, and with so much old experience and living
gusto, that weariness was excluded. And in the midst
he would suddenly straighten his bowed back, the stick

would fly abroad in demonstration, and the sharp thunder of his voice roll out a long itinerary for the dogs, so that you saw at last the use of that great wealth of names for every knowe and howe upon the hillside; and the dogs, having hearkened with lowered tails and raised faces, would run up their flags again to the masthead and spread themselves upon the indicated circuit. It used to fill me with wonder how they could follow and retain so long a story. But John denied these creatures all intelligence; they were the constant butt of his passion and contempt; it was just possible to work with the like of them, he said—not more than possible. And then he would expand upon the subject of the really good dogs that he had known, and the one really good dog that he had himself possessed. He had been offered forty pounds for it; but a good collie was worth more than that, more than anything, to a "herd"; he did the herd's work for him. "As for the like of them!" he would cry, and scornfully indicate the scouring tails of his assistants.

Once—I translate John's Lallan, for I cannot do it justice, being born *Britannis in montibus,* indeed, but alas! *inerudito sœculo*—once, in the days of his good dog, he had bought some sheep in Edinburgh, and on the way out, the road being crowded, two were lost. This was a reproach to John, and a slur upon the dog; and both were alive to their misfortune. Word came, after some days, that a farmer about Braid had found a pair of sheep; and thither went John and the dog to ask for restitution. But the farmer was a hard man and stood upon his rights. "How were they marked?" he asked; and since John had bought right and left from many sellers and had no notion of the marks—"Very well," said the farmer, "then it's only right that I should keep them."—"Well," said John, "it's a fact that I cannae tell the sheep; but if my dog can, will ye let me have them?" The farmer was honest as well as hard, and besides I daresay he had little fear of the ordeal; so he had all the sheep upon his farm into

one large park, and turned John's dog into their midst.
That hairy man of business knew his errand well; he
knew that John and he had bought two sheep and (to
their shame) lost them about Boroughmuirhead; he
knew besides (the Lord knows how, unless by listening)
that they were come to Braid for their recovery; and
without pause or blunder singled out, first one and then
another, the two waifs. It was that afternoon the forty
pounds were offered and refused. And the shepherd
and his dog—what do I say? the true shepherd and
his man—set off together by Fairmilehead in jocund
humour, and "smiled to ither" all the way home,
with the two recovered ones before them. So far, so
good; but intelligence may be abused. The dog, as he
is by little man's inferior in mind, is only by little
his superior in virtue; and John had another collie tale
of quite a different complexion. At the foot of the
moss behind Kirk Yetton (Caer Ketton, wise men
say) there is a scrog of low wood and a pool with a
dam for washing sheep. John was one day lying under
a bush in the scrog, when he was aware of a collie on
the far hillside skulking down through the deepest of
the heather with obtrusive stealth. He knew the dog;
knew him for a clever, rising practitioner from quite a
distant farm; one whom perhaps he had coveted as he
saw him masterfully steering flocks to market. But
what did the practitioner so far from home? and why
this guilty and secret manœuvring towards the pool?
—for it was towards the pool that he was heading.
John lay the closer under his bush, and presently saw
the dog come forth upon the margin, look all about to
see if he were anywhere observed, plunge in and repeatedly wash himself over head and ears, and then
(but now openly and with tail in air) strike homeward
over the hills. That same night word was sent his master, and the rising practitioner, shaken up from where
he lay, all innocence before the fire, was had out to a
dykeside and promptly shot; for alas! he was that
foulest of criminals under trust, a sheep-eater; and it

was from the maculation of sheep's blood that he had
come so far to cleanse himself in the pool behind Kirk
Yetton.

A trade that touches nature, one that lies at the
foundations of life, in which we have all had ancestors
employed, so that on a hint of it ancestral memories
revive, lends itself to literary use, vocal or written.
The fortune of a tale lies not alone in the skill of him
that writes, but as much, perhaps, in the inherited
experience of him who reads; and when I hear with a
particular thrill of things that I have never done or
seen, it is one of that innumerable army of my ancestors
rejoicing in past deeds. Thus novels begin to touch not
the fine *dilettanti* but the gross mass of mankind, when
they leave off to speak of parlours and shades of manner and still-born niceties of motive, and begin to deal
with fighting, sailoring, adventure, death, or child-
birth; and thus ancient outdoor crafts and occupations,
whether Mr. Hardy wields the shepherd's crook or
Count Tolstoi swings the scythe, lift romance into a
near neighbourhood with epic. These aged things have
on them the dew of man's morning; they lie near, not
so much to us, the semi-artificial flowerets, as to the
trunk and aboriginal taproot of the race. A thousand
interests spring up in the process of the ages, and a
thousand perish; that is now an eccentricity or a lost
art which was once the fashion of an empire; and those
only are perennial matters that rouse us to-day, and
that roused men in all epochs of the past. There is a
certain critic, not indeed of execution but of matter,
whom I dare be known to set before the best: a certain
low-browed, hairy gentleman, at first a percher in the
fork of trees, next (as they relate) a dweller in caves,
and whom I think I see squatting in cave-mouths, of a
pleasant afternoon, to munch his berries—his wife,
that accomplished lady, squatting by his side: his name
I never heard, but he is often described as Probably
Arboreal, which may serve for recognition. Each has
his own tree of ancestors, but at the top of all sits

Probably Arboreal; in all our veins there run some minims of his old, wild, tree-top blood; our civilised nerves still tingle with his rude terrors and pleasures; and to that which would have moved our common ancestor, all must obediently thrill.

We have not so far to climb to come to shepherds; and it may be I had one for an ascendant who has largely moulded me. But yet I think I owe my taste for that hillside business rather to the art and interest of John Todd. He it was that made it live for me, as the artist can make all things live. It was through him the simple strategy of massing sheep upon a snowy evening, with its attendant scampering of earnest, shaggy aides-de-camp, was an affair that I never wearied of seeing, and that I never weary of recalling to mind: the shadow of the night darkening on the hills, inscrutable black blots of snow shower moving here and there like night already come, huddles of yellow sheep and dartings of black dogs upon the snow, a bitter air that took you by the throat, unearthly harpings of the wind along the moors; and for centre-piece to all these features and influences, John winding up the brae, keeping his captain's eye upon all sides, and breaking, ever and again, into a spasm of bellowing that seemed to make the evening bleaker. It is thus that I still see him in my mind's eye, perched on a hump of the declivity not far from Halkerside, his staff in airy flourish, his great voice taking hold upon the hills and echoing terror to the lowlands; I, meanwhile, standing somewhat back, until the fit should be over, and, with a pinch of snuff, my friend relapse into his easy, even conversation.

VII

THE MANSE

I HAVE named, among many rivers that make music in my memory, that dirty Water of Leith. Often and often I desire to look upon it again; and the choice of a point of view is easy to me. It should be at a certain water-door, embowered in shrubbery. The river is there dammed back for the service of the flour-mill just below, so that it lies deep and darkling, and the sand slopes into brown obscurity with a glint of gold; and it has but newly been recruited by the borrowings of the snuff-mill just above, and these, tumbling merrily in, shake the pool to its black heart, fill it with drowsy eddies, and set the curded froth of many other mills solemnly steering to and fro upon the surface. Or so it was when I was young; for change, and the masons, and the pruning-knife, have been busy; and if I could hope to repeat a cherished experience, it must be on many and impossible conditions. I must choose, as well as the point of view, a certain moment in my growth, so that the scale may be exaggerated, and the trees on the steep opposite side may seem to climb to heaven, and the sand by the water-door, where I am standing, seem as low as Styx. And I must choose the season also, so that the valley may be brimmed like a cup with sunshine and the songs of birds—and the year of grace, so that when I turn to leave the riverside I may find the old manse and its inhabitants unchanged.

It was a place in that time like no other: the garden cut into provinces by a great hedge of beech, and overlooked by the church and the terrace of the churchyard, where the tombstones were thick, and after nightfall " spunkies " might be seen to dance at least by children; flower-plots lying warm in sunshine; laurels and the great yew making elsewhere a pleasing horror of shade; the smell of water rising from all round, with an added tang of paper-mills; the sound of water everywhere, and the sound of mills—the wheel and the dam singing their alternate strain; the birds on every bush and from every corner of the overhanging woods pealing out their notes until the air throbbed with them; and in the midst of this, the manse. I see it, by the standard of my childish stature, as a great and roomy house. In truth, it was not so large as I supposed, nor yet so convenient, and, standing where it did, it is difficult to suppose that it was healthful. Yet a large family of stalwart sons and tall daughters was housed and reared, and came to man and womanhood in that nest of little chambers; so that the face of the earth was peppered with the children of the manse, and letters with outlandish stamps became familiar to the local postman, and the walls of the little chambers brightened with the wonders of the East. The dullest could see this was a house that had a pair of hands in divers foreign places: a well-beloved house—its image fondly dwelt on by many travellers.

Here lived an ancestor of mine, who was a herd of men. I read him, judging with older criticism the report of childish observation, as a man of singular simplicity of nature; unemotional, and hating the display of what he felt; standing contented on the old ways; a lover of his life and innocent habits to the end. We children admired him: partly for his beautiful face and silver hair, for none more than children are concerned for beauty and, above all, for beauty in the old; partly for the solemn light in which we beheld him once a week, the observed of all observers, in the pulpit. But his strictness and distance, the effect, I now fancy, of old age, slow blood, and settled habit, oppressed us with a kind of terror. When not abroad he sat much alone, writing sermons or letters to his scattered family in a dark and cold room with a library of bloodless books—or so they seemed in those days, although I have some of them now on my own shelves and like well enough to read them; and these lonely hours wrapped him in the greater gloom for our imaginations. But the study had a redeeming grace in many Indian pictures, gaudily coloured and dear to young eyes. I cannot depict (for I have no such passions now) the greed with which I beheld them; and when I was once sent in to say a psalm to my grandfather, I went, quaking indeed with fear, but at the same time glowing with hope that, if I said it well, he might reward me with an Indian picture.

> " Thy foot He'll not let slide, nor will
> He slumber that thee keeps,"

it ran: a strange conglomerate of the unpronounceable, a sad model to set in childhood before one who was himself to be a versifier, and a task in recitation that really merited reward. And I must suppose the old man thought so too, and was either touched or amused by the performance; for he took me in his arms with most unwonted tenderness, and kissed me, and gave me a little kindly sermon for my psalm; so that, for that day, we were clerk and parson. I was struck by this reception into so tender a surprise that I forgot my disappointment. And indeed the hope was one of those that childhood forges for a pastime, and with no design upon reality. Nothing was more unlikely than that my grandfather should strip himself of one of those pictures, love-gifts and reminders of his absent sons; nothing more unlikely than that he should bestow it upon me. He had no idea of spoiling children, leaving all that to my aunt; he had fared hard himself, and blubbered under the rod in the last century; and his ways were still Spartan for the young. The last word I heard upon his lips was in this Spartan key. He had overwalked in the teeth of an east wind, and was now near the end of his many days. He sat by the dining-room fire, with his white hair, pale face, and bloodshot eyes, a somewhat awful figure; and my aunt had given him a dose of our good old Scots medicine, Dr. Gregory's powder. Now that remedy, as the work of a near kinsman of Rob Roy himself, may have a savour of romance for the imagination; but it comes uncouthly to the palate. The old gentleman had taken it with a wry face; and that being accomplished, sat with perfect simplicity, like a child's, munching a " barley-sugar kiss." But when my aunt, having the canister open in her hands, proposed to let me share in the sweets, he interfered at once. I had had no Gregory; then I should have no barley-sugar kiss: so he decided with a touch of irritation. And just then the phaeton coming opportunely to the kitchen door—for such was our unlordly fashion—I was taken for the last time from the presence of my grandfather.

Now I often wonder what I have inherited from this old minister. I must suppose, indeed, that he was fond of preaching sermons, and so am I, though I never heard it maintained that either of us loved to hear them. He sought health in his youth in the Isle of Wight, and I have sought it in both hemispheres; but whereas he found and kept it, I am still on the quest. He was a great lover of Shakespeare, whom he read aloud, I have been told, with taste; well, I love my Shakespeare also, and am persuaded I can read him well, though I own I never have been told so. He made embroidery, designing his own patterns, and in that kind of work I never made anything but a kettle-holder in Berlin wool, and an odd garter of knitting, which was as black as the chimney before I had done with it. He loved port, and nuts, and porter; and so do I, but they agreed better with my grandfather, which seems to me a breach of contract. He had chalk-stones in his fingers; and these, in good time, I may possibly inherit, but I would much rather have inherited his noble presence. Try as I please, I cannot join myself on with the reverend doctor; and all the while, no doubt, and even as I write the phrase, he moves in my blood, and whispers words to me, and sits efficient in the very knot and centre of my being. In his garden, as I played there, I learned the love of mills—or had I an ancestor a miller?—and a kindness for the neighbourhood of graves, as homely things not without their poetry—or had I an ancestor a sexton? But what of the garden where he played himself?—for that, too, was a scene of my education. Some part of me played there in the eighteenth century, and ran races under the green avenue at Pilrig; some part of me trudged up Leith Walk, which was still a country place, and sat on the High School benches, and was thrashed, perhaps, by Dr. Adam. The house where I spent my youth was not yet thought upon; but we made holiday parties among the cornfields on its site, and ate strawberries and cream near by at a gardener's. All this I had forgotten; only my grandfather remembered and once reminded me. I have forgotten, too, how we grew up, and took orders, and went to our first Ayrshire parish, and fell in love with and married a daughter of Burns's Dr. Smith— "Smith opens out his cauld harangues." I have forgotten, but I was there all the same, and heard stories of Burns at first hand.

And there is a thing stranger than all that; for this *homunculus* or part-man of mine that walked about the eighteenth century with Dr. Balfour in his youth, was in the way of meeting other *homunculi* or part-men, in the persons of my other ancestors. These were of a lower order, and doubtless we looked down upon them duly. But as I went to college with Dr. Balfour, I may have seen the lamp and oil man taking down the shutters from his shop beside the Tron—we may have had a rabbit-hutch or a bookshelf made for us by a certain carpenter in I know not what wynd of the old, smoky city; or, upon some holiday excursion, we may have looked into the windows of a cottage in a flower-garden and seen a certain weaver plying his

shuttle. And these were all kinsmen of mine upon the
other side; and from the eyes of the lamp and oil man
one-half of my unborn father, and one-quarter of myself, looked out upon us as we went by to college.
Nothing of all this would cross the mind of the young
student, as he posted up the Bridges with trim, stock-
inged legs, in that city of cocked hats and good Scots
still unadulterated. It would not cross his mind that
he should have a daughter; and the lamp and oil man,
just then beginning, by a not unnatural metastasis, to
bloom into a lighthouse-engineer, should have a grandson; and that these two, in the fulness of time, should
wed; and some portion of that student himself should
survive yet a year or two longer in the person of their
child.

But our ancestral adventures are beyond even the
arithmetic of fancy; and it is the chief recommendation
of long pedigrees, that we can follow backward the
careers of our *homunculi* and be reminded of our
antenatal lives. Our conscious years are but a moment
in the history of the elements that build us. Are you
a bank-clerk, and do you live at Peckham? It was
not always so. And though to-day I am only a man
of letters, either tradition errs or I was present when
there landed at St. Andrews a French barber-surgeon,
to tend the health and the beard of the great Cardinal
Beaton; I have shaken a spear in the Debatable
Land and shouted the slogan of the Elliots; I was
present when a skipper, plying from Dundee, smuggled
Jacobites to France after the '15; I was in a West India
merchant's office, perhaps next door to Bailie Nicol
Jarvie's, and managed the business of a plantation in
St. Kitt's; I was with my engineer-grandfather (the son
in-law of the lamp and oil man) when he sailed north
about Scotland on the famous cruise that gave us the
Pirate and the *Lord of the Isles;* I was with him, too,
on the Bell Rock, in the fog, when the *Smeaton* had
drifted from her moorings, and the Aberdeen men, pick
in hand, had seized upon the only boats, and he must

stoop and lap sea-water before his tongue could utter audible words; and once more with him when the Bell Rock beacon took a " thrawe," and his workmen fled into the tower, then nearly finished, and he sat un-moved reading in his Bible—or affecting to read—till one after another slunk back with confusion of coun-tenance to their engineer. Yes, parts of me have seen life, and met adventures, and sometimes met them well. And away in the still cloudier past, the threads that make me up can be traced by fancy into the bosoms of thousands and millions of ascendants: Picts who rallied round Macbeth and the old (and highly preferable) system of descent by females, fleërs from before the legions of Agricola, marchers in Pannonian morasses, star-gazers on Chaldæan plateaus; and, fur-thest of all, what face is this that fancy can see peering through the disparted branches? What sleeper in green tree-tops, what muncher of nuts, concludes my pedi-gree? Probably Arboreal in his habits. . . .

And I know not which is the more strange, that I should carry about with me some fibres of my minister-grandfather; or that in him, as he sat in his cool study, grave, reverend, contented gentleman, there was an aboriginal frisking of the blood that was not his; tree-top memories, like undeveloped negatives, lay dormant in his mind; tree-top instincts awoke and were trod down; and Probably Arboreal (scarce to be distin-guished from a monkey) gambolled and chattered in the brain of the old divine.

VIII

MEMOIRS OF AN ISLET

THOSE who try to be artists use, time after time, the matter of their recollections, setting and resetting little coloured memories of men and scenes, rigging up (it may be) some especial friend in the attire of a buccaneer, and decreeing armies to manœuvre, or murder to be done, on the playground of their youth. But the memories are a fairy gift which cannot be worn out in using. After a dozen services in various tales, the little sunbright pictures of the past still shine in the mind's eye with not a lineament defaced, not a tint impaired. *Glück und Unglück wird Gesang*, if Goethe pleases; yet only by endless avatars, the original reembodying after each. So that a writer, in time, begins to wonder at the perdurable life of these impressions; begins, perhaps, to fancy that he wrongs them when he weaves them in with fiction; and looking back on them with ever-growing kindness, puts them at last, substantive jewels, in a setting of their own.

One or two of these pleasant spectres I think I have laid. I used one but the other day: a little eyot of dense, freshwater sand, where I once waded deep in butterburrs, delighting to hear the song of the river on both sides, and to tell myself that I was indeed and at last upon an island. Two of my puppets lay there a summer's day, hearkening to the shearers at work in riverside fields and to the drums of the gray old garrison upon the neighbouring hill. And this was, I think, done rightly: the place was rightly peopled—and now belongs not to me but to my puppets—for a time at least. In time, perhaps, the puppets will grow faint;

the original memory swim up instant as ever; and I
shall once more lie in bed, and see the little sandy isle
in Allan Water as it is in nature, and the child (that
once was me) wading there in butterburrs; and wonder
at the instancy and virgin freshness of that memory;
and be pricked again, in season and out of season, by
the desire to weave it into art.

There is another isle in my collection, the memory of
which besieges me. I put a whole family there, in one
of my tales; and later on, threw upon its shores, and
condemned to several days of rain and shellfish on its
tumbled boulders, the hero of another. The ink is not
yet faded; the sound of the sentences is still in my
mind's ear; and I am under a spell to write of that
island again.

I

The little isle of Earraid lies close in to the south-
west corner of the Ross of Mull: the sound of Iona on
one side, across which you may see the isle and church
of Columba; the open sea to the other, where you
shall be able to mark, on a clear, surfy day, the breakers
running white on many sunken rocks. I first saw it,
or first remember seeing it, framed in the round bull's-
eye of a cabin port, the sea lying smooth along its
shores like the waters of a lake, the colourless, clear
light of the early morning making plain its heathery and
rocky hummocks. There stood upon it, in these days, a
single rude house of uncemented stones, approached
by a pier of wreckwood. It must have been very early,
for it was then summer, and in summer, in that latitude, day scarcely withdraws; but even at that hour
the house was making a sweet smoke of peats which
came to me over the bay, and the bare-legged daughters
of the cotter were wading by the pier. The same day
we visited the shores of the isle in the ship's boats;
rowed deep into Fiddler's Hole, sounding as we went;

and having taken stock of all possible accommodation, pitched on the northern inlet as the scene of operations. For it was no accident that had brought the lighthouse steamer to anchor in the Bay of Earraid. Fifteen miles away to seaward, a certain black rock stood environed by the Atlantic rollers, the outpost of the Torran reefs. Here was a tower to be built, and a star lighted, for the conduct of seamen. But as the rock was small, and hard of access, and far from land, the work would be one of years; and my father was now looking for a shore station, where the stones might be quarried and dressed, the men live, and the tender, with some degree of safety, lie at anchor.

I saw Earraid next from the stern-thwart of an Iona lugger, Sam Bough and I sitting there cheek by jowl, with our feet upon our baggage, in a beautiful, clear, northern summer eve. And behold! there was now a pier of stone, there were rows of sheds, railways, travelling-cranes, a street of cottages, an iron house for the resident engineer, wooden bothies for the men, a stage where the courses of the tower were put together experimentally, and behind the settlement a great gash in the hillside where granite was quarried. In the bay, the steamer lay at her moorings. All day long there hung about the place the music of chinking tools; and even in the dead of night, the watchman carried his lantern to and fro in the dark settlement, and could light the pipe of any midnight muser. It was, above all, strange to see Earraid on the Sunday, when the sound of the tools ceased and there fell a crystal quiet. All about the green compound men would be sauntering in their Sunday's best, walking with those lax joints of the reposing toiler, thoughtfully smoking, talking small, as if in honour of the stillness, or hearkening to the wailing of the gulls. And it was strange to see our Sabbath services, held, as they were, in one of the bothies, with Mr. Brebner reading at a table, and the congregation perched about in the double tier of sleeping bunks; and to hear the singing of the psalms, " the chapters," the inevitable Spurgeon's sermon, and the old, eloquent lighthouse prayer.

In fine weather, when by the spy-glass on the hill the sea was observed to run low upon the reef, there would be a sound of preparation in the very early morning; and before the sun had risen from behind Ben More, the tender would steam out of the bay. Over fifteen sea-miles of the great blue Atlantic rollers she ploughed her way, trailing at her tail a brace of wallowing stone-lighters. The open ocean widened upon either board, and the hills of the mainland began to go down on the horizon, before she came to her unhomely destination, and lay-to at last where the rock clapped its black head above the swell, with the tall iron barrack on its spider legs, and the truncated tower, and the cranes waving their arms, and the smoke of the engine-fire rising in the mid-sea. An ugly reef is this of the Dhu Heartach; no pleasant assemblage of shelves, and pools, and creeks, about which a child might play for a whole summer without weariness, like the Bell Rock or the Skerryvore, but one oval nodule of black-trap, sparsely bedabbled with an inconspicuous fucus, and alive in every crevice with a dingy insect between a slater and a bug. No other life was there but that of sea-birds, and of the sea itself, that here ran like a mill-race, and growled about the outer reef for ever, and ever and again, in the calmest weather, roared and spouted on the rock itself. Times were different upon Dhu Heartach when it blew, and the night fell dark, and the neighbour lights of Skerryvore and Rhu-val were quenched in fog, and the men sat prisoned high up in their iron drum, that then resounded with the lashing of the sprays. Fear sat with them in their sea-beleaguered dwelling; and the colour changed in anxious faces when some greater billow struck the barrack, and its pillars quivered and sprang under the blow. It was then that the foreman builder, Mr. Goodwillie, whom I see before me still in his rock-habit of undecipherable rags, would get his fiddle down and strike up human minstrelsy amid

the music of the storm. But it was in sunshine only
that I saw Dhu Heartach; and it was in sunshine, or
the yet lovelier summer afterglow, that the steamer
would return to Earraid, ploughing an enchanted sea;
the obedient lighters, relieved of their deck cargo, rid-
ing in her wake more quietly; and the steersman upon
each, as she rose on the long swell, standing tall and
dark against the shining west.

II

But it was in Earraid itself that I delighted chiefly.
The lighthouse settlement scarce encroached beyond its
fences; over the top of the first brae the ground was all
virgin, the world all shut out, the face of things unchanged by any of man's doings. Here was no living
presence, save for the limpets on the rocks, for some
old, gray, rain-beaten ram that I might rouse out of a
ferny den betwixt two boulders, or for the haunting and
the piping of the gulls. It was older than man; it
was found so by incoming Celts and seafaring Norsemen, and Columba's priests. The earthy savour of the
bog plants, the rude disorder of the boulders, the inimitable seaside brightness of the air, the brine and the
iodine, the lap of the billows among the weedy reefs,
the sudden springing up of a great run of dashing surf
along the sea-front of the isle, all that I saw and felt
my predecessors must have seen and felt with scarce a
difference. I steeped myself in open air and in past
ages.

" Delightful would it be to me to be in *Uchd Ailiun*
        On the pinnacle of a rock,
    That I might often see
        The face of the ocean;
    That I might hear the song of the wonderful birds,
        Source of happiness;
    That I might hear the thunder of the crowding waves
        Upon the rocks:
    At times at work without compulsion—

> This would be delightful;
> At times plucking dulse from the rocks;
> At times at fishing."

So, about the next island of Iona, sang Columba himself twelve hundred years before. And so might I have
sung of Earraid.

And all the while I was aware that this life of sea-
bathing and sun-burning was for me but a holiday. In
that year cannon were roaring for days together on
French battlefields; and I would sit in my isle (I call
it mine, after the use of lovers) and think upon the war,
and the loudness of these far-away battles, and the
pain of the men's wounds, and the weariness of their
marching. And I would think too of that other war
which is as old as mankind, and is indeed the life of
man: the unsparing war, the grinding slavery of competition; the toil of seventy years, dear-bought bread,
precarious honour, the perils and pitfalls, and the poor
rewards. It was a long look forward; the future sum-
moned me as with trumpet calls, it warned me back as
with a voice of weeping and beseeching; and I thrilled
and trembled on the brink of life, like a childish bather
on the beach.

There was another young man on Earraid in these
days, and we were much together, bathing, clambering
on the boulders, trying to sail a boat and spinning round
instead in the oily whirlpools of the roost. But the
most part of the time we spoke of the great uncharted
desert of our future; wondering together what should
there befall us; hearing with surprise the sound of our
own voices in the empty vestibule of youth. As far,
and as hard, as it seemed then to look forward to the
grave, so far it seems now to look backward upon these
emotions; so hard to recall justly that loath submission, as of the sacrificial bull, with which we stooped
our necks under the yoke of destiny. I met my old
companion but the other day; I cannot tell of course
what he was thinking; but, upon my part, I was
wondering to see us both so much at home, and so

composed and sedentary in the world; and how much we had gained, and how much we had lost, to attain to that composure; and which had been upon the whole our best estate: when we sat there prating sensibly like men of some experience, or when we shared our timorous and hopeful counsels in a western islet.

IX

THOMAS STEVENSON

CIVIL ENGINEER

THE death of Thomas Stevenson will mean not very
much to the general reader. His service to mankind took on forms of which the public knows little
and understands less. He came seldom to London, and
then only as a task, remaining always a stranger and
a convinced provincial; putting up for years at the
same hotel where his father had gone before him; faithful for long to the same restaurant, the same church,
and the same theatre, chosen simply for propinquity;
steadfastly refusing to dine out. He had a circle of his
own, indeed, at home; few men were more beloved in
Edinburgh, where he breathed an air that pleased him;
and wherever he went, in railway carriages or hotel
smoking-rooms, his strange, humorous vein of talk,
and his transparent honesty, raised him up friends and
admirers. But to the general public and the world of
London, except about the parliamentary committee-
rooms, he remained unknown. All the time, his lights
were in every part of the world, guiding the mariner;
his firm were consulting engineers to the Indian, the
New Zealand, and the Japanese Lighthouse Boards, so
that Edinburgh was a world centre for that branch of
applied science; in Germany, he had been called " the
Nestor of lighthouse illumination "; even in France,
where his claims were long denied, he was at last, on the
occasion of the late Exposition, recognised and medalled.
And to show by one instance the inverted nature of his
reputation, comparatively small at home, yet filling the

world, a friend of mine was this winter on a visit to the Spanish main, and was asked by a Peruvian if he "knew Mr. Stevenson the author, because his works were much esteemed in Peru?" My friend supposed the reference was to the writer of tales; but the Peruvian had never heard of *Dr. Jekyll;* what he had in his eye, what was esteemed in Peru, were the volumes of the engineer.

Thomas Stevenson was born at Edinburgh in the year 1818, the grandson of Thomas Smith, first engineer to the Board of Northern Lights, son of Robert Stevenson, brother of Alan and David; so that his nephew, David Alan Stevenson, joined with him at the time of his death in the engineership, is the sixth of the family who has held, successively or conjointly, that office. The Bell Rock, his father's great triumph, was finished before he was born; but he served under his brother Alan in the building of Skerryvore, the noblest of all extant deep-sea lights; and, in conjunction with his brother David, he added two—the Chickens and Dhu Heartach—to that small number of man's extreme outposts in the ocean. Of shore lights, the two brothers last named erected no fewer than twenty-seven; of beacons,* about twenty-five. Many harbours were successfully carried out: one, the harbour of Wick, the chief disaster of my father's life, was a failure; the sea proved too strong for man's arts; and after expedients hitherto unthought of, and on a scale hyper-cyclopean, the work must be deserted, and now stands a ruin in that bleak, God-forsaken bay, ten miles from John-o'-Groat's. In the improvement of rivers the brothers were likewise in a large way of practice over both England and Scotland, nor had any British engineer anything approaching their experience.

It was about this nucleus of his professional labours that all my father's scientific inquiries and inventions

---

* In Dr. Murray's admirable new dictionary I have remarked a flaw *sub voce* Beacon. In its express, technical sense, a beacon may be defined as "a founded, artificial sea-mark, not lighted."

centred; these proceeded from, and acted back upon, his daily business. Thus it was as a harbour engineer that he became interested in the propagation and reduction of waves; a difficult subject in regard to which he has left behind him much suggestive matter and some valuable approximate results. Storms were his sworn adversaries, and it was through the study of storms that he approached that of meteorology at large. Many who knew him not otherwise, knew—perhaps have in their gardens—his louvre-boarded screen for instruments. But the great achievement of his life was, of course, in optics as applied to lighthouse illumination. Fresnel had done much; Fresnel had settled the fixed light apparatus on a principle that still seems unimprovable; and when Thomas Stevenson stepped in and brought to a comparable perfection the revolving light, a not unnatural jealousy and much painful controversy rose in France. It had its hour; and, as I have told already, even in France it has blown by. Had it not, it would have mattered the less, since all through his life my father continued to justify his claim by fresh advances. New apparatus for lights in new situations was continually being designed with the same unwearied search after perfection, the same nice ingenuity of means; and though the holophotal revolving light perhaps still remains his most elegant contrivance, it is difficult to give it the palm over the much later condensing system, with its thousand possible modifications. The number and the value of these improvements entitle their author to the name of one of mankind's benefactors. In all parts of the world a safer landfall awaits the mariner. Two things must be said: and, first, that Thomas Stevenson was no mathematician. Natural shrewdness, a sentiment of optical laws, and a great intensity of consideration led him to just conclusions; but to calculate the necessary formulæ for the instruments he had conceived was often beyond him, and he must fall back on the help of others, notably on that of his cousin and lifelong intimate friend, *emeritus* Professor Swan,* of St. Andrews, and his later friend, Professor P. G. Tait. It is a curious enough circumstance, and a great encouragement to others, that a man so ill equipped should have succeeded in one of the most abstract and arduous walks of applied science. The second remark is one that applies to the whole family, and only particularly to Thomas Stevenson from the great number and importance of his inventions: holding as the Stevensons did a Government appointment, they regarded their original work as something due already to the nation, and none of them has ever taken out a patent. It is another cause of the comparative obscurity of the name: for a patent not only brings in money, it infallibly spreads reputation; and my father's instruments enter anonymously into a hundred light-rooms, and are passed anonymously over in a hundred reports, where the least considerable patent would stand out and tell its author's story.

But the life-work of Thomas Stevenson remains; what we have lost, what we now rather try to recall, is the friend and companion. He was a man of a somewhat antique strain: with a blended sternness and softness that was wholly Scottish and at first somewhat bewildering; with a profound essential melancholy of disposition and (what often accompanies it) the most humorous geniality in company; shrewd and childish; passionately attached, passionately prejudiced; a man of many extremes, many faults of temper, and no very stable foothold for himself among life's troubles. Yet he was a wise adviser; many men, and these not inconsiderable, took counsel with him habitually. "I sat at his feet," writes one of these, "when I asked his advice, and when the broad brow was set in thought and the firm mouth said his say, I always knew that no man could add to the worth of the conclusion." He had excellent taste, though whimsical and partial; collected old furniture and delighted specially in sun-

* William Swan, Professor of Natural Philosophy in the University of St. Andrews.

flowers long before the days of Mr. Wilde; took a lasting pleasure in prints and pictures; was a devout admirer of Thomson of Duddingston at a time when few shared the taste; and though he read little, was constant to his favourite books. He had never any Greek; Latin he happily re-taught himself after he had left school, where he was a mere consistent idler: happily, I say, for Lactantius, Vossius, and Cardinal Bona were his chief authors. The first he must have read for twenty years uninterruptedly, keeping it near him in his study, and carrying it in his bag on journeys. Another old theologian, Brown of Wamphray, was often in his hands. When he was indisposed, he had two books, *Guy Mannering* and *The Parent's Assistant*, of which he never wearied. He was a strong Conservative, or, as he preferred to call himself, a Tory; except in so far as his views were modified by a hot-headed chivalrous sentiment for women. He was actually in favour of a marriage law under which any woman might have a divorce for the asking, and no man on any ground whatever; and the same sentiment found another expression in a Magdalen Mission in Edinburgh, founded and largely supported by himself. This was but one of the many channels of his public generosity; his private was equally unstrained. The Church of Scotland, of which he held the doctrines (though in a sense of his own) and to which he bore a clansman's loyalty, profited often by his time and money; and though, from a morbid sense of his own unworthiness, he would never consent to be an office-bearer, his advice was often sought, and he served the Church on many committees. What he perhaps valued highest in his work were his contributions to the defence of Christianity; one of which, in particular, was praised by Hutchinson Stirling and reprinted at the request of Professor Crawford.

His sense of his own unworthiness I have called morbid; morbid, too, were his sense of the fleetingness of life and his concern for death. He had never accepted the conditions of man's life or his own character; and his inmost thoughts were ever tinged with the Celtic melancholy. Cases of conscience were sometimes grievous to him, and that delicate employment of a scientific witness cost him many qualms. But he found respite from these troublesome humours in his work, in his lifelong study of natural science, in the society of those he loved, and in his daily walks, which now would carry him far into the country with some congenial friend, and now keep him dangling about the town from one old book-shop to another, and scraping romantic acquaintance with every dog that passed. His talk, compounded of so much sterling sense and so much freakish humour, and clothed in language so apt, droll, and emphatic, was a perpetual delight to all who knew him before the clouds began to settle on his mind. His use of language was both just and picturesque; and when at the beginning of his illness he began to feel the ebbing of this power, it was strange and painful to hear him reject one word after another as inadequate, and at length desist from the search and leave his phrase unfinished rather than finish it without propriety. It was perhaps another Celtic trait that his affections and emotions, passionate as these were, and liable to passionate ups and downs, found the most eloquent expression both in words and gestures. Love, anger, and indignation shone through him and broke forth in imagery, like what we read of Southern races. For all these emotional extremes, and in spite of the melancholy ground of his character, he had upon the whole a happy life; nor was he less fortunate in his death, which at the last came to him unaware.

X

TALK AND TALKERS

"Sir, we had a good talk."—JOHNSON.
"As we must account for every idle word, so we must for every idle silence."—FRANKLIN.

I

THERE can be no fairer ambition than to excel in talk; to be affable, gay, ready, clear, and welcome; to have a fact, a thought, or an illustration, pat to every subject; and not only to cheer the flight of time among our intimates, but bear our part in that great international congress, always sitting, where public wrongs are first declared, public errors first corrected, and the course of public opinion shaped, day by day, a little nearer to the right. No measure comes before Parliament but it has been long ago prepared by the grand jury of the talkers; no book is written that has not been largely composed by their assistance. Literature in many of its branches is no other than the shadow of good talk; but the imitation falls far short of the original in life, freedom, and effect. There are always two to a talk, giving and taking, comparing experience and according conclusions. Talk is fluid, tentative, continually " in further search and progress "; while written words remain fixed, become idols even to the writer, found wooden dogmatisms, and preserve flies of obvious error in the amber of the truth. Last and chief, while literature, gagged with linsey-woolsey, can only deal with a fraction of the life of man, talk goes fancy free and may call a spade a spade. Talk has none of the freezing immunities of the pulpit. It cannot, even if it would, become merely æsthetic or merely classical like literature. A jest intervenes, the solemn humbug is dissolved in laughter, and speech runs forth out of the contemporary groove into the open fields of nature, cheery and cheering, like schoolboys out of school. And it is in talk alone that we can learn our period and ourselves. In short, the first duty of a man is to speak; that is his chief business in this world; and talk, which is the harmonious speech of two or more, is by far the most accessible of pleasures. It costs nothing in money; it is all profit; it completes our education, founds and fosters our friendships, and can be enjoyed at any age and in almost any state of health.

The spice of life is battle; the friendliest relations are still a kind of contest; and if we would not forego all that is valuable in our lot, we must continually face some other person, eye to eye, and wrestle a fall whether in love or enmity. It is still by force of body, or power of character or intellect, that we attain to worthy pleasures. Men and women contend for each other in the lists of love, like rival mesmerists; the active and adroit decide their challenges in the sports of the body; and the sedentary sit down to chess or conversation. All sluggish and pacific pleasures are, to the same degree, solitary and selfish; and every durable bond between human beings is founded in or heightened by some element of competition. Now, the relation that has the least root in matter is undoubtedly that airy one of friendship; and hence, I suppose, it is that good talk most commonly arises among friends. Talk is, indeed, both the scene and instrument of friendship. It is in talk alone that the friends can measure strength, and enjoy that amicable counter-assertion of personality which is the gauge of relations and the sport of life.

A good talk is not to be had for the asking. Humours must first be accorded in a kind of overture or prologue; hour, company and circumstance be suited; and then, at a fit juncture, the subject, the quarry of

two heated minds, spring up like a deer out of the wood.
Not that the talker had any of the hunter's pride,
though he has all and more than all his ardour. The
genuine artist follows the stream of conversation as an
angler follows the windings of a brook, not dallying
where he fails to " kill." He trusts implicitly to hazard;
and he is rewarded by continual variety, continual
pleasure, and those changing prospects of the truth that
are the best of education. There is nothing in a subject,
so called, that we should regard it as an idol, or follow
it beyond the promptings of desire. Indeed, there are
few subjects; and so far as they are truly talkable, more
than the half of them may be reduced to three: that I
am I, that you are you, and that there are other people
dimly understood to be not quite the same as either.
Wherever talk may range, it still runs half the time on
these eternal lines. The theme being set, each plays on
himself as on an instrument; asserts and justifies himself; ransacks his brain for instances and opinions, and
brings them forth new-minted, to his own surprise and
the admiration of his adversary. All natural talk is a
festival of ostentation; and by the laws of the game
each accepts and fans the vanity of the other. It is
from that reason that we venture to lay ourselves so
open, that we dare to be so warmly eloquent, and that
we swell in each other's eyes to such a vast proportion.
For talkers, once launched, begin to overflow the limits
of their ordinary selves, tower up to the height of their
secret pretensions, and give themselves out for the
heroes, brave, pious, musical, and wise, that in their most
shining moments they aspire to be. So they weave for
themselves with words and for a while inhabit a palace
of delights, temple at once and theatre, where they fill
the round of the world's dignities, and feast with the
gods, exulting in Kudos. And when the talk is over,
each goes his way, still flushed with vanity and admiration, still trailing clouds of glory; each declines
from the height of his ideal orgie, not in a moment, but
by slow declension. I remember, in the *entr'acte* of

an afternoon performance, coming forth into the sunshine in a beautiful green, gardened corner of a romantic city; and as I sat and smoked, the music moving in my blood, I seemed to sit there and evaporate
The Flying Dutchman (for it was that I had been
hearing) with a wonderful sense of life, warmth, well-
being, and pride; and the noises of the city, voices,
bells, and marching feet, fell together in my ears like a
symphonious orchestra. In the same way, the excitement of a good talk lives for a long while after in the
blood, the heart still hot within you, the brain still
simmering, and the physical earth swimming around
you with the colours of the sunset.

Natural talk, like ploughing, should turn up a large
surface of life, rather than dig mines into geological
strata. Masses of experience, anecdote, incident, cross-
lights, quotation, historical instances, the whole flotsam
and jetsam of two minds forced in and in upon the
matter in hand from every point of the compass, and
from every degree of mental elevation and abasement—
these are the material with which talk is fortified, the
food on which the talkers thrive. Such argument as is
proper to the exercise should still be brief and seizing.
Talk should proceed by instances; by the apposite, not
the expository. It should keep close along the lines of
humanity, near the bosoms and businesses of men, at
the level where history, fiction, and experience intersect
and illuminate each other. I am I, and you are you,
with all my heart; but conceive how these lean propositions change and brighten when, instead of words, the
actual you and I sit cheek by jowl, the spirit housed in
the live body, and the very clothes uttering voices to
corroborate the story in the face. Not less surprising
is the change when we leave off to speak of generalities
—the bad, the good, the miser, and all the characters of
Theophrastus—and call up other men, by anecdote or
instance, in their very trick and feature; or trading on
a common knowledge, toss each other famous names,
still glowing with the hues of life. Communication is

no longer by words, but by the instancing of whole
biographies, epics, systems of philosophy, and epochs
of history, in bulk. That which is understood excels
that which is spoken in quantity and quality alike;
ideas thus figured and personified, change hands, as
we may say, like coin; and the speakers imply without effort the most obscure and intricate thoughts.
Strangers who have a large common ground of reading
will, for this reason, come the sooner to the grapple of
genuine converse. It they know Othello and Napoleon,
Consuelo and Clarissa Harlowe, Vautrin and Steenie
Steenson, they can leave generalities and begin at once
to speak by figures.

Conduct and art are the two subjects that arise most
frequently and that embrace the widest range of facts.
A few pleasures bear discussion for their own sake, but
only those which are most social or most radically human; and even these can only be discussed among their
devotees. A technicality is always welcome to the ex-
pert, whether in athletics, art, or law; I have heard the
best kind of talk on technicalities from such rare and
happy persons as both know and love their business. No
human being ever spoke of scenery for above two minutes at a time, which makes me suspect we hear too
much of it in literature. The weather is regarded as
the very nadir and scoff of conversational topics. And
yet the weather, the dramatic element in scenery, is
far more tractable in language, and far more human
both in import and suggestion than the stable features
of the landscape. Sailors and shepherds, and the people
generally of coast and mountain, talk well of it; and it
is often excitingly presented in literature. But the tendency of all living talk draws it back and back into the
common focus of humanity. Talk is a creature of the
street and market-place, feeding on gossip; and its last
resort is still in a discussion on morals. That is the
heroic form of gossip; heroic in virtue of its high pretensions; but still gossip because it turns on personal-
ities. You can keep no man long, nor Scotsman at all,

off moral, or theological discussion. These are to all the world what law is to lawyers; they are everybody's technicalities; the medium through which all consider life, and the dialect in which they express their judgments. I knew three young men who walked together daily for some two months in a solemn and beautiful forest and in cloudless summer weather; daily they talked with unabated zest, and yet scarce wandered that whole time beyond two subjects—theology and love. And perhaps neither a court of love nor an assembly of divines would have granted their premises or welcomed their conclusions.

Conclusions, indeed, are not often reached by talk any more than by private thinking. That is not the profit. The profit is in the exercise, and above all in the experience; for when we reason at large on any subject, we review our state and history in life. From time to time, however, and specially, I think, in talking art, talk becomes effective, conquering like war, widening the boundaries of knowledge like an exploration. A point arises; the question takes a problematical, a baffling, yet a likely air; the talkers begin to feel lively presentiments of some conclusion near at hand; towards this they strive with emulous ardour, each by his own path, and struggling for first utterance; and then one leaps upon the summit of that matter with a shout, and almost at the same moment the other is beside him; and behold they are agreed. Like enough, the progress is illusory, a mere cat's cradle having been wound and unwound out of words. But the sense of joint discovery is none the less giddy and inspiring. And in the life of the talker such triumphs, though imaginary, are neither few nor far apart; they are attained with speed and pleasure, in the hour of mirth; and by the nature of the process, they are always worthily shared.

There is a certain attitude, combative at once and defe.ential, eager to fight yet most averse to quarrel, which marks out at once the talkable man. It is not eloquence, not fairness, not obstinacy, but a certain proportion of all of these that I love to encounter in my amicable adversaries. They must not be pontiffs holding doctrine, but huntsmen questing after elements of truth. Neither must they be boys to be instructed, but fellow-teachers with whom I may wrangle and agree on equal terms. We must reach some solution, some shadow of consent; for without that, eager talk becomes a torture. But we do not wish to reach it cheaply, or quickly, or without the tussle and effort wherein pleasure lies.

The very best talker, with me, is one whom I shall call Spring-Heel'd Jack.* I say so, because I never knew any one who mingled so largely the possible ingredients of converse. In the Spanish proverb, the fourth man necessary to compound a salad, is a madman to mix it: Jack is that madman. I know not which is more remarkable; the insane lucidity of his conclusions, the humorous eloquence of his language, or his power of method, bringing the whole of life into the focus of the subject treated, mixing the conversational salad like a drunken god. He doubles like the serpent, changes and flashes like the shaken kaleidoscope, transmigrates bodily into the views of others, and so, in the twinkling of an eye and with a heady rapture, turns questions inside out and flings them empty before you on the ground, like a triumphant conjuror. It is my common practice when a piece of conduct puzzles me, to attack it in the presence of Jack with such grossness, such partiality, and such wearing iteration, as at length shall spur him up in its defence. In a moment he transmigrates, dons the required character, and with moonstruck philosophy justifies the act in question. I can fancy nothing to compare with the *vim* of these impersonations, the strange scale of language, flying from Shakespeare to Kant, and from Kant to Major Dyngwell—

> " As fast as a musician scatters sounds
> Out of an instrument——"

* Robert Alan Mowbray Stevenson (1847-1900).

the sudden, sweeping generalisations, the absurd irrelevant particularities, the wit, wisdom, folly, humour,
eloquence, and pathos, each startling in its kind, and
yet all luminous in the admired disorder of their combination. A talker of a different calibre, though be-
longing to the same school, is Burly.* Burly is a man
of a great presence; he commands a larger atmosphere,
gives the impression of a grosser mass of character than
most men. It has been said of him that his presence
could be felt in a room you entered blindfold; and
the same, I think, has been said of other powerful
constitutions condemned to much physical inaction.
There is something boisterous and piratic in Burly's
manner of talk which suits well enough with this impression. He will roar you down, he will bury his face
in his hands, he will undergo passions and revolt and
agony; and meanwhile his attitude of mind is really
both conciliatory and receptive; and after Pistol has
been out-Pistol'd, and the welkin rung for hours, you
begin to perceive a certain subsidence in these spring
torrents, points of agreement issue, and you end arm-in-
arm, and in a glow of mutual admiration. The outcry
only serves to make your final union the more unexpected and precious. Throughout there has been
perfect sincerity, perfect intelligence, a desire to hear
although not always to listen, and an unaffected eagerness to meet concessions. You have, with Burly, none
of the dangers that attend debate with Spring-Heel'd
Jack, who may at any moment turn his powers of
transmigration on yourself, create for you a view you
never held, and then furiously fall on you for holding it.
These, at least, are my two favourites, and both are
loud, copious, intolerant talkers. This argues that I
myself am in the same category; for if we love talking
at all, we love a bright, fierce adversary, who will hold
his ground, foot by foot, in much our own manner, sell
his attention dearly, and give us our full measure of the
dust and exertion of battle. Both these men can be

* W. E. Henley (1849-1903).

beat from a position, but it takes six hours to do it; a
high and hard adventure, worth attempting. With both
you can pass days in an enchanted country of the mind,
with people, scenery, and manners of its own; live a life
apart, more arduous, active, and glowing than any real
existence; and come forth again when the talk is over,
as out of a theatre or a dream, to find the east wind still
blowing and the chimney-pots of the old battered city
still around you. Jack has the far finer mind, Burly
the far more honest; Jack gives us the animated poetry,
Burly the romantic prose, of similar themes; the one
glances high like a meteor and makes a light in darkness; the other, with many changing hues of fire, burns
at the sea-level, like a conflagration; but both have the
same humour and artistic interests, the same un-
quenched ardour in pursuit, the same gusts of talk
and thunderclaps of contradiction.

Cockshot * is a different article, but vastly entertaining and has been meat and drink to me for many a long
evening. His manner is dry, brisk, and pertinacious,
and the choice of words not much. The point about him
is his extraordinary readiness and spirit. You can propound nothing but he has either a theory about it ready-
made, or will have one instantly on the stocks, and
proceed to lay its timbers and launch it in your
presence. " Let me see," he will say. " Give me a
moment, I *should* have some theory for that." A
blither spectacle than the vigour with which he sets
about the task, it were hard to fancy. He is possessed
by a demoniac energy, welding the elements for his life,
and bending ideas, as an athlete bends a horseshoe, with
a visible and lively effort. He has, in theorising, a compass, an art; what I would call the synthetic gusto;
something of a Herbert Spencer, who should see the fun
of the thing. You are not bound, and no more is he, to
place your faith in these brand-new opinions. But some
of them are right enough, durable even for life; and the
poorest serve for a cock-shy—as when idle people after

* Fleeming Jenkin (1833-85).

picnics, float a bottle on a pond and have an hour's
diversion ere it sinks. Whichever they are, serious
opinions or humours of the moment, he still defends
his ventures with indefatigable wit and spirit, hitting
savagely himself, but taking punishment like a man.
He knows and never forgets that people talk, first of
all, for the sake of talking; conducts himself in the ring,
to use the old slang, like a thorough " glutton," and
honestly enjoys a telling facer from his adversary.
Cockshot is bottled effervescency, the sworn foe of
sleep. Three-in-the-morning Cockshot, says a victim.
His talk is like the driest of all imaginable dry cham-
pagnes. Sleight of hand and inimitable quickness are
the qualities by which he lives. Athelred,* on the other
hand, presents you with the spectacle of a sincere and
somewhat slow nature thinking aloud. He is the most
unready man I ever knew to shine in conversation. You
may see him sometimes wrestle with a refractory jest
for a minute or two together, and perhaps fail to throw
it in the end. And there is something singularly engaging, often instructive, in the simplicity with which he
thus exposes the process as well as the result, the works
as well as the dial of the clock. Withal he has his hours
of inspiration. Apt words come to him as if by accident,
and, coming from deeper down, they smack the more
personally, they have the more of fine old crusted humanity, rich in sediment and humour. There are sayings of his in which he has stamped himself into the
very grain of the language; you would think he must
have worn the words next his skin and slept with them.
Yet it is not as a sayer of particular good things that
Athelred is most to be regarded, rather as the stalwart
woodman of thought. I have pulled on a light cord
often enough, while he has been wielding the broad-axe;
and between us, on this unequal division, many a spe-
cious fallacy has fallen. I have known him to battle the
same question night after night for years, keeping it in
the reign of talk, constantly applying it and re-applying

* Sir Walter Grindlay Simpson, Bart. (1843-98).

it to life with humorous or grave intention, and all the while, never hurrying, nor flagging, nor taking an unfair advantage of the facts. Jack at a given moment, when arising, as it were, from the tripod, can be more radiantly just to those from whom he differs; but then the tenor of his thoughts is even calumnious; while Athelred, slower to forge excuses, is yet slower to condemn, and sits over the welter of the world, vacillating but still judicial, and still faithfully contending with his doubts.

Both the last talkers deal much in points of conduct and religion studied in the " dry light " of prose. Indirectly and as if against his will the same elements from time to time appear in the troubled and poetic talk of Opalstein.* His various and exotic knowledge, complete although unready sympathies, and fine, full, discriminative flow of language, fit him out to be the best of talkers; so perhaps he is with some, not *quite* with me—*proxime accessit*, I should say. He sings the praises of the earth and the arts, flowers and jewels, wine and music, in a moonlight, serenading manner, as to the light guitar; even wisdom comes from his tongue like singing; no one is, indeed, more tuneful in the upper notes. But even while he sings the song of the Sirens, he still hearkens to the barking of the Sphinx. Jarring Byronic notes interrupt the flow of his Horatian humours. His mirth has nothing of the tragedy of the world for its perpetual background; and he feasts like Don Giovanni to a double orchestra, one lightly sounding for the dance, one pealing Beethoven in the distance. He is not truly reconciled either with life or with himself; and this instant war in his members sometimes divides the man's attention. He does not always, perhaps not often, frankly surrender himself in conversation. He brings into the talk other thoughts than those which he expresses; you are conscious that he keeps an eye on something else, that he does not shake off the world, nor quite forget himself. Hence arise occasional disappointments; even an occasional unfairness for his

* John Addington Symonds (1840-93).

companions, who find themselves one day giving too much, and the next, when they are wary out of season, giving perhaps too little. Purcel is in another class from any I have mentioned. He is no debater, but appears in conversation, as occasion rises, in two distinct characters, one of which I admire and fear, and the other love. In the first, he is radiantly civil and rather silent, sits on a high, courtly hilltop, and from that vantage-ground drops you his remarks like favours. He seems not to share in our sublunary contentions; he wears no sign of interest; when on a sudden there falls in a crystal of wit, so polished that the dull do not perceive it, but so right that the sensitive are silenced. True talk should have more body and blood, should be louder, vainer, and more declaratory of the man; the true talker should not hold so steady an advantage over whom he speaks with; and that is one reason out of a score why I prefer my Purcel in his second character, when he unbends into a strain of graceful gossip, singing like the fireside kettle. In these moods he has an elegant homeliness that rings of the true Queen Anne. I know another person who attains, in his moments, to the insolence of a Restoration comedy, speaking, I declare, as Congreve wrote; but that is a sport of nature, and scarce falls under the rubic, for there is none, alas! to give him answer.

One last remark occurs: It is the mark of genuine conversation that the sayings can scarce be quoted with their full effect beyond the circle of common friends. To have their proper weight they should appear in a biography, and with the portrait of the speaker. Good talk is dramatic; it is like an impromptu piece of acting where each should represent himself to the greatest advantage; and that is the best kind of talk where each speaker is most fully and candidly himself, and where, if you were to shift the speeches round from one to another, there would be the greatest loss in significance and perspicuity. It is for this reason that talk depends so wholly on our

company. We should like to introduce Falstaff and
Mercutio, or Falstaff and Sir Toby; but Falstaff in talk
with Cordelia seems even painful. Most of us, by the
Protean quality of man, can talk to some degree with
all; but the true talk, that strikes out all the slumbering best of us, comes only with the peculiar brethren
of our spirits, is founded as deep as love in the constitution of our being, and is a thing to relish with all
our energy, while yet we have it, and to be grateful
for for ever.

XI

TALK AND TALKERS *

II

IN the last paper there was perhaps too much about mere debate; and there was nothing said at all about that kind of talk which is merely luminous and restful, a higher power of silence, the quiet of the evening shared by ruminating friends. There is something, aside from personal preference, to be alleged in support of this omission. Those who are no chimney-corenerers, who rejoice in the social thunderstorm, have a ground in reason for their choice. They get little rest indeed; but restfulness is a quality for cattle; the virtues are all active, life is alert, and it is in repose that men prepare themselves for evil. On the other hand, they are bruised into a knowledge of themselves and others; they have in a high degree the fencer's pleasure in dexterity displayed and proved; what they get they get upon life's terms, paying for it as they go; and once the talk is launched, they are assured of honest dealing from an adversary eager like themselves. The aboriginal man within us, the cave-dweller, still lusty as when he fought tooth and nail for roots and berries, scents this kind of equal battle from afar; it is like his old primæval days upon the crags, a return to the sincerity of savage life from the comfortable fictions of the civilised. And if it be delightful to the Old Man, it is none the less profitable to his younger brother, the conscientious gentleman. I feel never quite

* This sequel was called forth by an excellent article in *The Spectator.*

sure of your urbane and smiling coteries; I fear they
indulge a man's vanities in silence, suffer him to encroach, encourage him on to be an ass, and send him
forth again, not merely contemned for the moment, but
radically more contemptible than when he entered. But
if I have a flushed, blustering fellow for my opposite,
bent on carrying a point, my vanity is sure to have its
ears rubbed, once at least, in the course of the debate.
He will not spare me when we differ; he will not fear to
demonstrate my folly to my face.

For many natures there is not much charm in the
still, chambered society, the circle of bland countenances, the digestive silence, the admired remark, the
flutter of affectionate approval. They demand more
atmosphere and exercise; " a gale upon their spirits," as
our pious ancestors would phrase it; to have their wits
well breathed in an uproarious Valhalla. And I suspect
that the choice, given their character and faults, is one
to be defended. The purely wise are silenced by facts;
they talk in a clear atmosphere, problems lying around
them like a view in nature; if they can be shown to be
somewhat in the wrong, they digest the reproof like a
thrashing, and make better intellectual blood. They
stand corrected by a whisper; a word or a glance re-
minds them of the great eternal law. But it is not so
with all. Others in conversation seek rather contact
with their fellow-men than increase of knowledge or
clarity of thought. The drama, not the philosophy, of
life is the sphere of their intellectual activity. Even
when they pursue truth, they desire as much as possible
of what we may call human scenery along the road they
follow. They dwell in the heart of life; the blood sounding in their ears, their eyes laying hold of what delights
them with a brutal avidity that makes them blind to
all besides, their interest riveted on people, living, loving, talking, tangible people. To a man of this description, the sphere of argument seems very pale and
ghostly. By a strong expression, a perturbed countenance, floods of tears, an insult which his conscience

obliges him to swallow, he is brought round to knowledge which no syllogism would have conveyed to him.
His own experience is so vivid, he is so superlatively
conscious of himself, that if, day after day, he is allowed
to hector and hear nothing but approving echoes, he
will lose his hold on the soberness of things and take
himself in earnest for a god. Talk might be to such
an one the very way of moral ruin; the school where
he might learn to be at once intolerable and ridiculous.

This character is perhaps commoner than philosophers
suppose. And for persons of that stamp to learn much
by conversation, they must speak with their superiors,
not in intellect, for that is a superiority that must be
proved, but in station. If they cannot find a friend to
bully them for their good, they must find either an old
man, a woman, or some one so far below them in the
artificial order of society, that courtesy may be particularly exercised.

The best teachers are the aged. To the old our
mouths are always partly closed; we must swallow our
obvious retorts and listen. They sit above our heads,
on life's raised daïs, and appeal at once to our respect
and pity. A flavour of the old school, a touch of something different in their manner—which is freer and
rounder, if they come of what is called a good family,
and often more timid and precise if they are of the
middle class—serves, in these days, to accentuate the
difference of age and add a distinction to gray hairs.
But their superiority is founded more deeply than by
outward marks or gestures. They are before us in the
march of man; they have more or less solved the irking
problem; they have battled through the equinox of life;
in good and evil they have held their course; and now,
without open shame, they near the crown and harbour.
It may be we have been struck with one of fortune's
darts; we can scarce be civil, so cruelly is our spirit
tossed. Yet long before we were so much as thought
upon, the like calamity befell the old man or woman
that now, with pleasant humour, rallies us upon our

inattention, sitting composed in the holy evening of man's life, in the clear shining after rain. We grow ashamed of our distresses, new and hot and coarse, like villainous roadside brandy; we see life in aerial perspective, under the heavens of faith; and out of the worst, in the mere presence of contented elders, look forward and take patience. Fear shrinks before them " like a thing reproved," not the flitting and ineffectual fear of death, but the instant, dwelling terror of the responsibilities and revenges of life. Their speech, indeed, is timid; they report lions in the path; they counsel a meticulous footing; but their serene, marred faces are more eloquent and tell another story. Where they have gone, we will go also, not very greatly fearing; what they have endured unbroken, we also, God helping us, will make a shift to bear.

Not only is the presence of the aged in itself remedial, but their minds are stored with antidotes, wisdom's simples, plain considerations overlooked by youth. They have matter to communicate, be they never so stupid. Their talk is not merely literature, it is great literature; classic in virtue of the speaker's detachment, studded, like a book of travel, with things we should not otherwise have learnt. In virtue, I have said, of the speaker's detachment—and this is why, of two old men, the one who is not your father speaks to you with the more sensible authority; for in the paternal relation the oldest have lively interests and remain still young. Thus I have known two young men great friends; each swore by the other's father; the father of each swore by the other lad; and yet each pair of parent and child were perpetually by the ears. This is typical: it reads like the germ of some kindly comedy.

The old appear in conversation in two characters: the critically silent and the garrulous anecdotic. The last is perhaps what we look for; it is perhaps the more instructive. An old gentleman, well on in years, sits handsomely and naturally in the bow window of his age, scanning experience with reverted eye; and,

chirping and smiling, communicates the accidents and
reads the lesson of his long career. Opinions are
strengthened, indeed, but they are also weeded out in
the course of years. What remains steadily present to
the eye of the retired veteran in his hermitage, what
still ministers to his content, what still quickens his old
honest heart—these are "the real long-lived things" that
Whitman tells us to prefer. Where youth agrees with
age, not where they differ, wisdom lies; and it is when
the young disciple finds his heart to beat in tune with his
gray-bearded teacher's that a lesson may be learned. I
have known one old gentleman, whom I may name, for
he is now gathered to his stock—Robert Hunter, Sheriff
of Dumbarton, and author of an excellent law-book still
re-edited and republished. Whether he was originally
big or little is more than I can guess. When I knew
him he was all fallen away and fallen in; crooked and
shrunken; buckled into a stiff waistcoat for support;
troubled by ailments, which kept him hobbling in and
out of the room; one foot gouty; a wig for decency, not
for deception, on his head; close shaved, except under
his chin—and for that he never failed to apologise, for
it went sore against the traditions of his life. You can
imagine how he would fare in a novel by Miss Mather;
yet this rag of a Chelsea veteran lived to his last year
in the plenitude of all that is best in man, brimming
with human kindness, and staunch as a Roman soldier
under his manifold infirmities. You could not say that
he had lost his memory, for he would repeat Shakespeare
and Webster and Jeremy Taylor and Burke by the page
together; but the parchment was filled up, there was no
room for fresh inscriptions, and he was capable of repeating the same anecdote on many successive visits.
His voice survived in its full power, and he took a pride
in using it. On his last voyage as Commissioner of
Lighthouses, he hailed a ship at sea and made himself
clearly audible without a speaking trumpet, ruffling the
while with a proper vanity in his achievement. He had
a habit of eking out his words with interrogative hems,

which was puzzling and a little wearisome, suited ill
with his appearance, and seemed a survival from some
former stage of bodily portliness. Of yore, when he was
a great pedestrian and no enemy to good claret, he may
have pointed with these minute guns his allocutions to
the bench. His humour was perfectly equable, set beyond the reach of fate; gout, rheumatism, stone and
gravel might have combined their forces against that
frail tabernacle, but when I came round on Sunday
evening, he would lay aside Jeremy Taylor's *Life of
Christ* and greet me with the same open brow, the same
kind formality of manner. His opinions and sympathies
dated the man almost to a decade. He had begun
life, under his mother's influence, as an admirer of
Junius, but on maturer knowledge had transferred his
admiration to Burke. He cautioned me, with entire
gravity, to be punctilious in writing English; never to
forget that I was a Scotsman, that English was a foreign
tongue, and that if I attempted the colloquial, I should
certainly be shamed: the remark was apposite, I suppose, in the days of David Hume. Scott was too new
for him; he had known the author—known him, too, for
a Tory; and to the genuine classic a contemporary is
always something of a trouble. He had the old, serious
love of the play; had even, as he was proud to tell,
played a certain part in the history of Shakespearian
revivals, for he had successfully pressed on Murray, of
the old Edinburgh Theatre, the idea of producing
Shakespeare's fairy pieces with great scenic display.
A moderate in religion, he was much struck in the last
years of his life by a conversation with two young lads,
revivalists. " H'm," he would say—" new to me. I
have had—h'm—no such experience." It struck him,
not with pain, rather with a solemn philosophic interest,
that he, a Christian as he hoped, and a Christian of
so old a standing, should hear these young fellows talking of his own subject, his own weapons that he had
fought the battle of life with—" and—h'm—not understand." In this wise and graceful attitude he did justice

to himself and others, reposed unshaken in his old beliefs, and recognised their limits without anger or alarm.
His last recorded remark, on the last night of his life,
was after he had been arguing against Calvinism with
his minister and was interrupted by an intolerable pang.
"After all," he said, "of all the 'isms, I know none so
bad as rheumatism." My own last sight of him was
some time before, when we dined together at an inn;
he had been on circuit, for he stuck to his duties like a
chief part of his existence; and I remember it as the
only occasion on which he ever soiled his lips with slang
—a thing he loathed. We were both Roberts; and as
we took our places at table, he addressed me with a
twinkle: "We are just what you would call two bob."
He offered me port, I remember, as the proper milk of
youth; spoke of "twenty-shilling notes"; and throughout the meal was full of old-world pleasantry and
quaintness, like an ancient boy on a holiday. But what
I recall chiefly was his confession that he had never read
Othello to an end. Shakespeare was his continual study.
He loved nothing better than to display his knowledge
and memory by adducing parallel passages from Shakespeare, passages where the same word was employed,
or the same idea differently treated. But *Othello* had
beaten him. "That noble gentleman and that noble
lady—h'm—too painful for me." The same night the
hoardings were covered with posters, "Burlesque of
Othello," and the contrast blazed up in my mind like a
bonfire. An unforgettable look it gave me into that
kind man's soul. His acquaintance was indeed a liberal
and pious education. All the humanities were taught
in that bare dining-room beside his gouty footstool.
He was a piece of good advice; he was himself the instance that pointed and adorned his various talk. Nor
could a young man have found elsewhere a place so set
apart from envy, fear, discontent, or any of the passions that debase; a life so honest and composed; a
soul like an ancient violin, so subdued to harmony,
responding to a touch in music—as in that dining-room,

with Mr. Hunter chatting at the eleventh hour, under
the shadow of eternity, fearless and gentle.

The second class of old people are not anecdotic; they
are rather hearers than talkers, listening to the young
with an amused and critical attention. To have this
sort of intercourse to perfection, I think we must go to
old ladies. Women are better hearers than men, to
begin with; they learn, I fear in anguish, to bear with
the tedious and infantile vanity of the other sex; and
we will take more from a woman than even from the
oldest man in the way of biting comment. Biting comment is the chief part, whether for profit or amusement,
in this business. The old lady that I have in my eye
is a very caustic speaker, her tongue, after years of
practice, in absolute command, whether for silence or
attack. If she chance to dislike you, you will be
tempted to curse the malignity of age. But if you
chance to please even slightly, you will be listened to
with a particular laughing grace of sympathy, and from
time to time chastised, as if in play, with a parasol as
heavy as a pole-axe. It requires a singular art, as well
as the vantage-ground of age, to deal these stunning
corrections among the coxcombs of the young. The pill
is disguised in sugar of wit; it is administered as a compliment—if you had not pleased, you would not have
been censured; it is a personal affair—a hyphen, a
trait d'union, between you and your censor; age's phi-
landering, for her pleasure and your good. Incontest-
ably the young man feels very much of a fool; but he
must be a perfect Malvolio, sick with self-love, if he
cannot take an open buffet and still smile. The correction of silence is what kills; when you know you have
transgressed, and your friend says nothing and avoids
your eye. If a man were made of gutta-percha, his
heart would quail at such a moment. But when the
word is out, the worst is over; and a fellow with any
good-humour at all may pass through a perfect hail of
witty criticism, every bare place on his soul hit to
the quick with a shrewd missile, and reappear, as if

after a dive, tingling with a fine moral reaction, and ready with a shrinking readiness, one-third loath, for a repetition of the discipline.

There are few women, not well sunned and ripened, and perhaps toughened, who can thus stand apart from a man and say the true thing with a kind of genial cruelty. Still there are some—and I doubt if there be any man who can return the compliment. The class of man represented by Vernon Whitford in *The Egoist* says, indeed, the true thing, but he says it stockishly. Vernon is a noble fellow, and makes, by the way, a noble and instructive contrast to Daniel Deronda; his conduct is the conduct of a man of honour; but we agree with him, against our consciences, when he remorsefully considers " its astonishing dryness." He is the best of men, but the best of women manage to combine all that and something more. Their very faults assist them; they are helped even by the falseness of their position in life. They can retire into the fortified camp of the proprieties. They can touch a subject and suppress it. The most adroit employ a somewhat elaborate reserve as a means to be frank, much as they wear gloves when they shake hands. But a man has the full responsibility of his freedom, cannot evade a question, can scarce be silent without rudeness, must answer for his words upon the moment, and is not seldom left face to face with a damning choice, between the more or less dishonourable wriggling of Deronda and the downright woodenness of Vernon Whitford.

But the superiority of women is perpetually menaced; they do not sit throned on infirmities like the old; they are suitors as well as sovereigns; their vanity is engaged, their affections are too apt to follow, and hence much of the talk between the sexes degenerates into something unworthy of the name. The desire to please, to shine with a certain softness of lustre and, to draw a fascinating picture of oneself, banishes from conversation all that is sterling and most of what is humorous. As soon as a strong current of mutual admiration begins to flow, the human interest triumphs entirely over the intellectual, and the commerce of words, consciously or not, becomes secondary to the commercing of eyes. But even where this ridiculous danger is avoided, and a man and woman converse equally and honestly, something in their nature or their education falsifies the strain. An instinct prompts them to agree; and where that is impossible, to agree to differ. Should they neglect the warning, at the first suspicion of an argument, they find themselves in different hemispheres. About any point of business or conduct, any actual affair demanding settlement, a woman will speak and listen, hear and answer arguments, not only with natural wisdom, but with candour and logical honesty. But if the subject of debate be something in the air, an abstraction, an excuse for talk, a logical Aunt Sally, then may the male debater instantly abandon hope; he may employ reason, adduce facts, be supple, be smiling, be angry, all shall avail him nothing; what the woman said first, that (unless she has forgotten it) she will repeat at the end. Hence, at the very junctures when a talk between men grows brighter and quicker and begins to promise to bear fruit, talk between the sexes is menaced with dissolution. The point of difference, the point of interest, is evaded by the brilliant woman, under a shower of irrelevant conversational rockets; it is bridged by the discreet woman with a rustle of silk, as she passes smoothly forward to the nearest point of safety. And this sort of prestidigitation, juggling the dangerous topic out of sight until it can be reintroduced with safety in an altered shape, is a piece of tactics among the true drawing-room queens.

The drawing-room is, indeed, an artificial place; it is so by our choice and for our sins. The subjection of women; the ideal imposed upon them from the cradle, and worn, like a hair-shirt, with so much constancy; their motherly, superior tenderness to man's vanity and self-importance; their managing arts—the arts of a civilised slave among good-natured barbarians—are all painful ingredients and all help to falsify relations. It is not till we get clear of that amusing artificial scene that genuine relations are founded, or ideas honestly compared. In the garden, on the road or the hillside, or *tête-à-tête* and apart from interruptions, occasions arise when we may learn much from any single woman; and nowhere more often than in married life. Marriage is one long conversation, chequered by disputes. The disputes are valueless; they but ingrain the difference; the heroic heart of woman prompting her at once to nail her colours to the mast. But in the intervals, almost unconsciously and with no desire to shine, the whole material of life is turned over and over, ideas are struck out and shared, the two persons more and more adapt their notions one to suit the other, and in process of time, without sound of trumpet, they conduct each other into new worlds of thought.

XII

THE CHARACTER OF DOGS

THE civilisation, the manners, and the morals of
dogkind are to a great extent subordinated to
those of his ancestral master, man. This animal, in
many ways so superior, has accepted a position of in-
feriority, shares the domestic life, and humours the
caprices of the tyrant. But the potentate, like the British in India, pays small regard to the character of his
willing client, judges him with listless glances, and condemns him in a byword. Listless have been the looks
of his admirers, who have exhausted idle terms of praise,
and buried the poor soul below exaggerations. And yet
more idle and, if possible, more unintelligent has been
the attitude of his express detractors; those who are very
fond of dogs " but in their proper place "; who say
" poo' fellow, poo' fellow," and are themselves far
poorer; who whet the knife of the vivisectionist or heat
his oven; who are not ashamed to admire " the creature's
instinct "; and flying far beyond folly, have dared to
resuscitate the theory of animal machines. The " dog's
instinct " and the " automaton-dog," in this age of
psychology and science, sound like strange anachron-
isms. An automaton he certainly is; a machine working independently of his control, the heart like the mill-
wheel, keeping all in motion, and the consciousness, like
a person shut in the mill garret, enjoying the view out
of the window and shaken by the thunder of the stones;
an automaton in one corner of which a living spirit is
confined: an automaton like man. Instinct again he
certainly possesses. Inherited aptitudes are his, inherited frailties. Some things he at once views and

understands, as though he were awakened from a sleep, as though he came " trailing clouds of glory." But with him, as with man, the field of instinct is limited; its utterances are obscure and occasional; and about the far larger part of life both the dog and his master must conduct their steps by deduction and observation.

The leading distinction between dog and man, after and perhaps before the different duration of their lives, is that the one can speak and that the other cannot. The absence of the power of speech confines the dog in the development of his intellect. It hinders him from many speculations, for words are the beginning of metaphysic. At the same blow it saves him from many superstitions, and his silence has won for him a higher name for virtue than his conduct justifies. The faults of the dog are many. He is vainer than man, singularly greedy of notice, singularly intolerant of ridicule, suspicious like the deaf, jealous to the degree of frenzy, and radically devoid of truth. The day of an intelligent small dog is passed in the manufacture and the laborious communication of falsehood; he lies with his tail, he lies with his eye, he lies with his protesting paw; and when he rattles his dish or scratches at the door his purpose is other than appears. But he has some apology to offer for the vice. Many of the signs which form his dialect have come to bear an arbitrary meaning, clearly understood both by his master and himself; yet when a new want arises he must either invent a new vehicle of meaning or wrest an old one to a different purpose; and this necessity frequently recurring must tend to lessen his idea of the sanctity of symbols. Meanwhile the dog is clear in his own conscience, and draws, with a human nicety, the distinction between formal and essential truth. Of his punning perversions, his legitimate dexterity with symbols, he is even vain; but when he has told and been detected in a lie, there is not a hair upon his body but confesses guilt. To a dog of gentlemanly feeling theft and falsehood are disgraceful vices. The canine, like the human, gentleman demands in his misdemeanours Montaigne's "*je ne sais quoi de gén-éreux.*" He is never more than half ashamed of having barked or bitten; and for those faults into which he has been led by the desire to shine before a lady of his race, he retains, even under physical correction, a share of pride. But to be caught lying, if he understands it, instantly uncurls his fleece.

Just as among dull observers he preserves a name for truth, the dog has been credited with modesty. It is amazing how the use of language blunts the faculties of man—that because vainglory finds no vent in words, creatures supplied with eyes have been unable to detect a fault so gross and obvious. If a small spoiled dog were suddenly to be endowed with speech, he would prate interminably, and still about himself; when we had friends, we should be forced to lock him in a garret; and what with his whining jealousies and his foible for falsehood, in a year's time he would have gone far to weary out our love. I was about to compare him to Sir Willoughby Patterne, but the Patternes have a manlier sense of their own merits; and the parallel, besides, is ready. Hans Christian Andersen, as we behold him in his startling memoirs, thrilling from top to toe with an excruciating vanity, and scouting even along the street for shadows of offence—here was the talking dog. It is just this rage for consideration that has betrayed the dog into his satellite position as the friend of man. The cat, an animal of franker appetites, preserves his independence. But the dog, with one eye ever on the audience, has been wheedled into slavery, and praised and patted into the renunciation of his nature. Once he ceased hunting and became man's plate-licker, the Rubicon was crossed. Thenceforth he was a gentleman of leisure; and except the few whom we keep working, the whole race grew more and more self-conscious, mannered, and affected. The number of things that a small dog does naturally is strangely small. Enjoying better spirits and not crushed under material cares, he is far more theatrical than average man. His whole life, if he be a dog of any pretension to gallantry, is spent in a vain show, and in the hot pursuit of admiration. Take out your puppy for a walk, and you will find the little ball of fur clumsy, stupid, bewildered, but natural. Let but a few months pass, and when you repeat the process you will find nature buried in convention. He will do nothing plainly; but the simplest processes of our material life will all be bent into the forms of an elaborate and mysterious etiquette. Instinct, says the fool, has awakened. But it is not so. Some dogs—some, at the very least—if they be kept separate from others, remain quite natural; and these, when at length they meet with a companion of experience, and have the game explained to them, distinguish themselves by the severity of their devotion to its rules. I wish I were allowed to tell a story which would radiantly illuminate the point; but men, like dogs, have an elaborate and mysterious etiquette. It is their bond of sympathy that both are the children of convention.

The person, man or dog, who has a conscience is eternally condemned to some degree of humbug; the sense of the law in their members fatally precipitates either towards a frozen and affected bearing. And the converse is true; and in the elaborate and conscious manners of the dog, moral opinions and the love of the ideal stand confessed. To follow for ten minutes in the street some swaggering, canine cavalier, is to receive a lesson in dramatic art and the cultured conduct of the body; in every act and gesture you see him true to a refined conception; and the dullest cur, beholding him, pricks up his ear and proceeds to imitate and parody that charming ease. For to be a high-mannered and high-minded gentleman, careless, affable, and gay, is the inborn pretension of the dog. The large dog, so much lazier, so much more weighed upon with matter, so majestic in repose, so beautiful in effort, is born with the dramatic means to wholly represent the part. And it is more pathetic and perhaps more instructive to consider the small dog in his conscientious and imperfect efforts to outdo Sir Philip Sidney. For the ideal of the dog is feudal and religious; the ever-present polytheism, the whip-bearing Olympus of mankind, rules them on the one hand; on the other, their singular difference of size and strength among themselves effectually prevents the appearance of the democratic notion. Or we might more exactly compare their society to the curious spectacle presented by a school—ushers, monitors, and big and little boys—qualified by one circumstance, the introduction of the other sex. In each, we should observe a somewhat similar tension of manner, and somewhat similar points of honour. In each the larger animal keeps a contemptuous good humour; in each the smaller annoys him with wasp-like impudence, certain of practical immunity; in each we shall find a double life producing double characters, and an excursive and noisy heroism combined with a fair amount of practical timidity. I have known dogs, and I have known school heroes that, set aside the fur, could hardly have been told apart; and if we desire to understand the chivalry of old, we must turn to the school playfields or the dungheap where the dogs are trooping.

Woman, with the dog, has been long enfranchised. Incessant massacre of female innocents has changed the proportion of the sexes and perverted their relations. Thus, when we regard the manners of the dog, we see a romantic and monogamous animal, once perhaps as delicate as the cat, at war with impossible conditions. Man has much to answer for; and the part he plays is yet more damnable and parlous than Corin's in the eyes of Touchstone. But his intervention has at least created an imperial situation for the rare surviving ladies. In that society they reign without a rival: conscious queens; and in the only instance of a canine wife-beater that has ever fallen under my notice, the criminal was somewhat excused by the circumstances of his story. He is a little, very alert, well-bred, intelligent Skye, as black as a hat, with a wet bramble for a nose and two cairngorms for eyes. To the human

observer, he is decidedly well-looking; but to the ladies
of his race he seems abhorrent. A thorough elaborate
gentleman, of the plume and sword-knot order, he was
born with a nice sense of gallantry to women. He took
at their hands the most outrageous treatment; I have
hard him bleating like a sheep, I have seen him streaming blood, and his ear tattered like a regimental banner;
and yet he would scorn to make reprisals. Nay more,
when a human lady upraised the contumelious whip
against the very dame who had been so cruelly mis-
using him, my little great-heart gave but one hoarse
cry and fell upon the tyrant tooth and nail. This is
the tale of a soul's tragedy. After three years of un-
availing chivalry, he suddenly, in one hour, threw off
the yoke of obligation; had he been Shakespeare he
would then have written *Troilus and Cressida* to brand
the offending sex; but being only a little dog, he began
to bite them. The surprise of the ladies whom he attacked indicated the monstrosity of his offence; but he
had fairly beaten off his better angel, fairly committed
moral suicide; for almost in the same hour, throwing
aside the last rags of decency, he proceeded to attack
the aged also. The fact is worth remark, showing,
as it does, that ethical laws are common both to dogs
and men; and that with both a single deliberate viola-
tion of the conscience loosens all. "But while the lamp
holds on to burn," says the paraphrase, "the greatest
sinner may return." I have been cheered to see symptoms of effectual penitence in my sweet ruffian; and by
the handling that he accepted uncomplainingly the other
day from an indignant fair one, I begin to hope the
period of *Sturm und Drang* is closed.

All these little gentlemen are subtle casuists. The
duty to the female dog is plain; but where competing
duties rise, down they will sit and study them out, like
Jesuit confessors. I knew another little Skye, somewhat plain in manner and appearance, but a creature
compact of amiability and solid wisdom. His family
going abroad for a winter, he was received for that

period by an uncle in the same city. The winter over, his own family home again, and his own house (of which he was very proud) reopened, he found himself in a dilemma between two conflicting duties of loyalty and gratitude. His old friends were not to be neglected, but it seemed hardly decent to desert the new. This was how he solved the problem. Every morning, as soon as the door was opened, off posted Coolin to his uncle's, visited the children in the nursery, saluted the whole family, and was back at home in time for breakfast and his bit of fish. Nor was this done without a sacrifice on his part, sharply felt; for he had to forego the particular honour and jewel of his day—his morning's walk with my father. And, perhaps from this cause, he gradually wearied of and relaxed the practice, and at length returned entirely to his ancient habits. But the same decision served him in another and more distressing case of divided duty, which happened not long after. He was not at all a kitchen dog, but the cook had nursed him with unusual kindness during the distemper; and though he did not adore her as he adored my father—although (born snob) he was critically conscious of her position as " only a servant " —he still cherished for her a special gratitude. Well, the cook left, and retired some streets away to lodgings of her own; and there was Coolin in precisely the same situation with any young gentleman who has had the inestimable benefit of a faithful nurse. The canine conscience did not solve the problem with a pound of tea at Christmas. No longer content to pay a flying visit, it was the whole forenoon that he dedicated to his solitary friend. And so, day by day, he continued to comfort her solitude until (for some reason which I could never understand and cannot approve) he was kept locked up to break him of the graceful habit. Here, it is not the similarity, it is the difference, that is worthy of remark; the clearly marked degrees of gratitude and the proportional duration of his visits. Anything further removed from instinct it were hard to

fancy; and one is even stirred to a certain impatience
with a character so destitute of spontaneity, so passion-
less in justice, and so priggishly obedient to the voice
of reason.

There are not many dogs like this good Coolin, and
not many people. But the type is one well marked,
both in the human and the canine family. Gallantry
was not his aim, but a solid and somewhat oppressive
respectability. He was a sworn foe to the unusual and
the conspicuous, a praiser of the golden mean, a kind
of city uncle modified by Cheeryble. And as he was
precise and conscientious in all the steps of his own
blameless course, he looked for the same precision and
an even greater gravity in the bearing of his deity,
my father. It was no sinecure to be Coolin's idol: he
was exacting like a rigid parent; and at every sign of
levity in the man whom he respected, he announced
loudly the death of virtue and the proximate fall of the
pillars of the earth.

I have called him a snob; but all dogs are so, though
in varying degrees. It is hard to follow their snobbery
among themselves; for though I think we can perceive
distinctions of rank, we cannot grasp what is the criterion. Thus in Edinburgh, in a good part of the town,
there were several distinct societies or clubs that met
in the morning to—the phrase is technical—to " rake
the backets " in a troop. A friend of mine, the master
of three dogs, was one day surprised to observe that
they had left one club and joined another; but whether
it was a rise or a fall, and the result of an invitation
or an expulsion, was more than he could guess. And
this illustrates pointedly our ignorance of the real life
of dogs, their social ambitions and their social hier-
archies. At least, in their dealings with men they are
not only conscious of sex, but of the difference of station. And that in the most snobbish manner; for the
poor man's dog is not offended by the notice of the rich,
and keeps all his ugly feeling for those poorer or more
ragged than his master. And again, for every station

they have an ideal of behaviour, to which the master, under pain of derogation, will do wisely to conform. How often has not a cold glance of an eye informed me that my dog was disappointed; and how much more gladly would he not have taken a beating than to be thus wounded in the seat of piety!

I knew one disrespectable dog. He was far liker a cat; cared little or nothing for men, with whom he merely co-existed as we do with cattle, and was entirely devoted to the art of poaching. A house would not hold him, and to live in a town was what he refused. He led, I believe, a life of troubled but genuine pleasure, and perished beyond all question in a trap. But this was an exception, a marked reversion to the ancestral type; like the hairy human infant. The true dog of the nineteenth century, to judge by the remainder of my fairly large acquaintance, is in love with respectability. A street-dog was once adopted by a lady. While still an Arab, he had done as Arabs do, gambolling in the mud, charging into butchers' stalls, a cat-hunter, a sturdy beggar, a common rogue and vagabond; but with his rise into society he laid aside these inconsistent pleasures. He stole no more, he hunted no more cats; and conscious of his collar, he ignored his old companions. Yet the canine upper class was never brought to recognise the upstart, and from that hour, except for human countenance, he was alone. Friendless, shorn of his sports and the habits of a life time, he still lived in a glory of happiness, content with his acquired respectability, and with no care but to support it solemnly. Are we to condemn or praise this self-made dog? We praise his human brother. And thus to conquer vicious habits is as rare with dogs as with men. With the more part, for all their scruple-mongering and moral thought, the vices that are born with them remain invincible throughout; and they live all their years, glorying in their virtues, but still the slaves of their defects. Thus the sage Coolin was a thief to the last; among a thousand peccadilloes, a whole goose and a

whole cold leg of mutton lay upon his conscience; but
Woggs,* whose soul's shipwreck in the matter of gallantry I have recounted above, has only twice been
known to steal, and has often nobly conquered the
temptation. The eighth is his favourite commandment.
There is something painfully human in these unequal
virtues and moral frailties of the best. Still more painful is the bearing of those " stammering professors " in
the house of sickness and under the terror of death. It
is beyond a doubt to me that, somehow or other, the
dog connects together, or confounds, the uneasiness of
sickness and the consciousness of guilt. To the pains of
the body he often adds the tortures of the conscience;
and at these times his haggard protestations form, in
regard to the human deathbed, a dreadful parody or
parallel.

I once supposed that I had found an inverse relation
between the double etiquette which dogs obey; and that
those who were most addicted to the showy street life
among other dogs were less careful in the practice of
home virtues for the tyrant man. But the female dog,
that mass of carneying affections, shines equally in
either sphere; rules her rough posse of attendant swains
with unwearying tact and gusto; and with her master
and mistress pushes the arts of insinuation to their
crowning point. The attention of man and the regard
of other dogs flatter (it would thus appear) the same
sensibility; but perhaps, if we could read the canine
heart, they would be found to flatter it in very different
degrees. Dogs live with man as courtiers round a mon-
arch, steeped in the flattery of his notice and enriched
with sinecures. To push their favour in this world of
pickings and caresses is, perhaps, the business of their
lives; and their joys may lie outside. I am in despair
at our persistent ignorance. I read in the lives of our

* Walter, Watty, Woggy, Woggs, Wogg, and lastly Bogue;
under which last name he fell in battle some twelve months ago.
Glory was his aim and he attained it; for his icon, by the hand
of Caldecott, now lies among the treasures of the nation at the
British Museum.

companions the same processes of reason, the same antique and fatal conflicts of the right against the wrong, and of unbitted nature with too rigid custom; I see them with our weakness, vain, false, inconstant against appetite, and with our one stalk of virtue, devoted to the dream of an ideal; and yet, as they hurry by me on the street with tail in air, or come singly to solicit my regard, I must own the secret purport of their lives is still inscrutable to man. Is man the friend, or is he the patron only? Have they indeed forgotten nature's voice? or are those moments snatched from courtiership when they touch noses with the tinker's mongrel, the brief reward and pleasure of their artificial lives? Doubtless, when man shares with his dog the toils of a profession and the pleasures of an art, as with the shepherd or the poacher, the affection warms and strengthens till it fills the soul. But doubtless, also, the masters are, in many cases, the object of a merely interested cultus, sitting aloft like Louis Quatorze, giving and receiving flattery and favour; and the dogs, like the majority of men, have but foregone their true existence and become the dupes of their ambition.

XIII

"A PENNY PLAIN AND TWOPENCE COLOURED"

THESE words will be familiar to all students of
Skelt's Juvenile Drama. That national monument, after having changed its name to Park's, to
Webb's, to Redington's, and last of all to Pollock's,
has now become, for the most part, a memory. Some
of its pillars, like Stonehenge, are still afoot, the rest
clean vanished. It may be the Museum numbers a full
set; and Mr. Ionides perhaps, or else her gracious
Majesty, may boast their great collections; but to the
plain private person they are become, like Raphaels,
unattainable. I have, at different times, possessed
*Aladdin, The Red Rover, The Blind Boy, The Old Oak
Chest, The Wood Dœmon, Jack Sheppard, The Miller
and his Men, Der Freischütz, The Smuggler, The Forest
of Bondy, Robin Hood, The Waterman, Richard I., My
Poll and my Partner Joe, The Inchcape Bell* (imperfect), and *Three-Fingered Jack, the Terror of Jamaica;*
and I have assisted others in the illumination of *The
Maid of the Inn* and *The Battle of Waterloo*. In this
roll-call of stirring names you read the evidences of a
happy childhood; and though not half of them are still
to be procured of any living stationer, in the mind of
their once happy owner all survive, kaleidoscopes of
changing pictures, echoes of the past.

There stands, I fancy, to this day (but now how
fallen!) a certain stationer's shop at a corner of the
wide thoroughfare that joins the city of my childhood
with the sea. When, upon any Saturday, we made a

114

party to behold the ships, we passed that corner; and since in those days I loved a ship as a man loves Burgundy or daybreak, this of itself had been enough to hallow it. But there was more than that. In the Leith Walk window, all the year round, there stood displayed a theatre in working order, with a " forest set," a " combat," and a few " robbers carousing " in the slides; and below and about, dearer tenfold to me! the plays themselves, those budgets of romance, lay tumbled one upon another. Long and often have I lingered there with empty pockets. One figure, we shall say, was visible in the first plate of characters, bearded, pistol in hand, or drawing to his ear the clothyard arrow; I would spell the name: was it Macaire, or Long Tom Coffin, or Grindoff, 2d dress? O, how I would long to see the rest! how—if the name by chance were hidden—I would wonder in what play he figured, and what immortal legend justified his attitude and strange apparel! And then to go within, to announce yourself as an intending purchaser, and, closely watched, be suffered to undo those bundles and breathlessly devour those pages of gesticulating villains, epileptic combats, bosky forests, palaces and war-ships, frowning fortresses and prison vaults—it was a giddy joy. That shop, which was dark and smelt of Bibles, was a loadstone rock for all that bore the name of boy. They could not pass it by, nor, having entered, leave it. It was a place besieged; the shopmen, like the Jews rebuilding Salem, had a double task. They kept us at the stick's end, frowned us down, snatched each play out of our hand ere we were trusted with another; and incredible as it may sound, used to demand of us upon our entrance, like banditti, if we came with money or with empty hand. Old Mr. Smith himself, worn out with my eternal vacillation, once swept the treasures from before me, with the cry: " I do not believe, child, that you are an intending purchaser at all! " These were the dragons of the garden; but for such joys of paradise we could have faced the Terror of Jamaica himself. Every sheet we fingered was another lightning glance into obscure, delicious story; it was like wallowing in the raw stuff of story-books. I know nothing to compare with it save now and then in dreams, when I am privileged to read in certain unwrit stories of adventure, from which I awake to find the world all vanity. The *crux* of Buridan's donkey was as nothing to the uncertainty of the boy as he handled and lingered and doated on these bundles of delight; there was a physical pleasure in the sight and touch of them which he would jealously prolong; and when at length the deed was done, the play selected, and the impatient shopman had brushed the rest into the gray portfolio, and the boy was forth again, a little late for dinner, the lamps springing into light in the blue winter's even, and *The Miller*, or *The Rover*, or some kindred drama clutched against his side—on what gay feet he ran, and how he laughed aloud in exultation! I can hear that laughter still. Out of all the years of my life, I can recall but one home-coming to compare with these, and that was on the night when I brought back with me the *Arabian Entertainments* in the fat, old, double-columned volume with the prints. I was just well into the story of the Hunchback, I remembered, when my clergyman-grandfather (a man we counted pretty stiff) came in behind me. I grew blind with terror. But instead of ordering the book away, he said he envied me. Ah, well he might!

The purchase and the first half-hour at home, that was the summit. Thenceforth the interest declined by little and little. The fable, as set forth in the play-book, proved to be not worthy of the scenes and characters: what fable would not? Such passages as: "Scene 6. The Hermitage. Night set scene. Place back of scene 1, No. 2, at back of stage and hermitage, Fig. 2, out of set piece, R. H. in a slanting direction"—such passages, I say, though very practical, are hardly to be called good reading. Indeed, as literature, these dramas did not much appeal to me. I forget the very outline of the plots. Of *The Blind Boy*, beyond the fact that he was a most injured prince and once, I think, abducted, I know nothing. And *The Old Oak Chest*, what was it all about? that proscript (1st dress), that prodigious number of banditti, that old woman with the broom, and the magnificent kitchen in the third act (was it in the third?)—they are all fallen in a deliquium, swim faintly in my brain, and mix and vanish.

I cannot deny that joy attended the illumination; nor can I quite forgive that child who, wilfully foregoing pleasure, stoops to " twopence coloured." With crimson lake (hark to the sound of it—crimson lake!—the horns of elf-land are not richer on the ear)—with crimson lake and Prussian blue a certain purple is to be compounded which, for cloaks especially, Titian could not equal. The latter colour with gamboge, a hated name although an exquisite pigment, supplied a green of such a savoury greenness that to-day my heart regrets it. Nor can I recall without a tender weakness the very aspect of the water where I dipped my brush. Yes, there was pleasure in the painting. But when all was painted, it is needless to deny it, all was spoiled. You might, indeed, set up a scene or two to look at; but to cut the figures out was simply sacrilege; nor could any child twice court the tedium, the worry, and the long-drawn disenchantment of an actual performance. Two days after the purchase the honey had been sucked. Parents used to complain; they thought I wearied of my play. It was not so: no more than a person can be said to have wearied of his dinner when he leaves the bones and dishes; I had got the marrow of it and said grace.

Then was the time to turn to the back of the play-book and to study that enticing double file of names, where poetry, for the true child of Skelt, reigned happy and glorious like her Majesty the Queen. Much as I have travelled in these realms of gold, I have yet seen, upon that map or abstract, names of El Dorados that still haunt the ear of memory, and are still but names.

The Floating Beacon—why was that denied me? or *The Wreck Ashore? Sixteen-String Jack,* whom I did not even guess to be a highwayman, troubled me awake and haunted my slumbers; and there is one sequence of three from that enchanted calendar that I still at times recall, like a loved verse of poetry: *Lodoiska, Silver Palace, Echo of Westminster Bridge.* Names, bare names, are surely more to children than we poor, grown-up, obliterated fools remember.

The name of Skelt itself has always seemed a part and parcel of the charm of his productions. It may be different with the rose, but the attraction of this paper drama sensibly declined when Webb had crept into the rubric: a poor cuckoo, flaunting in Skelt's nest. And now we have reached Pollock, sounding deeper gulfs. Indeed, this name of Skelt appears so stagey and piratic, that I will adopt it boldly to design these qualities. Skeltery, then, is a quality of much art. It is even to be found, with reverence be it said, among the works of nature. The stagey is its generic name; but it is an old, insular, home-bred staginess; not French, domestically British; not of to-day, but smacking of O. Smith, Fitzball, and the great age of melodrama; a peculiar fragrance haunting it; uttering its unimportant message in a tone of voice that has the charm of fresh antiquity. I will not insist upon the art of Skelt's purveyors. These wonderful characters that once so thrilled our soul with their bold attitude, array of deadly engines, and incomparable costume, to-day look somewhat pallidly; the extreme hard favour of the heroine strikes me, I had almost said with pain; the villain's scowl no longer thrills me like a trumpet; and the scenes themselves (those once unparalleled landscapes, seem the efforts of a prentice hand. So much of fault we find; but on the other side the imperial critic rejoices to remark the presence of a great unity of gusto; of those direct clap-trap appeals, which a man is dead and buriable when he fails to answer; of the footlight glamour, the ready-made, bare-faced, transpontine picturesque, a thing not one with cold reality, but how much dearer to the mind!

The scenery of Skeltdom—or, shall we say, the Kingdom of Transpontus?—had a prevailing character. Whether it set forth Poland as in *The Blind Boy*, or Bohemia with *The Miller and his Men*, or Italy with *The Old Oak Chest*, still it was Transpontus. A botanist could tell it by the plants. The hollyhock was all pervasive, running wild in deserts; the dock was common, and the bending reed; and over-shadowing these were poplar, palm, potato tree, and *Quercus Skeltica*—brave growths. The caves were all embowelled in the Surreyside formation; the soil was all betrodden by the light pump of T. P. Cooke. Skelt, to be sure, had yet another, an oriental string: he held the gorgeous East in fee; and in the new quarter of Hyères, say, in the garden of the Hotel des Îles d'Or, you may behold these blessed visions realised. But on these I will not dwell; they were an outwork; it was in the occidental scenery that Skelt was all himself. It had a strong flavour of England; it was a sort of indigestion of England and drop-scenes, and I am bound to say was charming. How the roads wander, how the castle sits upon the hill, how the sun eradiates from behind the cloud, and how the congregated clouds themselves uproll, as stiff as bolsters! Here is the cottage interior, the usual first flat, with the cloak upon the nail, the rosaries of onions, the gun and powder-horn and corner-cupboard; here is the inn (this drama must be nautical, I foresee Captain Luff and Bold Bob Bowsprit) with the red curtain, pipes, spittoons, and eight-day clock; and there again is that impressive dungeon with the chains, which was so dull to colour. England, the hedgerow elms, the thin brick houses, windmills, glimpses of the navigable Thames—England, when at last I came to visit it, was only Skelt made evident: to cross the border was, for the Scotsman, to come home to Skelt; there was the inn-sign and there the horse-trough, all foreshadowed in the faithful Skelt. If, at the ripe age of fourteen years, I bought a certain cudgel, got a friend to load it, and thenceforward walked the tame ways of the earth my own ideal, radiating pure romance—still I was but a puppet in the hand of Skelt; the original of that regretted bludgeon, and surely the antitype of all the bludgeon kind, greatly improved from Cruikshank, had adorned the hand of' Jonathan Wild, pl. 1. "This is mastering me," as Whitman cries, upon some lesser provocation. What am I? what are life, art, letters, the world, but what my Skelt has made them? He stamped himself upon my immaturity. The world was plain before I knew him, a poor penny world; but soon it was all coloured with romance. If I go to the theatre to see a good old melodrama, 'tis but Skelt a little faded. If I visit a bold scene in nature, Skelt would have been bolder; there had been certainly a castle on that mountain, and the hollow tree—that set piece—I seem to miss it in the foreground. Indeed, out of this cut-and-dry, dull, swaggering, obtrusive, and infantile art, I seem to have learned the very spirit of my life's enjoyment; met there the shadows of the characters I was to read about and love in a late future; got the romance of *Der Freischütz* long ere I was to hear of Weber or the mighty Formes; acquired a gallery of scenes and characters with which, in the silent theatre of the brain, I might enact all novels and romances; and took from these rude cuts an enduring and transforming pleasure. Reader—and yourself?

A word of moral: it appears that B. Pollock, late J. Redington, No. 73 Hoxton Street, not only publishes twenty-three of these old stage favourites, but owns the necessary plates and displays a modest readiness to issue other thirty-three. If you love art, folly, or the bright eyes of children, speed to Pollock's, or to Clarke's of Garrick Street. In Pollock's list of publicanda I perceive a pair of my ancient aspirations: *Wreck Ashore* and *Sixteen-String Jack;* and I cherish the belief that when these shall see once more the light of day, B. Pollock will remember this apologist. But, indeed, I have a dream at times that is not all a dream. I seem to myself to wander in a ghostly street—E. W., I think, the postal district—close below the fool's-cap of St. Paul's, and yet within easy hearing of the echo of the Abbey bridge. There in a dim shop, low in the roof and smelling strong of glue and footlights, I find myself in quaking treaty with great Skelt himself, the aboriginal, all dusty from the tomb. I buy, with what a choking heart—I buy them all, all but the pantomimes; I pay my mental money, and go forth; and lo! the packets are dust.

XIV

A GOSSIP ON A NOVEL OF DUMAS'S

THE books that we re-read the oftenest are not always those that we admire the most; we choose
and we revisit them for many and various reasons, as
we choose and revisit human friends. One or two of
Scott's novels, Shakespeare, Molière, Montaigne, *The
Egoist*, and the *Vicomte de Bragelonne*, form the inner
circle of my intimates. Behind these comes a good
troop of dear acquaintances; *The Pilgrim's Progress* in
the front rank, *The Bible in Spain* not far behind.
There are besides a certain number that look at me
with reproach as I pass them by on my shelves: books
that I once thumbed and studied: houses which were
once like home to me, but where I now rarely visit. I
am on these sad terms (and blush to confess it) with
Wordsworth, Horace, Burns, and Hazlitt. Last of all,
there is the class of book that has its hour of bril-
liancy—glows, sings, charms, and then fades again into
insignificance until the fit return. Chief of those who
thus smile and frown on me by turns, I must name
Virgil and Herrick, who, were they but

" Their sometime selves the same throughout the year,"

must have stood in the first company with the six
names of my continual literary intimates. To these
six, incongruous as they seem, I have long been faithful, and hope to be faithful to the day of death. I
have never read the whole of Montaigne, but I do not
like to be long without reading some of him, and
my delight in what I do read never lessens. Of

Shakespeare I have read all but *Richard III., Henry VI., Titus Andronicus,* and *All's Well that Ends Well;* and these, having already made all suitable endeavour, I now know that I shall never read—to make up for which unfaithfulness I could read much of the rest for ever. Of Molière—surely the next greatest name of Christendom—I could tell a very similar story; but in a little corner of a little essay these princes are too much out of place, and I prefer to pay my fealty and pass on. How often I have read *Guy Mannering, Rob Roy,* or *Redgauntlet,* I have no means of guessing, having begun young. But it is either four or five times that I have read *The Egoist,* and either five or six that I have read the *Vicomte de Bragelonne.*

Some, who would accept the others, may wonder that I should have spent so much of this brief life of ours over a work so little famous as the last. And, indeed, I am surprised myself; not at my own devotion, but the coldness of the world. My acquaintance with the *Vicomte* began, somewhat indirectly, in the year of grace 1863, when I had the advantage of studying certain illustrated dessert plates in a hotel at Nice. The name of d'Artagnan in the legends I already saluted like an old friend, for I had met it the year before in a work of Miss Yonge's. My first perusal was in one of those pirated editions that swarmed at that time out of Brussels, and ran to such a troop of neat and dwarfish volumes. I understood but little of the merits of the book; my strongest memory is of the execution of d'Eyméric and Lyodot—a strange testimony to the dulness of a boy, who could enjoy the rough-and-tumble in the Place de Grève, and forget d'Artagnan's visits to the two financiers. My next reading was in winter-time, when I lived alone upon the Pentlands. I would return in the early night from one of my patrols with the shepherd; a friendly face would meet me in the door, a friendly retriever scurry upstairs to fetch my slippers; and I would sit down with the *Vicomte* for a long, silent, solitary lamplight evening by the fire.

And yet I know not why I call it silent, when it was enlivened with such a clatter of horse-shoes, and such a rattle of musketry, and such a stir of talk; or why I call those evenings solitary in which I gained so many friends. I would rise from my book and pull the blind aside, and see the snow and the glittering hollies chequer a Scottish garden, and the winter moonlight brighten the white hills. Thence I would turn again to that crowded and sunny field of life in which it was so easy to forget myself, my cares, and my surroundings: a place busy as a city, bright as a theatre, thronged with memorable faces, and sounding with delightful speech. I carried the thread of that epic into my slumbers, I woke with it unbroken, I rejoiced to plunge into the book again at breakfast, it was with a pang that I must lay it down and turn to my own labours; for no part of the world has ever seemed to me so charming as these pages, and not even my friends are quite so real, perhaps quite so dear, as d'Artagnan.

Since then I have been going to and fro at very brief intervals in my favourite book; and I have now just risen from my last (let me call it my fifth) perusal, having liked it better and admired it more seriously than ever. Perhaps I have a sense of ownership, being so well known in these six volumes. Perhaps I think that d'Artagnan delights to have me read of him, and Louis Quatorze is gratified, and Fouquet throws me a look, and Aramis, although he knows I do not love him, yet plays to me with his best graces, as to an old patron of the show. Perhaps, if I am not careful, something may befall me like what befell George IV. about the battle of Waterloo, and I may come to fancy the *Vicomte* one of the first, and Heaven knows the best, of my own works. At least, I avow myself a partisan; and when I compare the popularity of the *Vicomte* with that of *Monte Cristo,* or its own elder brother, the *Trois Mousquetaires,* I confess I am both pained and puzzled.

To those who have already made acquaintance with

the titular hero in the pages of *Vingt Ans Après,* perhaps the name may act as a deterrent. A man might well stand back if he supposed he were to follow, for six volumes, so well-conducted, so fine-spoken, and withal so dreary a cavalier as Bragelonne. But the fear is idle. I may be said to have passed the best years of my life in these six volumes, and my acquaintance with Raoul has never gone beyond a bow; and when he, who has so long pretended to be alive, is at last suffered to pretend to be dead, I am sometimes reminded of a saying in an earlier volume: " *Enfin, dit Miss Stewart* "—and it was of Bragelonne she spoke—" *enfin il a fait quelquechose: c'est, ma foi! bien heureux.*" I am reminded of it, as I say; and the next moment, when Athos dies of his death, and my dear d'Artagnan bursts into his storm of sobbing, I can but deplore my flippancy.

Or perhaps it is La Vallière that the reader of *Vingt Ans Après* is inclined to flee. Well, he is right there too, though not so right. Louise is no success. Her creator has spared no pains; she is well-meant, not ill-designed, sometimes has a word that rings out true; sometimes, if only for a breath, she may even engage our sympathies. But I have never envied the King his triumph. And so far from pitying Bragelonne for his defeat, I could wish him no worse (not for lack of malice, but imagination) than to be wedded to that lady. Madame enchants me; I can forgive that royal minx her most serious offences; I can thrill and soften with the King on that memorable occasion when he goes to upbraid and remains to flirt; and when it comes to the " *Allons, aimez-moi donc,*" it is my heart that melts in the bosom of de Guiche. Not so with Louise. Readers cannot fail to have remarked that what an author tells us of the beauty or the charm of his creatures goes for nought; that we know instantly better; that the heroine cannot open her mouth but what, all in a moment, the fine phrases of preparation fall from round her like the robes from Cinderella, and she stands

before us, self-betrayed, as a poor, ugly, sickly wench,
or perhaps a strapping market-woman. Authors, at
least, know it well; a heroine will too often start the
trick of " getting ugly "; and no disease is more difficult
to cure. I said authors; but indeed I had a side eye to
one author in particular, with whose works I am very
well acquainted, though I cannot read them, and who
has spent many vigils in this cause, sitting beside his
ailing puppets and (like a magician) wearying his art to
restore them to youth and beauty. There are others
who ride too high for these misfortunes. Who doubts
the loveliness of Rosalind? Arden itself was not more
lovely. Who ever questioned the perennial charm of
Rose Jocelyn, Lucy Desborough, or Clara Middleton?
fair women with fair names, the daughters of George
Meredith. Elizabeth Bennet has but to speak, and I
am at her knees. Ah! these are the creators of desirable women. They would never have fallen in the
mud with Dumas and poor La Vallière. It is my only
consolation that not one of all of them, except the
first, could have plucked at the moustache of d'Artagnan.

Or perhaps, again, a proportion of readers stumble
at the threshold. In so vast a mansion there were sure
to be back stairs and kitchen offices where no one
would delight to linger; but it was at least unhappy
that the vestibule should be so badly lighted; and until, in the seventeenth chapter, d'Artagnan sets off to
seek his friends, I must confess, the book goes heavily
enough. But, from thenceforward, what a feast is
spread! Monk kidnapped; d'Artagnan enriched;
Mazarin's death; the ever delectable adventure of Belle
Isle, wherein Aramis outwits d'Artagnan, with its epi-
logue (vol. v. chap. xxviii.), where d'Artagnan regains
the moral superiority; the love adventures at Fontainebleau, with St. Aignan's story of the dryad and the
business of de Guiche, de Wardes, and Manicamp;
Aramis made general of the Jesuits; Aramis at the
Bastille; the night talk in the forest of Sénart; Belle

Isle again, with the death of Porthos; and last, but not least, the taming of d'Artagnan the untamable, under the lash of the young King. What other novel has such epic variety and nobility of incident? often, if you will, impossible; often of the order of an Arabian story; and yet all based in human nature. For if you come to that, what novel has more human nature? not studied with the microscope, but seen largely, in plain daylight, with the natural eye? What novel has more good sense, and gaiety, and wit, and unflagging, admirable literary skill? Good souls, I suppose, must sometimes read it in the blackguard travesty of a translation. But there is no style so untranslatable; light as a whipped trifle, strong as silk; wordy like a village tale; pat like a general's despatch; with every fault, yet never tedious; with no merit, yet inimitably right. And, once more, to make an end of commendations, what novel is inspired with a more unstrained or a more wholesome morality?

Yes; in spite of Miss Yonge, who introduced me to the name of d'Artagnan only to dissuade me from a nearer knowledge of the man, I have to add morality. There is no quite good book without a good morality; but the world is wide, and so are morals. Out of two people who have dipped into Sir Richard Burton's *Thousand and One Nights,* one shall have been offended by the animal details; another to whom these were harmless, perhaps even pleasing, shall yet have been shocked in his turn by the rascality and cruelty of all the characters. Of two readers, again, one shall have been pained by the morality of a religious memoir, one by that of the *Vicomte de Bragelonne.* And the point is that neither need be wrong. We shall always shock each other both in life and art; we cannot get the sun into our pictures, nor the abstract right (if there be such a thing) into our books; enough if, in the one, there glimmer some hint of the great light that blinds us from heaven; enough, if, in the other, there shine, even upon foul details, a spirit of magnanimity. I

would scarce send to the *Vicomte* a reader who was in
quest of what we may call puritan morality. The
ventripotent mulatto, the great eater, worker, earner,
and waster, the man of much and witty laughter, the
man of the great heart and alas! of the doubtful honesty, is a figure not yet clearly set before the world;
he still awaits a sober and yet genial portrait; but with
whatever art that may be touched, and whatever indulgence, it will not be the portrait of a precisian.
Dumas was certainly not thinking of himself, but of
Planchet, when he put into the mouth of d'Artagnan's
old servant this excellent profession: " *Monsieur, j'étais
une de ces bonnes pâtes d'hommes que Dieu a fait pour
s'animer pendant un certain temps et pour trouver
bonnes toutes choses qui accompagnent leur séjour sur
la terre.*" He was thinking, as I say, of Planchet, to
whom the words are aptly fitted; but they were fitted
also to Planchet's creator; and perhaps this struck him
as he wrote, for observe what follows: " *D'Artagnan
s'assit alors près de la fenêtre, et, cette philosophie de
Planchet lui ayant paru solide, il y rêva.*" In a man
who finds all things good, you will scarce expect much
zeal for negative virtues: the active alone will have a
charm for him; abstinence, however wise, however kind,
will always seem to such a judge entirely mean and
partly impious. So with Dumas. Chastity is not near
his heart; nor yet, to his own sore cost, that virtue of
frugality which is the armour of the artist. Now, in
the *Vicomte*, he had much to do with the contest of
Fouquet and Colbert. Historic justice should be all
upon the side of Colbert, of official honesty, and fiscal
competence. And Dumas knew it well: three times at
least he shows his knowledge; once it is but flashed
upon us and received with the laughter of Fouquet himself, in the jesting controversy in the gardens of Saint
Mandé; once it is touched on by Aramis in the forest
of Sénart; in the end, it is set before us clearly in one
dignified speech of the triumphant Colbert. But in
Fouquet, the waster, the lover of good cheer and wit and

art, the swift transactor of much business, "*l'homme de bruit, l'homme de plaisir, l'homme qui n'est que parceque les autres sont,*" Dumas saw something of himself and drew the figure the more tenderly. It is to me even touching to see how he insists on Fouquet's honour; not seeing, you might think, that unflawed honour is impossible to spendthrifts; but rather, perhaps, in the light of his own life, seeing it too well, and clinging the more to what was left. Honour can survive a wound; it can live and thrive without a member. The man rebounds from his disgrace; he begins fresh foundations on the ruins of the old; and when his sword is broken, he will do valiantly with his dagger. So it is with Fouquet in the book; so it was with Dumas on the battlefield of life.

To cling to what is left of any damaged quality is virtue in the man; but perhaps to sing its praises is scarcely to be called morality in the writer. And it is elsewhere, it is in the character of d'Artagnan, that we must look for that spirit of morality, which is one of the chief merits of the book, makes one of the main joys of its perusal, and sets it high above more popular rivals. Athos, with the coming of years, has declined too much into the preacher, and the preacher of a sapless creed; but d'Artagnan has mellowed into a man so witty, rough, kind, and upright, that he takes the heart by storm. There is nothing of the copy-book about his virtues, nothing of the drawing-room in his fine, natural civility; he will sail near the wind; he is no district visitor—no Wesley or Robespierre; his conscience is void of all refinement whether for good or evil; but the whole man rings true like a good sovereign. Readers who have approached the *Vicomte*, not across country, but by the legitimate, five-volumed avenue of the *Mousquetaires* and *Vingt Ans Après*, will not have forgotten d'Artagnan's ungentlemanly and perfectly improbable trick upon Milady. What a pleasure it is, then, what a reward, and how agreeable a lesson, to see the old captain humble himself to the son of the man

whom he had personated! Here, and throughout, if I
am to choose virtues for myself or my friends, let me
choose the virtues of d'Artagnan. I do not say there
is no character as well drawn in Shakespeare; I do say
there is none that I love so wholly. There are many
spiritual eyes that seem to spy upon our actions—eyes
of the dead and the absent, whom we imagine to behold
us in our most private hours, and whom we fear and
scruple to offend: our witnesses and judges. And among
these, even if you should think me childish, I must
count my d'Artagnan—not d'Artagnan of the memoirs
whom Thackeray pretended to prefer—a preference, I
take the freedom of saying, in which he stands alone;
not the d'Artagnan of flesh and blood, but him of the
ink and paper; not Nature's, but Dumas's. And this
is the particular crown and triumph of the artist—not
to be true merely, but to be lovable; not simply to con-
vince, but to enchant.

There is yet another point in the *Vicomte* which I
find incomparable. I can recall no other work of the
imagination in which the end of life is represented with
so nice a tact. I was asked the other day if Dumas
made me laugh or cry. Well, in this my late fifth reading of the *Vicomte*, I did laugh once at the small Coque-
lin de Volière business, and was perhaps a thought
surprised at having done so; to make up for it, I smiled
continually. But for tears, I do not know. If you put
a pistol to my throat, I must own the tale trips upon a
very airy foot—within a measurable distance of unreality; and for those who like the big guns to be discharged and the great passions to appear authentically,
it may even seem inadequate from first to last. Not
so to me; I cannot count that a poor dinner, or a poor
book, where I meet with those I love; and, above all,
in this last volume, I find a singular charm of spirit.
It breathes a pleasant and a tonic sadness, always
brave, never hysterical. Upon the crowded, noisy life
of this long tale, evening gradually falls; and the lights
are extinguished, and the heroes pass away one by one.

One by one they go, and not a regret embitters their departure; the young succeed them in their places, Louis Quatorze is swelling larger and shining broader, another generation and another France dawn on the horizon; but for us and these old men whom we have loved so long, the inevitable end draws near and is welcome. To read this well is to anticipate experience. Ah, if only when these hours of the long shadows fall for us in reality and not in figure, we may hope to face them with a mind as quiet!

But my paper is running out; the siege guns are firing on the Dutch frontier; and I must say adieu for the fifth time to my old comrade fallen on the field of glory. *Adieu*—rather *au revoir!* Yet a sixth time, dearest d'Artagnan, we shall kidnap Monk and take horse together for Belle Isle.

XV

A GOSSIP ON ROMANCE

IN anything fit to be called by the name of reading,
the process itself should be absorbing and voluptu-
ous, we should gloat over a book, be rapt clean out of
ourselves, and rise from the perusal, our mind filled
with the busiest, kaleidoscopic dance of images, incapable of sleep or of continuous thought. The words,
if the book be eloquent, should run thenceforward in
our ears like the noise of breakers, and the story, if it
be a story, repeat itself in a thousand coloured pictures
to the eye. It was for this last pleasure that we read
so closely, and loved our books so dearly, in the bright,
troubled period of boyhood. Eloquence and thought,
character and conversation, were but obstacles to brush
aside as we dug blithely after a certain sort of incident, like a pig for truffles. For my part, I liked a
story to begin with an old wayside inn where, "towards the close of the year 17—," several gentlemen
in three-cocked hats were playing bowls. A friend of
mine preferred the Malabar coast in a storm, with a
ship beating to windward, and a scowling fellow of
Herculean proportions striding along the beach; he, to
be sure, was a pirate. This was further afield than my
home-keeping fancy loved to travel, and designed altogether for a larger canvas than the tales that I affected. Give me a highwayman and I was full to the
brim; a Jacobite would do, but the highwayman was my
favourite dish. I can still hear that merry clatter of
the hoofs along the moonlit lane; night and the coming
of day are still related in my mind with the doings
of John Rann or Jerry Abershaw; and the words

"postchaise," the "great North Road," "ostler," and "nag" still sound in my ears like poetry. One and all, at least, and each with his particular fancy, we read storybooks in childhood, not for eloquence or character or thought, but for some quality of the brute incident. That quality was not mere bloodshed or wonder. Although each of these was welcome in its place, the charm for the sake of which we read depended on something different from either. My elders used to read novels aloud; and I can still remember four different passages which I heard, before I was ten, with the same keen and lasting pleasure. One I discovered long afterwards to be the admirable opening of *What will he Do with It*: it was no wonder I was pleased with that. The other three still remain unidentified. One is a little vague; it was about a dark, tall house at night, and people groping on the stairs by the light that escaped from the open door of a sick-room. In another, a lover left a ball, and went walking in a cool, dewy park, whence he could watch the lighted windows and the figures of the dancers as they moved. This was the most sentimental impression I think I had yet received, for a child is somewhat deaf to the sentimental. In the last, a poet, who had been tragically wrangling with his wife, walked forth on the sea-beach on a tempestuous night and witnessed the horrors of a wreck.* Different as they are, all these early favourites have a common note—they have all a touch of the romantic.

Drama is the poetry of conduct, romance the poetry of circumstance. The pleasure that we take in life is of two sorts—the active and the passive. Now we are conscious of a great command over our destiny; anon we are lifted up by circumstance, as by a breaking wave, and dashed we know not how into the future. Now we are pleased by our conduct, anon merely pleased by our surroundings. It would be hard to say which

* Since traced by many obliging correspondents to the gallery of Charles Kingsley.

of these modes of satisfaction is the more effective, but
the latter is surely the more constant. Conduct is three
parts of life, they say; but I think they put it high.
There is a vast deal in life and letters both which is not
immoral, but simply non-moral; which either does not
regard the human will at all, or deals with it in obvious and healthy relations; where the interest turns,
not upon what a man shall choose to do, but on how he
manages to do it; not on the passionate slips and
hesitations of the conscience, but on the problems of
the body and of the practical intelligence, in clean,
open air adventure, the shock of arms or the di-
plomacy of life. With such material as this it is
impossible to build a play, for the serious theatre
exists solely on moral grounds, and is a standing proof
of the dissemination of the human conscience. But it
is possible to build, upon this ground, the most joyous
of verses, and the most lively, beautiful, and buoyant
tales.

One thing in life calls for another; there is a fitness
in events and places. The sight of a pleasant arbour
puts it in our mind to sit there. One place suggests
work, another idleness, a third early rising and long
rambles in the dew. The effect of night, of any flowing
water, of lighted cities, of the peep of day, of ships, of
the open ocean, calls up in the mind an army of anony-
mous desires and pleasures. Something, we feel, should
happen; we know not what, yet we proceed in quest of
it. And many of the happiest hours of life fleet by us
in this vain attendance on the genius of the place and
moment. It is thus that tracts of young fir, and low
rocks that reach into deep soundings, particularly torture and delight me. Something must have happened in
such places, and perhaps ages back, to members of my
race; and when I was a child I tried in vain to invent
appropriate games for them, as I still try, just as vainly,
to fit them with the proper story. Some places speak
distinctly. Certain dank gardens cry aloud for a murder; certain old houses demand to be haunted; certain

coasts are set apart for shipwreck. Other spots again seem to abide their destiny, suggestive and impenetrable, "miching mallecho." The inn at Burford Bridge, with its arbours and green garden and silent, eddying river—though it is known already as the place where Keats wrote some of his *Endymion* and Nelson parted from his Emma—still seems to wait the coming of the appropriate legend. Within these ivied walls, behind these old green shutters, some further business smoulders, waiting for its hour. The old Hawes Inn at the Queen's Ferry makes a similar call upon my fancy. There it stands, apart from the town, beside the pier, in a climate of its own, half inland, half marine—in front, the ferry bubbling with the tide and the guardship swinging to her anchor; behind, the old garden with the trees. Americans seek it already for the sake of Lovel and Oldbuck, who dined there at the beginning of the *Antiquary*. But you need not tell me —that is not all; there is some story, unrecorded or not yet complete, which must express the meaning of that inn more fully. So it is with names and faces; so it is with incidents that are idle and inconclusive in themselves, and yet seem like the beginning of some quaint romance, which the all-careless author leaves untold. How many of these romances have we not seen determined at their birth; how many people have met us with a look of meaning in their eye, and sunk at once into trivial acquaintances; to how many places have we not drawn near, with express intimations—" here my destiny awaits me "—and we have but dined there and passed on! I have lived both at the Hawes and Burford in a perpetual flutter, on the heels, as it seemed, of some adventure that should justify the place; but though the feeling had me to bed at night and called me again at morning in one unbroken round of pleasure and suspense, nothing befell me in either worth remark. The man or the hour had not yet come; but some day, I think, a boat shall put off from the Queen's Ferry, fraught with a dear cargo, and some frosty night a horseman, on a tragic errand, rattle with his whip upon the green shutters of the inn at Burford.*

Now, this is one of the natural appetites with which any lively literature has to count. The desire for knowledge, I had almost added the desire for meat, is not more deeply seated than this demand for fit and striking incident. The dullest of clowns tells, or tries to tell, himself a story, as the feeblest of children uses invention in his play; and even as the imaginative grown person, joining in the game, at once enriches it with many delightful circumstances, the great creative writer shows us the realisation and the apotheosis of the day-dreams of common men. His stories may be nourished with the realities of life, but their true mark is to satisfy the nameless longings of the reader, and to obey the ideal laws of the day-dream. The right kind of thing should fall out in the right kind of place; the right kind of thing should follow; and not only the characters talk aptly and think naturally, but all the circumstances in a tale answer one to another like notes in music. The threads of a story come from time to time together and make a picture in the web; the characters fall from time to time into some attitude to each other or to nature, which stamps the story home like an illustration. Crusoe recoiling from the footprint, Achilles shouting over against the Trojans, Ulysses bending the great bow, Christian running with his fingers in his ears, these are each culminating moments in the legend, and each has been printed on the mind's eye for ever. Other things we may forget; we may forget the words, although they are beautiful; we may forget the author's comment, although perhaps it was ingenious and true; but these epoch-making scenes, which put the last mark of truth upon a story and fill up, at one blow, our capacity for sympathetic pleasure, we

* Since the above was written I have tried to launch the boat with my own hands in *Kidnapped*. Some day perhaps, I may try a rattle at the shutters.

so adopt into the very bosom of our mind that neither time nor tide can efface or weaken the impression. This, then, is the plastic part of literature: to embody character, thought, or emotion in some act or attitude that shall be remarkably striking to the mind's eye. This is the highest and hardest thing to do in words; the thing which, once accomplished, equally delights the schoolboy and the sage, and makes, in its own right, the quality of epics. Compared with this, all other purposes in literature, except the purely lyrical or the purely philosophic, are bastard in nature, facile of execution, and feeble in result. It is one thing to write about the inn at Burford, or to describe scenery with the word-painters; it is quite another to seize on the heart of the suggestion and make a country famous with a legend. It is one thing to remark and to dissect, with the most cutting logic, the complications of life, and of the human spirit; it is quite another to give them body and blood in the story of Ajax or of Hamlet. The first is literature, but the second is something besides, for it is likewise art.

English people of the present day are apt, I know not why, to look somewhat down on incident, and reserve their admiration for the clink of teaspoons and the accents of the curate. It is thought clever to write a novel with no story at all, or at least with a very dull one. Reduced even to the lowest terms, a certain interest can be communicated by the art of narrative; a sense of human kinship stirred; and a kind of monotonous fitness, comparable to the words and air of *Sandy's Mull*, preserved among the infinitesimal occurrences recorded. Some people work, in this manner, with even a strong touch. Mr. Trollope's inimitable clergymen naturally arise to the mind in this connection. But even Mr. Trollope does not confine himself to chronicling small beer. Mr. Crawley's collision with the Bishop's wife, Mr. Melnotte dallying in the deserted banquet-room, are typical incidents, epically conceived, fitly embodying a crisis. Or again look at Thackeray.

If Rawdon Crawley's blow were not delivered, *Vanity Fair* would cease to be a work of art. That scene is the chief ganglion of the tale; and the discharge of energy from Rawdon's fist is the reward and consolation of the reader. The end of *Esmond* is a yet wider excursion from the author's customary fields; the scene at Castlewood is pure Dumas; the great and wily English borrower has here borrowed from the great, unblushing French thief; as usual, he has borrowed admirably well, and the breaking of the sword rounds off the best of all his books with a manly, martial note. But perhaps nothing can more strongly illustrate the necessity for marking incident than to compare the living fame of *Robinson Crusoe* with the discredit of *Clarissa Harlowe*. *Clarissa* is a book of a far more startling import, worked out, on a great canvas, with inimitable courage and unflagging art. It contains wit, character, passion, plot, conversations full of spirit and insight, letters sparkling with unstrained humanity; and if the death of the heroine be somewhat frigid and artificial, the last days of the hero strike the only note of what we now call Byronism, between the Elizabethans and Byron himself. And yet a little story of a shipwrecked sailor, with not a tenth part of the style nor a thousandth part of the wisdom, exploring none of the arcana of humanity and deprived of the perennial interest of love, goes on from edition to edition, ever young, while *Clarissa* lies upon the shelves unread. A friend of mine, a Welsh blacksmith, was twenty-five years old and could neither read nor write, when he heard a chapter of *Robinson* read aloud in a farm kitchen. Up to that moment he had sat content, huddled in his ignorance, but he left that farm another man. There were day-dreams, it appeared, divine day-dreams, written and printed and bound, and to be bought for money and enjoyed at pleasure. Down he sat that day, painfully learned to read Welsh, and returned to borrow the book. It had been lost, nor could he find another copy but one that was in English.

Down he sat once more, learned English, and at length, and with entire delight, read *Robinson*. It is like the story of a love-chase. If he had heard a letter from *Clarissa*, would he have been fired with the same chivalrous ardour? I wonder. Yet *Clarissa* has every quality that can be shown in prose, one alone excepted —pictorial or picture-making romance. While *Robinson* depends, for the most part and with the overwhelming majority of its readers, on the charm of circumstance.

In the highest achievements of the art of words, the dramatic and the pictorial, the moral and romantic interest, rise and fall together by a common and organic law. Situation is animated with passion, passion clothed upon with situation. Neither exists for itself, but each inheres indissolubly with the other. This is high art; and not only the highest art possible in words, but the highest art of all, since it combines the greatest mass and diversity of the elements of truth and pleasure. Such are epics, and the few prose tales that have the epic weight. But as from a school of works, aping the creative, incident and romance are ruthlessly discarded, so may character and drama be omitted or subordinated to romance. There is one book, for example, more generally loved than Shakespeare, that captivates in childhood and still delights in age—I mean the *Arabian Nights*—where you shall look in vain for moral or for intellectual interest. No human face or voice greets us among that wooden crowd of kings and genies, sorcerers and beggarmen. Adventure, on the most naked terms, furnishes forth the entertainment and is found enough. Dumas approaches perhaps nearest of any modern to these Arabian authors in the purely material charm of some of his romances. The early part of *Monte Cristo,* down to the finding of the treasure, is a piece of perfect story-telling; the man never breathed who shared these moving incidents without a tremor; and yet Faria is a thing of packthread and Dantès little more than a name. The sequel is one long-drawn error, gloomy, bloody, unnatural, and dull; but as for these early chapters, I do not believe there is another volume extant where you can breathe the same unmingled atmosphere of romance. It is very thin and light, to be sure, as on a high mountain; but it is brisk and clear and sunny in proportion. I saw the other day, with envy, an old and a very clever lady setting forth on a second or third voyage into *Monte Cristo*. Here are stories which powerfully affect the reader, which can be reperused at any age, and where the characters are no more than puppets. The bony fist of the showman visibly propels them; their springs are an open secret; their faces are of wood, their bellies filled with bran; and yet we thrillingly partake of their adventures. And the point may be illustrated still further. The last interview between Lucy and Richard Feverel is pure drama; more than that, it is the strongest scene, since Shakespeare, in the English tongue. Their first meeting by the river, on the other hand, is pure romance; it has nothing to do with character; it might happen to any other boy and maiden, and be none the less delightful for the change. And yet I think he would be a bold man who should choose between these passages. Thus, in the same book, we may have two scenes, each capital in its order: in the one, human passion, deep calling unto deep, shall utter its genuine voice; in the second, according circumstances, like instruments in tune, shall build up a trivial but desirable incident, such as we love to prefigure for ourselves; and in the end, in spite of the critics, we may hesitate to give the preference to either. The one may ask more genius— I do not say it does; but at least the other dwells as clearly in the memory.

True romantic art, again, makes a romance of all things. It reaches into the highest abstraction of the ideal; it does not refuse the most pedestrian realism. *Robinson Crusoe* is as realistic as it is romantic; both qualities are pushed to an extreme, and neither suffers. Nor does romance depend upon the material importance of the incidents. To deal with strong and deadly elements, banditti, pirates, war, and murder, is to conjure with great names, and, in the event of failure, to double the disgrace. The arrival of Haydn and Consuelo at the Canon's villa is a very trifling incident; yet we may read a dozen boisterous stories from beginning to end, and not receive so fresh and stirring an impression of adventure. It was the scene of Crusoe at the wreck, if I remember rightly, that so bewitched my blacksmith. Nor is the fact surprising. Every single article the castaway recovers from the hulk is "a joy for ever" to the man who reads of them. They are the things that should be found, and the bare enumeration stirs the blood. I found a glimmer of the same interest the other day in a new book, *The Sailor's Sweetheart*, by Mr. Clark Russell. The whole business of the brig *Morning Star* is very rightly felt and spiritedly written; but the clothes, the books, and the money satisfy the reader's mind like things to eat. We are dealing here with the old cut-and-dry, legitimate interest of treasure trove. But even treasure trove can be made dull. There are few people who have not groaned under the plethora of goods that fell to the lot of the *Swiss Family Robinson*, that dreary family. They found article after article, creature after creature, from milk-kine to pieces of ordnance, a whole consignment; but no informing taste had presided over the selection, there was no smack or relish in the invoice; and these riches left the fancy cold. The box of goods in Verne's *Mysterious Island* is another case in point: there was no gusto and no glamour about that; it might have come from a shop. But the two hundred and seventy-eight Australian sovereigns on board the *Morning Star* fell upon me like a surprise that I had expected; whole vistas of secondary stories, besides the one in hand, radiated forth from that discovery, as they radiate from a striking particular life; and I was made for the moment as happy as a reader has the right to be.

To come at all at the nature of this quality of
romance, we must bear in mind the peculiarity of our
attitude to any art. No art produces illusion; in the
theatre we never forget that we are in the theatre; and
while we read a story, we sit wavering between two
minds, now merely clapping our hands at the merit of
the performance, now condescending to take an active
part in fancy with the characters. This last is the
triumph of romantic story-telling: when the reader consciously plays at being the hero, the scene is a good
scene. Now in character-studies the pleasure that we
take is critical; we watch, we approve, we smile at
incongruities, we are moved to sudden heats of sympathy with courage, suffering, or virtue. But the characters are still themselves, they are not us; the more
clearly they are depicted, the more widely do they
stand away from us, the more imperiously do they
thrust us back into our place as a spectator. I cannot identify myself with Rawdon Crawley or with Eu-
gène de Rastignac, for I have scarce a hope or fear in
common with them. It is not character but incident
that woos us out of our reserve. Something happens as
we desire to have it happen to ourselves; some situation, that we have long dallied with in fancy, is realised in the story with enticing and appropriate details.
Then we forget the characters; then we push the hero
aside; then we plunge into the tale in our own person
and bathe in fresh experience; and then, and then only,
do we say we have been reading a romance. It is not
only pleasurable things that we imagine in our day-
dreams; there are lights in which we are willing to con-
template even the idea of our own death; ways in which
it seems as if it would amuse us to be cheated, wounded,
or calumniated. It is thus possible to construct a story,
even of tragic import, in which every incident, detail, and
trick of circumstance shall be welcome to the reader's
thoughts. Fiction is to the grown man what play is to
the child; it is there that he changes the atmosphere
and tenor of his life; and when the game so chimes with

his fancy that he can join in it with all his heart, when it pleases him with every turn, when he loves to recall it and dwells upon its recollection with entire delight, fiction is called romance.

Walter Scott is out and away the king of the romantics. *The Lady of the Lake* has no indisputable claim to be a poem beyond the inherent fitness and desirability of the tale. It is just such a story as a man would make up for himself, walking, in the best health and temper, through just such scenes as it is laid in. Hence it is that a charm dwells undefinable among these slovenly verses, as the unseen cuckoo fills the mountains with his note; hence, even after we have flung the book aside, the scenery and adventures remain present to the mind, a new and green possession, not unworthy of that beautiful name, *The Lady of the Lake*, or that direct, romantic opening—one of the most spirited and poetical in literature—"The stag at eve had drunk his fill." The same strength and the same weaknesses adorn and disfigure the novels. In that ill-written, ragged book, *The Pirate*, the figure of Cleveland—cast up by the sea on the resounding foreland of Dunrossness—moving, with the blood on his hands and the Spanish words on his tongue among the simple islanders—singing a serenade under the window of his Shetland mistress—is conceived in the very highest manner of romantic invention. The words of his song, "Through groves of palm," sung in such a scene and by such a lover, clench, as in a nutshell, the emphatic contrast upon which the tale is built. In *Guy Mannering*, again, every incident is delightful to the imagination; and the scene when Harry Bertram lands at Ellangowan is a model instance of romantic method.

"'I remember the tune well,' he says, 'though I cannot guess what should at present so strongly recall it to my memory.' He took his flageolet from his pocket and played a simple melody. Apparently the tune awoke the corresponding associations of a damsel. . . . She immediately took up the song—

"'Are these the links of Forth, she said;
    Or are they the crooks of Dee,
  Or the bonny woods of Warroch Head
    That I so fain would see?'

"'By heaven!' said Bertram, 'it is the very ballad.'"

On this quotation two remarks fall to be made. First, as an instance of modern feeling for romance, this famous touch of the flageolet and the old song is selected by Miss Braddon for omission. Miss Braddon's idea of a story, like Mrs. Todgers's idea of a wooden leg, were something strange to have expounded. As a matter of personal experience, Meg's appearance to old Mr. Bertram on the road, the ruins of Derncleugh, the scene of the flageolet, and the Dominie's recognition of Harry, are the four strong notes that continue to ring in the mind after the book is laid aside. The second point is still more curious. The reader will observe a mark of excision in the passage as quoted by me. Well, there is how it runs in the original: "A damsel, who, close behind a fine spring about half-way down the descent and which had once supplied the castle with water, was engaged in bleaching linen." A man who gave in such copy would be discharged from the staff of a daily paper. Scott has forgotten to prepare the reader for the presence of the "damsel"; he has forgotten to mention the spring and its relation to the ruin; and now, face to face with his omission, instead of trying back and starting fair, crams all this matter, tail foremost, into a single shambling sentence. It is not merely bad English, or bad style; it is abominably bad narrative besides.

Certainly the contrast is remarkable; and it is one that throws a strong light upon the subject of this paper. For here we have a man of the finest creative instinct touching with perfect certainty and charm the romantic junctures of his story; and we find him utterly careless, almost, it would seem, incapable, in the technical matter of style, and not only frequently weak, but frequently wrong in points of drama. In character parts, indeed, and particularly in the Scots, he was delicate, strong, and truthful; but the trite, obliterated features of too many of his heroes have already wearied two generations of readers. At times his characters will speak with something far beyond propriety —with a true heroic note; but on the next page they will be wading wearily forward with an ungrammatical and undramatic rigmarole of words. The man who could conceive and write the character of Elspeth of the Craigburnfoot, as Scott has conceived and written it, had not only splendid romantic, but splendid tragic gifts. How comes it, then, that he could so often fob us off with languid, inarticulate twaddle?

It seems to me that the explanation is to be found in the very quality of his surprising merits. As his books are play to the reader, so were they play to him. He conjured up the romantic with delight, but he had hardly patience to describe it. He was a great daydreamer, a seer of fit and beautiful and humorous visions, but hardly a great artist; hardly, in the manful sense, an artist at all. He pleased himself, and so he pleases us. Of the pleasures of his art he tasted fully; but of its toils and vigils and distresses never man knew less. A great romantic—an idle child.

XVI

A HUMBLE REMONSTRANCE*

I

WE have recently enjoyed a quite peculiar pleasure: hearing, in some detail, the opinions, about
the art they practise, of Mr. Walter Besant and Mr.
Henry James; two men certainly of very different
calibre: Mr. James so precise of outline, so cunning of
fence, so scrupulous of finish, and Mr. Besant so genial,
so friendly, with so persuasive and humorous a vein of
whim: Mr. James the very type of the deliberate artist,
Mr. Besant the impersonation of good nature. That
such doctors should differ will excite no great surprise;
but one point in which they seem to agree fills me, I
confess, with wonder. For they are both content to
talk about the " art of fiction "; and Mr. Besant, waxing
exceedingly bold, goes on to oppose this so-called " art
of fiction " to the " art of poetry." By the art of poetry
he can mean nothing but the art of verse, an art of
handicraft, and only comparable with the art of prose.
For that heat and height of sane emotion which we agree
to call by the name of poetry, is but a libertine and
vagrant quality; present, at times, in any art, more
often absent from them all; too seldom present in the
prose novel, too frequently absent from the ode and
epic. Fiction is in the same case; it is no substantive
art, but an element which enters largely into all the

* This paper, which does not otherwise fit the present volume,
is reprinted here as the proper continuation of the last.—R.L.S.

arts but architecture. Homer, Wordsworth, Phidias, Hogarth, and Salvini, all deal in fiction; and yet I do not suppose that either Hogarth or Salvini, to mention but these two, entered in any degree into the scope of Mr. Besant's interesting lecture or Mr. James's charming essay. The art of fiction, then, regarded as a definition, is both too ample and too scanty. Let me suggest another; let me suggest that what both Mr. James and Mr. Besant had in view was neither more nor less than the art of narrative.

But Mr. Besant is anxious to speak solely of "the modern English novel," the stay and bread-winner of Mr. Mudie; and in the author of the most pleasing novel on that roll, *All Sorts and Conditions of Men,* the desire is natural enough. I can conceive then, that he would hasten to propose two additions, and read thus: the art of *fictitious* narrative *in prose.*

Now the fact of the existence of the modern English novel is not to be denied; materially, with its three volumes, leaded type, and gilded lettering, it is easily distinguishable from other forms of literature; but to talk at all fruitfully of any branch of art, it is needful to build our definitions on some more fundamental ground than binding. Why, then, are we to add "in prose"? *The Odyssey* appears to me the best of romances; *The Lady of the Lake* to stand high in the second order; and Chaucer's tales and prologues to contain more of the matter and art of the modern English novel than the whole treasury of Mr. Mudie. Whether a narrative be written in blank verse or the Spenserian stanza, in the long period of Gibbon or the chipped phrase of Charles Reade, the principles of the art of narrative must be equally observed. The choice of a noble and swelling style in prose affects the problem of narration in the same way, if not to the same degree, as the choice of measured verse; for both imply a closer synthesis of events, a higher key of dialogue, and a more picked and stately strain of words. If you are to refuse *Don Juan,* it is hard to see why you should include *Zanoni* or (to bracket works of very different value) *The Scarlet Letter;* and by what discrimination are you to open your doors to *The Pilgrim's Progress* and close them on *The Faery Queen?* To bring things closer home, I will here propound to Mr. Besant a conundrum. A narrative called *Paradise Lost* was written in English verse by one John Milton; what was it then? It was next translated by Chateaubriand into French prose; and what was it then? Lastly, the French translation was, by some inspired compatriot of George Gilfillan (and of mine) turned bodily into an English novel; and, in the name of clearness, what was it then?

But, once more, why should we add " fictitious "? The reason why is obvious. The reason why not, if something more recondite, does not want for weight. The art of narrative, in fact, is the same, whether it is applied to the selection and illustration of a real series of events or of an imaginary series. Boswell's *Life of Johnson* (a work of cunning and inimitable art) owes its success to the same technical manœuvres as (let us say) *Tom Jones:* the clear conception of certain characters of man, the choice and presentation of certain incidents out of a great number that offered, and the invention (yes, invention) and preservation of a certain key in dialogue. In which these things are done with the more art—in which the greater air of nature— readers will differently judge. Boswell's is, indeed, a very special case, and almost a generic; but it is not only in Boswell, it is in every biography with any salt of life, it is in every history where events and men, rather than ideas, are presented—in Tacitus, in Carlyle, in Michelet, in Macauley—that the novelist will find many of his own methods most conspicuously and adroitly handled. He will find besides that he, who is free—who has the right to invent or steal a missing incident, who has the right, more precious still, of wholesale omission—is frequently defeated, and, with all his advantages, leaves a less strong impression of reality and passion. Mr. James utters his mind with a becoming fervour on the sanctity of truth to the novelist; on a more careful examination truth will seem a word of very debatable propriety, not only for the labours of the novelist, but for those of the historian. No art—to use the daring phrase of Mr. James—can successfully " compete with life "; and the art that seeks to do so is condemned to perish *montibus aviis*. Life goes before us, infinite in complication; attended by the most various and surprising meteors; appealing at once to the eye, to the ear, to the mind—the seat of wonder, to the touch—so thrillingly delicate, and to the belly—so imperious when starved. It combines and employs in its manifestation the method and material, not of one art only, but of all the arts. Music is but an arbitrary trifling with a few of life's majestic chords; painting is but a shadow of its pageantry of light and colour; literature does but drily indicate that wealth of incident, of moral obligation, of virtue, vice, action, rapture, and agony, with which it teems. To " compete with life," whose sun we cannot look upon, whose passions and diseases waste and slay us—to compete with the flavour of wine, the beauty of the dawn, the scorching of fire, the bitterness of death and separation—here is, indeed, a projected escalade of heaven; here are, indeed, labours for a Hercules in a dress coat, armed with a pen and a dictionary to depict the passions, armed with a tube of superior flake-white to paint the portrait of the insufferable sun. No art is true in this sense: none can " compete with life ": not even history, built indeed of indisputable facts, but these facts robbed of their vivacity and sting; so that even when we read of the sack of a city or the fall of an empire, we are surprised, and justly commend the author's talent, if our pulse be quickened. And mark, for a last differentia, that this quickening of the pulse is, in almost every case, purely agreeable; that these phantom reproductions of experience, even at their most acute, convey decided pleasure; while experience itself, in the cockpit of life, can torture and slay.

What, then, is the object, what the method, of an art, and what the source of its power? The whole secret is that no art does " compete with life." Man's one method, whether he reasons or creates, is to half-shut his eyes against the dazzle and confusion of reality. The arts, like arithmetic and geometry, turn away their eyes from the gross, coloured and mobile nature at our feet, and regard instead a certain figmentary abstraction. Geometry will tell us of a circle, a thing never seen in nature; asked about a green circle or an iron circle, it lays its hand upon its mouth. So with the arts. Painting, ruefully comparing sunshine and flake-white, gives up truth of colour, as it had already given up relief and movement; and instead of vying with nature, arranges a scheme of harmonious tints. Literature, above all in its most typical mood, the mood of narrative, similarly flees the direct challenge and pursues instead an independent and creative aim. So far as it imitates at all, it imitates not life but speech: not the facts of human destiny, but the emphasis and the suppressions with which the human actor tells of them. The real art that dealt with life directly was that of the first men who told their stories round the savage camp-fire. (Our art is occupied, and bound to be occupied, not so much in making stories true as in making them typical; not so much in capturing the lineaments of each fact, as in marshalling all of them towards a common end.) For the welter of impressions, all forcible but all discreet, which life presents, it substitutes a certain artificial series of impressions, all indeed most feebly represented, but all aiming at the same effect, all eloquent of the same ideas, all chiming together like consonant notes in music or like the graduated tints in a good picture. From all its chapters, from all its pages, from all its sentences, the well-written novel echoes and re-echoes its one creative and controlling thought; to this must every incident and character contribute; the style must have been pitched in unison with this; and if there is anywhere a word that looks another way, the book would be stronger, clearer, and (I had almost said) fuller without it. Life is monstrous, infinite, illogical, abrupt, and poignant; a work of art, in comparison, is neat, finite, self-contained, rational, flowing, and emasculate. Life imposes by brute energy, like inarticulate thunder; art catches the ear, among the far louder noises of experience, like an air artificially made by a discreet musician. A proposition of geometry does not compete with life; and a proposition of geometry is a fair and luminous parallel for a work of art. Both are reasonable, both untrue to the crude fact; both inhere in nature, neither represents it. The novel, which is a work of art, exists, not by its resemblances to life, which are forced and material, as a shoe must still consist of leather, but by its immeasurable difference from life, which is designed and significant, and is both the method and the meaning of the work.

The life of man is not the subject of novels, but the inexhaustible magazine from which subjects are to be selected; the name of these is legion; and with each new subject—for here again I must differ by the whole width of heaven from Mr. James—the true artist will vary his method and change the point of attack. That which was in one case an excellence, will become a defect in another; what was the making of one book, will in the next be impertinent or dull. First each novel, and then each class of novels, exists by and for itself. I will take, for instance, three main classes, which are fairly distinct: first, the novel of adventure, which appeals to certain almost sensual and quite illogical tendencies in man; second, the novel of character, which appeals to our intellectual appreciation of man's foibles and mingled and inconstant motives; and third, the dramatic novel, which deals with the same stuff as the serious theatre, and appeals to our emotional nature and moral judgment.

And first for the novel of adventure. Mr. James
refers, with singular generosity of praise, to a little book
about a quest for hidden treasure; but he lets fall, by
the way, some rather startling words. In this book he
misses what he calls the " immense luxury " of being
able to quarrel with his author. The luxury, to most
of us, is to lay by our judgment, to be submerged by the
tale as by a billow, and only to awake, and begin to
distinguish and find fault, when the piece is over and
the volume laid aside. Still more remarkable is Mr.
James's reason. He cannot criticise the author, as he
goes, " because," says he, comparing it with another
work, " *I have been a child, but I have never been on
a quest for buried treasure.*" Here is, indeed, a wilful
paradox; for if he has never been on a quest for buried
treasure, it can be demonstrated that he has never been
a child. There never was a child (unless Master James)
but has hunted gold, and been a pirate, and a military
commander, and a bandit of the mountains; but has
fought, and suffered shipwreck and prison, and imbrued
its little hands in gore, and gallantly retrieved the lost
battle, and triumphantly protected innocence and
beauty. Elsewhere in his essay Mr. James has pro-
tested with excellent reason against too narrow a conception of experience; for the born artist, he contends,
the "faintest hints of life " are converted into revela-
tions; and it will be found true, I believe, in a majority
of cases, that the artist writes with more gusto and
effect of those things which he has only wished to do,
than of those which he has done. Desire is a wonderful telescope, and Pisgah the best observatory. Now,
while it is true that neither Mr. James nor the author
of the work in question has ever, in the fleshly sense,
gone questing after gold, it is probable that both have
ardently desired and fondly imagined the details of such
a life in youthful day-dreams; and the author, count-
ing upon that, and well aware (cunning and low-minded
man!) that this class of interest, having been frequently
treated, finds a readily accessible and beaten road to

the sympathies of the reader, addressed himself throughout to the building up and circumstantiation of this boyish dream. Character to the boy is a sealed book; for him, a pirate is a beard, a pair of wide trousers, and a liberal complement of pistols. The author, for the sake of circumstantiation and because he was himself more or less grown up, admitted character, within certain limits, into his design; but only within certain limits. Had the same puppets figured in a scheme of another sort, they had been drawn to very different purpose; for in this elementary novel of adventure, the characters need to be presented with but one class of qualities—the warlike and formidable. So as they appear insidious in deceit and fatal in the combat, they have served their end. Danger is the matter with which this class of novel deals; fear, the passion with which it idly trifles; and the characters are portrayed only so far as they realise the sense of danger and provoke the sympathy of fear. To add more traits, to be too clever, to start the hare of moral or intellectual interest while we are running the fox of material interest, is not to enrich but to stultify your tale. The stupid reader will only be offended, and the clever reader lose the scent.

The novel of character has this difference from all others: that it requires no coherency of plot, and for this reason, as in the case of *Gil Blas*, it is sometimes called the novel of adventure. It turns on the humours of the persons represented; these are, to be sure, embodied in incidents, but the incidents themselves, being tributary, need not march in a progression; and the characters may be statically shown. As they enter, so they may go out; they must be consistent, but they need not grow. Here Mr. James will recognise the note of much of his own work: he treats, for the most part, the statics of character, studying it at rest or only gently moved; and, with his usual delicate and just artistic instinct, he avoids those stronger passions which would deform the attitudes he loves to study, and change his sitters from the humorists of ordinary life to the brute forces and bare types of more emotional moments. In his recent *Author of Beltraffio*, so just in conception, so nimble and neat in workmanship, strong passion is indeed employed; but observe that it is not displayed. Even in the heroine the working of the passion is suppressed; and the great struggle, the true tragedy, the *scène-à-faire*, passes unseen behind the panels of a locked door. The delectable invention of the young visitor is introduced, consciously or not, to this end: that Mr. James, true to his method, might avoid the scene of passion. I trust no reader will suppose me guilty of undervaluing this little masterpiece. I mean merely that it belongs to one marked class of novel, and that it would have been very differently conceived and treated had it belonged to that other marked class, of which I now proceed to speak.

I take pleasure in calling the dramatic novel by that name, because it enables me to point out by the way a strange and peculiarly English misconception. It is sometimes supposed that the drama consists of incident. It consists of passion, which gives the actor his opportunity; and that passion must progressively increase, or the actor, as the piece proceeded, would be unable to carry the audience from a lower to a higher pitch of interest and emotion. A good serious play must therefore be founded on one of the passionate *cruces* of life, where duty and inclination come nobly to the grapple; and the same is true of what I call, for that reason, the dramatic novel. I will instance a few worthy specimens, all of our own day and language: Meredith's *Rhoda Fleming*, that wonderful and painful book, long out of print,* and hunted for at bookstalls like an Aldine; Hardy's *Pair of Blue Eyes;* and two of Charles Reade's, *Griffith Gaunt* and *The Double Marriage*, originally called *White Lies*, and founded (by an accident quaintly favourable to my nomenclature) on a play by

* Now no longer so, thank Heaven!

Maquet, the partner of the great Dumas. In this kind
of novel the closed door of *The Author of Beltraffio*
must be broken open; passion must appear upon the
scene and utter its last word; passion is the be-all and
the end-all, the plot and the solution, the protagonist
and the *deus ex machina* in one. The characters may
come anyhow upon the stage: we do not care; the point
is, that, before they leave it, they shall become trans-
figured and raised out of themselves by passion. It may
be part of the design to draw them with detail; to depict
a full-length character, and then behold it melt and
change in the furnace of emotion. But there is no
obligation of the sort; nice portraiture is not required;
and we are content to accept mere abstract types, so
they be strongly and sincerely moved. A novel of this
class may be even great, and yet contain no individual
figure; it may be great, because it displays the workings
of the perturbed heart and the impersonal utterance of
passion; and with an artist of the second class it is,
indeed, even more likely to be great, when the issue
has thus been narrowed and the whole force of the
writer's mind directed to passion alone. Cleverness
again, which has its fair field in the novel of character,
is debarred all entry upon this more solemn theatre.
A far-fetched motive, an ingenious evasion of the issue,
a witty instead of a passionate turn, offend us like an
insincerity. All should be plain, all straightforward to
the end. Hence, it is that, in *Rhoda Fleming*, Mrs. Lovel
raises such resentment in the reader; her motives are
too flimsy, her ways are too equivocal, for the weight
and strength of her surroundings. Hence the hot indignation of the reader when Balzac, after having begun
the *Duchesse de Langeais* in terms of strong if somewhat
swollen passion, cuts the knot by the derangement of
the hero's clock. Such personages and incidents belong
to the novel of character; they are out of place in the
high society of the passions; when the passions are
introduced in art at their full height, we look to see
them, not baffled and impotently striving, as in life, but

towering above circumstance and acting substitutes for fate.

And here I can imagine Mr. James, with his lucid sense, to intervene. To much of what I have said he would apparently demur; in much he would, somewhat impatiently, acquiesce. It may be true; but it is not what he desired to say or to hear said. He spoke of the finished picture and its worth when done; I, of the brushes, the palette, and the north light. He uttered his views in the tone and for the ear of good society; I, with the emphasis and technicalities of the obtrusive student. But the point, I may reply, is not merely to amuse the public, but to offer helpful advice to the young writer. And the young writer will not so much be helped by genial pictures of what an art may aspire to at its highest, as by a true idea of what it must be on the lowest terms. The best that we can say to him is this: Let him choose a motive, whether of character or passion; carefully construct his plot so that every incident is an illustration of the motive, and every property employed shall bear to it a near relation of congruity or contrast; avoid a sub-plot, unless, as sometimes in Shakespeare, the sub-plot be a reversion or complement of the main intrigue; suffer not his style to flag below the level of the argument; pitch the key of conversation, not with any thought of how men talk in parlours, but with a single eye to the degree of passion he may be called on to express; and allow neither himself in the narrative, nor any character in the course of the dialogue, to utter one sentence that is not part and parcel of the business of the story or the discussion of the problem involved. Let him not regret if this shortens his book; it will be better so; for to add irrelevant matter is not to lengthen but to bury. Let him not mind if he miss a thousand qualities, so that he keeps unflaggingly in pursuit of the one he has chosen. Let him not care particularly if he miss the tone of conversation, the pungent material detail of the day's manners, the reproduction of the atmosphere and

the environment. These elements are not essential:
a novel may be excellent, and yet have none of them;
a passion or a character is so much the better depicted
as it rises clearer from material circumstance. In this
age of the particular, let him remember the ages of the
abstract, the great books of the past, the brave men that
lived before Shakespeare and before Balzac. And as
the root of the whole matter, let him bear in mind that
his novel is not a transcript of life, to be judged by
its exactitude; but a simplification of some side or
point of life, to stand or fall by its significant simplicity.
For although, in great men, working upon great motives,
what we observe and admire is often their complexity,
yet underneath appearances the truth remains unchanged: that simplification was their method, and that
simplicity is their excellence.

II

Since the above was written another novelist has entered repeatedly the lists of theory: one well worthy of
mention, Mr. W. D. Howells; and none ever couched a
lance with narrower convictions. His own work and
those of his pupils and masters singly occupy his mind;
he is the bond-slave, the zealot of his school; he dreams
of an advance in art like what there is in science; he
thinks of past things as radically dead; he thinks a
form can be outlived: a strange immersion in his own
history; a strange forgetfulness of the history of the
race! Meanwhile, by a glance at his own works (could
he see them with the eager eyes of his readers) much of
this illusion would be dispelled. For while he holds all
the poor little orthodoxies of the day—no poorer and no
smaller than those of yesterday or to-morrow, poor and
small, indeed, only so far as they are exclusive—the
living quality of much that he has done is of a contrary, I had almost said of a heretical, complexion. A
man, as I read him, of an originally strong romantic

bent—a certain glow of romance still resides in many of his books, and lends them their distinction. As by accident he runs out and revels in the exceptional; and it is then, as often as not, that his reader rejoices —justly, as I contend. For in all this excessive eagerness to be centrally human, is there not one central human thing that Mr. Howells is too often tempted to neglect: I mean himself? A poet, a finished artist, a man in love with the appearances of life, a cunning reader of the mind, he has other passions and aspirations than those he loves to draw. And why should he suppress himself and do such reverence to the Lemuel Barkers? The obvious is not of necessity the normal; fashion rules and deforms; the majority fall tamely into the contemporary shape, and thus attain, in the eyes of the true observer, only a higher power of insignificance; and the danger is lest, in seeking to draw the normal, a man should draw the null, and write the novel of society instead of the romance of man.

RANDOM MEMORIES

THESE papers appeared originally as follows:

I. *Scribner's Magazine*, January, 1888.
II. *Scribner's Magazine*, February, 1888.
III. *Scribner's Magazine*, March, 1888.
IV. *Scribner's Magazine*, April, 1888.
V. *Scribner's Magazine*, October, 1888.
VI. *Scribner's Magazine*, November, 1888.
VII. *Scribner's Magazine*, December, 1888.
VIII. The last paper was drafted in 1893 or 1894 towards a projected new series of essays for *Scribner's Magazine*.

RANDOM MEMORIES

I

A CHAPTER ON DREAMS

THE past is all of one texture—whether feigned or suffered—whether acted out in three dimensions, or only witnessed in that small theatre of the brain which we keep brightly lighted all night long, after the jets are down, and darkness and sleep reign undisturbed in the remainder of the body. There is no distinction on the face of our experiences; one is vivid indeed, and one dull, and one pleasant, and another agonising to remember, but which of them is what we call true, and which a dream, there is not one hair to prove. The past stands on a precarious footing; another straw split in the field of metaphysic, and behold us robbed of it. There is scarce a family that can count four generations but lays a claim to some dormant title or some castle and estate: a claim not prosecutable in any court of law, but flattering to the fancy and a great alleviation of idle hours. A man's claim to his own past is yet less valid. A paper might turn up (in proper story-book fashion) in the secret drawer of an old ebony secretary, and restore your family to its ancient honours, and reinstate mine in a certain West Indian islet (not far from St. Kitt's, as beloved tradition hummed in my young ears) which was once ours, and is now unjustly someone else's, and for that matter (in the state of the sugar trade) is not worth anything to anybody. I do not say that these revolutions are likely; only no man can deny that they are possible; and the past, on the other hand, is lost for ever: our old days and deeds, our old selves, too, and the very world in which these scenes were acted, all brought down to the same faint residuum as a last night's dream, to some incontinuous images, and an echo in the chambers of the brain. Not an hour, not a mood, not a glance of the eye, can we revoke; it is all gone, past conjuring. And yet conceive us robbed of it, conceive that little thread of memory that we trail behind us broken at the pocket's edge; and in what naked nullity should we be left! for we only guide ourselves, and only know ourselves, by these air-painted pictures of the past.

Upon these grounds, there are some among us who claimed to have lived longer and more richly than their neighbours; when they lay asleep they claim they were still active; and among the treasures of memory that all men review for their amusement, these count in no second place the harvests of their dreams. There is one of this kind whom I have in my eye, and whose case is perhaps unusual enough to be described. He was from a child an ardent and uncomfortable dreamer. When he had a touch of fever at night, and the room swelled and shrank, and his clothes, hanging on a nail, now loomed up instant to the bigness of a church, and now drew away into a horror of infinite distance and infinite littleness, the poor soul was very well aware of what must follow, and struggled hard against the approaches of that slumber which was the beginning of sorrows. But his struggles were in vain; sooner or later the night-hag would have him by the throat, and pluck him, strangling and screaming, from his sleep. His dreams were at times commonplace enough, at times very strange: at times they were almost formless, he would be haunted, for instance, by nothing more definite than a certain hue of brown, which he did not mind in the least while he was awake, but feared and loathed while he was dreaming; at times, again, they took on

every detail of circumstance, as when once he supposed
he must swallow the populous world, and awoke screaming with the horror of the thought. The two chief
troubles of his very narrow existence—the practical and
everyday trouble at school tasks and the ultimate and
airy one of hell and judgment—were often confounded
together into one appalling nightmare. He seemed to
himself to stand before the Great White Throne; he was
called on, poor little devil, to recite some form of words,
on which his destiny depended; his tongue stuck, his
memory was blank, hell gaped for him; and he would
awake, clinging to the curtain-rod with his knees to his
chin.

These were extremely poor experiences, on the whole;
and at that time of life my dreamer would have very
willingly parted with his power of dreams. But
presently, in the course of his growth, the cries and
physical contortions passed away, seemingly for ever;
his visions were still for the most part miserable, but
they were more constantly supported; and he would
awake with no more extreme symptom than a flying
heart, a freezing scalp, cold sweats, and the speechless
midnight fear. His dreams, too, as befitted a mind
better stocked with particulars, became more circum-
stantial, and had more the air and continuity of life.
The look of the world beginning to take hold on his
attention, scenery came to play a part in his sleeping
as well as in his waking thoughts, so that he would take
long, uneventful journeys and see strange towns and
beautiful places as he lay in bed. And, what is more
significant, an odd taste that he had for the Georgian
costume and for stories laid in that period of English
history, began to rule the features of his dreams; so that
he masqueraded there in a three-cornered hat, and was
much engaged with Jacobite conspiracy between the
hour for bed and that for breakfast. About the same
time, he began to read in his dreams—tales, for the
most part, and for the most part after the manner of
G. P. R. James, but so incredibly more vivid and

moving than any printed book, that he has ever since been malcontent with literature.

And then, while he was yet a student, there came to him a dream-adventure which he has no anxiety to repeat; he began, that is to say, to dream in sequence and thus to lead a double life—one of the day, one of the night—one that he had every reason to believe was the true one, another that he had no means of proving to be false. I should have said he studied, or was by way of studying, at Edinburgh College, which (it may be supposed) was how I came to know him. Well, in his dream-life, he passed a long day in the surgical theatre, his heart in his mouth, his teeth on edge, seeing monstrous malformations and the abhorred dexterity of surgeons. In a heavy, rainy, foggy evening he came forth into the South Bridge, turned up the High Street, and entered the door of a tall *land*, at the top of which he supposed himself to lodge. All night long, in his wet clothes, he climbed the stairs, stair after stair in endless series, and at every second flight a flaring lamp with a reflector. All night long, he brushed by single persons passing downward—beggarly women of the street, great, weary, muddy labourers, poor scarecrows of men, pale parodies of women—but all drowsy and weary like himself, and all single, and all brushing against him as they passed. In the end, out of a northern window, he would see day beginning to whiten over the Firth, give up the ascent, turn to descend, and in a breath be back again upon the streets, in his wet clothes, in the wet, haggard dawn, trudging to another day of monstrosities and operations. Time went quicker in the life of dreams, some seven hours (as near as he can guess) to one; and it went, besides, more intensely, so that the gloom of these fancied experiences clouded the day, and he had not shaken off their shadow ere it was time to lie down and to renew them. I cannot tell how long it was that he endured this discipline; but it was long enough to leave a great black blot upon his memory, long enough to send him, trembling for his reason, to

the doors of a certain doctor; whereupon with a simple
draught he was restored to the common lot of man.

The poor gentleman has since been troubled by
nothing of the sort; indeed, his nights were for some
while like any other man's, now blank, now chequered
with dreams, and these sometimes charming, sometimes
appalling, but except for an occasional vividness, of no
extraordinary kind. I will just note one of these occasions, ere I pass on to what makes my dreamer truly
interesting. It seemed to him that he was in the first
floor of a rough hill-farm. The room showed some poor
efforts at gentility, a carpet on the floor, a piano, I
think, against the wall; but, for all these refinements,
there was no mistaking he was in a moorland place,
among hillside people, and set in miles of heather. He
looked down from the window upon a bare farm-yard,
that seemed to have been long disused. A great, uneasy
stillness lay upon the world. There was no sign of the
farm-folk or of any live-stock, save for an old, brown,
curly dog of the retriever breed, who sat close in against
the wall of the house and seemed to be dozing. Something about this dog disquieted the dreamer; it was
quite a nameless feeling, for the beast looked right
enough—indeed, he was so old and dull and dusty and
broken down, that he should rather have awakened
pity; and yet the conviction came and grew upon the
dreamer that this was no proper dog at all, but something hellish. A great many dozing summer flies
hummed about the yard; and presently the dog thrust
forth his paw, caught a fly in his open palm, carried it
to his mouth like an ape, and looking suddenly up at
the dreamer in the window, winked to him with one eye.
The dream went on, it matters not how it went; it was
a good dream as dreams go; but there was nothing in
the sequel worthy of that devilish brown dog. And the
point of interest for me lies partly in that very fact:
that having found so singular an incident, my imperfect dreamer should prove unable to carry the tale to
a fit end and fall back on indescribable noises and

indiscriminate horrors. It would be different now; he knows his business better!

For, to approach at last the point: This honest fellow had long been in the custom of setting himself to sleep with tales, and so had his father before him; but these were irresponsible inventions, told for the teller's pleasure, with no eye to the crass public or the thwart reviewer: tales where a thread might be dropped, or one adventure quitted for another, on fancy's least suggestion. So that the little people who manage man's internal theatre had not as yet received a very rigorous training; and played upon their stage like children who should have slipped into the house and found it empty, rather than like drilled actors performing a set piece to a huge hall of faces. But presently my dreamer began to turn his former amusement of story-telling to (what is called) account; by which I mean that he began to write and sell his tales. Here was he, and here were the little people who did that part of his business, in quite new conditions. The stories must now be trimmed and pared and set upon all fours, they must run from a beginning to an end and fit (after a manner) with the laws of life; the pleasure, in one word, had become a business; and that not only for the dreamer, but for the little people of his theatre. These understood the change as well as he. When he lay down to prepare himself for sleep, he no longer sought amusement, but printable and profitable tales; and after he had dozed off in his box-seat, his little people continued their evolutions with the same mercantile designs. All other forms of dream deserted him but two: he still occasionally reads the most delightful books, he still visits at times the most delightful places; and it is perhaps worthy of note that to these same places, and to one in particular, he returns at intervals of months and years, finding new field-paths, visiting new neighbours, beholding that happy valley under new effects of noon and dawn and sunset. But all the rest of the family of visions is quite lost to him: the common, mangled

version of yesterday's affairs, the raw-head-and-bloody-
bones nightmare, rumoured to be the child of toasted
cheese—these and their like are gone; and, for the most
part, whether awake or asleep, he is simply occupied—
he or his little people—in consciously making stories for
the market. This dreamer (like many other persons)
has encountered some trifling vicissitudes of fortune.
When the bank begins to send letters and the butcher
to linger at the back gate, he sets to belabouring his
brains after a story, for that is his readiest money-
winner; and, behold! at once the little people begin to
bestir themselves in the same quest, and labour all night
long, and all night long set before him truncheons of
tales upon their lighted theatre. No fear of his being
frightened now; the flying heart and the frozen scalp
are things bygone; applause, growing applause, growing
interest, growing exultation in his own cleverness (for
he takes all the credit), and at last a jubilant leap to
wakefulness, with the cry, "I have it, that'll do!"
upon his lips: with such and similar emotions he sits
at these nocturnal dramas, with such outbreaks, like
Claudius in the play, he scatters the performance in
the midst. Often enough the waking is a disappointment; he has been too deep asleep, as I explain the
thing; drowsiness has gained his little people, they have
gone stumbling and maundering through their parts;
and the play, to the awakened mind, is seen to be a
issue of absurdities. And yet how often have these
sleepless Brownies done him honest service, and given
him, as he sat idly taking his pleasure in the boxes,
better tales than he could fashion for himself.

Here is one, exactly as it came to him. It seemed he
was the son of a very rich and wicked man, the owner
of broad acres and a most damnable temper. The
dreamer (and that was the son) had lived much abroad,
on purpose to avoid his parent; and when at length he
returned to England, it was to find him married again
to a young wife, who was supposed to suffer cruelly and
to loathe her yoke. Because of this marriage (as the

dreamer indistinctly understood) it was desirable for father and son to have a meeting; and yet both being proud and both angry, neither would condescend upon a visit. Meet they did accordingly, in a desolate, sandy country by the sea, and there they quarrelled, and the son, stung by some intolerable insult, struck down the father dead. No suspicion was aroused; the dead man was found and buried, and the dreamer succeeded to the broad estates, and found himself installed under the same roof with his father's widow, for whom no provision had been made. These two lived very much alone, as people may after a bereavement, sat down to table together, shared the long evenings, and grew daily better friends; until it seemed to him of a sudden that she was prying about dangerous matters, that she had conceived a notion of his guilt, that she watched him and tried him with questions. He drew back from her company as men draw back from a precipice suddenly discovered; and yet so strong was the attraction that he would drift again and again into the old intimacy, and again and again be startled back by some suggestive question or some inexplicable meaning in her eye. So they lived at cross purposes, a life full of broken dialogue, challenging glances, and suppressed passion until, one day, he saw the woman slipping from the house in a veil, followed her to the station, followed her in the train to the seaside country, and out over the sand-hills to the very place where the murder was done. There she began to grope among the bents, he watching her, flat upon his face; and presently she had something in her hand—I cannot remember what it was, but it was deadly evidence against the dreamer—and as she held it up to look at it, perhaps from the shock of the discovery, her foot slipped, and she hung at some peril on the brink of the tall sand-wreaths. He had no thought but to spring up and rescue her; and there they stood face to face, she with that deadly matter openly in her hand—his very presence on the spot another link of proof. It was plain she was about to speak, but th

was more than he could bear—he could bear to be lost,
but not to talk of it with his destroyer; and he cut her
short with trivial conversation. Arm in arm, they returned together to the train, talking he knew not what,
made the journey back in the same carriage, sat down
to dinner, and passed the evening in the drawing-room
as in the past. But suspense and fear drummed in the
dreamer's bosom. "She has not denounced me yet"—
so his thoughts ran—"when will she denounce me?
Will it be to-morrow?" And it was not to-morrow,
nor the next day, nor the next; and their life settled
back on the old terms, only that she seemed kinder than
before, and that, as for him, the burthen of his suspense and wonder grew daily more unbearable, so that
he wasted away like a man with a disease. Once, indeed, he broke all bounds of decency, seized an occasion
when she was abroad, ransacked her room, and at last,
hidden away among her jewels, found the damning evidence. There he stood, holding this thing, which was
his life, in the hollow of his hand, and marvelling at her
inconsequent behaviour, that she should seek, and keep,
and yet not use it; and then the door opened, and behold
herself. So, once more, they stood, eye to eye, with the
evidence between them; and once more she raised to
him a face brimming with some communication; and
once more he shied away from speech and cut her off.
But before he left the room, which he had turned up-
side down, he laid back his death-warrant where he had
found it; and at that, her face lighted up. The next
thing he heard, she was explaining to her maid, with
some ingenious falsehood, the disorder of her things.
Flesh and blood could bear the strain no longer; and I
think it was the next morning (though chronology is
always hazy in the theatre of the mind) that he burst
from his reserve. They had been breakfasting together
in one corner of a great, parqueted, sparely furnished
room of many windows; all the time of the meal she had
tortured him with sly allusions; and no sooner were the
servants gone and these two protagonists alone together,

than he leaped to his feet. She too sprang up, with a
pale face; with a pale face, she heard him as he raved
out his complaint: Why did she torture him so? she
knew all, she knew he was no enemy to her; why did
she not denounce him at once? what signified her whole
behaviour? why did she torture him? and yet again,
why did she torture him? And when he had done, she
fell upon her knees, and with outstretched hands: " Do
you not understand? " she cried. " I love you! "

Hereupon, with a pang of wonder and mercantile delight, the dreamer awoke. His mercantile delight was
not of long endurance; for it soon became plain that
in this spirited tale there were unmarketable elements;
which is just the reason why you have it here so briefly
told. But his wonder has still kept growing; and I
think the reader's will also, if he consider it ripely. For
now he sees why I speak of the little people as of substantive inventors and performers. To the end they had
kept their secret. I will go bail for the dreamer (having
excellent grounds for valuing his candour) that he had
no guess whatever at the motive of the woman—the
hinge of the whole well-invented plot—until the instant
of that highly dramatic declaration. It was not his
tale; it was the little people's! And observe: not only
was the secret kept, the story was told with really guile-
ful craftsmanship. The conduct of both actors is (in
the cant phrase) psychologically correct, and the emotion aptly graduated up to the surprising climax. I
am awake now, and I know this trade; and yet I cannot
better it. I am awake, and I live by this business;
and yet I could not outdo—could not perhaps equal—
that crafty artifice (as of some old, experienced carpenter of plays, some Dennery or Sardou) by which the
same situation is twice presented and the two actors
twice brought face to face over the evidence, only once
it is in her hand, once in his—and these in their due
order, the least dramatic first. The more I think of it,
the more I am moved to press upon the world my
question: Who are the Little People? They are near

connections of the dreamer's, beyond doubt; they share
in his financial worries and have an eye to the bank-
book; they share plainly in his training; they have
plainly learned like him to build the scheme of a considerate story and to arrange emotion in progressive
order; only I think they have more talent; and one
thing is beyond doubt, they can tell him a story piece
by piece, like a serial, and keep him all the while in
ignorance of where they aim. Who are they, then? and
who is the dreamer?

Well, as regards the dreamer, I can answer that, for
he is no less a person than myself;—as I might have
told you from the beginning, only that the critics murmur over my consistent egotism;—and as I am posi-
tively forced to tell you now, or I could advance but
little farther with my story. And for the Little People,
what shall I say they are but just my Brownies, God
bless them! who do one-half my work for me while I
am fast asleep, and in all human likelihood, do the rest
for me as well, when I am wide awake and fondly suppose I do it for myself. That part which is done while
I am sleeping is the Brownies' part beyond contention;
but that which is done while I am up and about is by
no means necessarily mine, since all goes to show the
Brownies have a hand in it even then. Here is a doubt
that much concerns my conscience. For myself—what
I call I, my conscience ego, the denizen of the pineal
gland unless he has changed his residence since
Descartes, the man with the conscience and the variable
bank-account, the man with the hat and the boots, and
the privilege of voting and not crying his candidate at
the general elections—I am sometimes tempted to suppose he is no story-teller at all, but a creature as matter
of fact as any cheesemonger or any cheese, and a realist
bemired up to the ears in actuality; so that, by that
account, the whole of my published fiction should be
the single-handed product of some Brownie, some
Familiar, some unseen collaborator, whom I keep locked
in a back garret, while I get all the praise and he but a

share (which I cannot prevent him getting) of the
pudding. I am an excellent adviser, something like
Molière's servant; I pull back and I cut down; and I
dress the whole in the best words and sentences that I
can find and make; I hold the pen, too; and I do the
sitting at the table, which is about the worst of it; and
when all is done, I make up the manuscript and pay
for the registration; so that, on the whole, I have some
claim to share, though not so largely as I do, in the
profits of our common enterprise.

I can but give an instance or so of what part is done
sleeping and what part awake, and leave the reader to
share what laurels there are, at his own nod, between
myself and my collaborators; and to do this I will first
take a book that a number of persons have been polite
enough to read, the *Strange Case of Dr. Jekyll and Mr.
Hyde.* I had long been trying to write a story on this
subject, to find a body, a vehicle, for that strong sense
of man's double being, which must at times come in
upon and overwhelm the mind of every thinking creature. I had even written one, *The Travelling Companion,* which was returned by an editor on the plea
that it was a work of genius and indecent, and which I
burned the other day on the ground that it was not a
work of genius, and that *Jekyll* had supplanted it. Then
came one of those financial fluctuations to which (with
an elegant modesty) I have hitherto referred in the
third person. For two days I went about racking my
brains for a plot of any sort; and on the second night I
dreamed the scene at the window, and a scene afterwards split in two, in which Hyde, pursued for some
crime, took the powder and underwent the change in the
presence of his pursuers. All the rest was made awake,
and consciously, although I think I can trace in much
of it the manner of my Brownies. The meaning of the
tale is therefore mine, and had long pre-existed in my
garden of Adonis, and tried one body after another in
vain; indeed, I do most of the morality, worse luck!
and my Brownies have not a rudiment of what we call

a conscience. Mine, too, is the setting, mine the characters. All that was given me was the matter of three scenes, and the central idea of a voluntary change becoming involuntary. Will it be thought ungenerous, after I have been so liberally ladling out praise to my unseen collaborators, if I here toss them over, bound hand and foot, into the arena of the critics? For the business of the powders, which so many have censured, is, I am relieved to say, not mine at all but the Brownies'. Of another tale, in case the reader should have glanced at it, I may say a word: the not very defensible story of *Olalla*. Here the court, the mother, the mother's niche, Olalla, Olalla's chamber, the meetings on the stair, the broken window, the ugly scene of the bite, were all given me in bulk and detail as I have tried to write them; to this I added only the external scenery (for in my dream I never was beyond the court), the portrait, the characters of Felipe and the priest, the moral, such as it is, and the last pages, such as, alas! they are. And I may even say that in this case the moral itself was given me; for it arose immediately on a comparison of the mother and the daughter, and from the hideous trick of atavism in the first. Sometimes a parabolic sense is still more undeniably present in a dream; sometimes I cannot but suppose my Brownies have been aping Bunyan, and yet in no case with what would possibly be called a moral in a tract; never with the ethical narrowness; conveying hints instead of life's larger limitations and that sort of sense which we seem to perceive in the arabesque of time and space.

For the most part, it will be seen, my Brownies are somewhat fantastic, like their stories hot and hot, full of passion and the picturesque, alive with animating incident; and they have no prejudice against the supernatural. But the other day they gave me a surprise, entertaining me with a love-story, a little April comedy, which I ought certainly to hand over to the author of *A Chance Acquaintance*, for he could write it as it should be written, and I am sure (although I mean to try) that I cannot.—But who would have supposed that a Brownie of mine should invent a tale for Mr. Howells?

II

THE LANTERN-BEARERS

I

THESE boys congregated every autumn about a
certain easterly fisher-village, where they tasted in
a high degree the glory of existence. The place was
created seemingly on purpose for the diversion of young
gentlemen. A street or two of houses, mostly red and
many of them tiled; a number of fine trees clustered
about the manse and the kirkyard, and turning the chief
street into a shady alley; many little gardens more than
usually bright with flowers; nets a-drying, and fisher-
wives scolding in the backward parts; a smell of fish,
a genial smell of seaweed; whiffs of blowing sand at the
street corners; shops with golf-balls and bottled lolli-
pops; another shop with penny pickwicks (that remarkable cigar) and the *London Journal*, dear to me for
its startling pictures, and a few novels, dear for their
suggestive names: such, as well as memory serves me,
were the ingredients of the town. These, you are to
conceive posted on a spit between two sandy bays, and
sparsely flanked with villas—enough for the boys to
lodge in with their subsidiary parents, not enough (not
yet enough) to cocknify the scene: a haven in the rocks
in front: in front of that, a file of grey islets: to the
left, endless links and sand-wreaths, a wilderness of
hiding-holes, alive with popping rabbits and soaring
gulls; to the right, a range of seaward crags, one rugged
brow beyond another; the ruins of a mighty and ancient
fortress on the brink of one; coves between—now
charmed into sunshine quiet, now whistling with wind

and clamorous with bursting surges; the dens and sheltered hollows redolent of thyme and southernwood, the air at the cliff's edge brisk and clean and pungent of the sea—in front of all, the Bass Rock, tilted seaward like a doubtful bather, the surf ringing it with white, the solan-geese hanging round its summit like a great and glittering smoke. This choice piece of sea-board was sacred, besides, to the wrecker; and the Bass, in the eye of fancy, still flew the colours of King James; and in the ear of fancy the arches of Tantallon still rang with horse-shoe iron, and echoed to the commands of Bell-the-Cat.

There was nothing to mar your days, if you were a boy summering in that part, but the embarrassment of pleasure. You might golf if you wanted; but I seem to have been better employed. You might secrete yourself in the Lady's Walk, a certain sunless dingle of elders, all mossed over by the damp as green as grass, and dotted here and there by the stream-side with roofless walls, the cold homes of anchorites. To fit themselves for life, and with a special eye to acquire the art of smoking, it was even common for the boys to harbour there; and you might have seen a single penny pickwick, honestly shared in lengths with a blunt knife, bestrew the glen with these apprentices. Again, you might join our fishing-parties, where we sat perched as thick as solan-geese, a covey of little anglers, boy and girl, angling over each other's heads, to the much entanglement of lines and loss of podleys and consequent shrill recrimination—shrill as the geese themselves. Indeed, had that been all, you might have done this often; but though fishing be a fine pastime, the podley is scarce to be regarded as a dainty for the table; and it was a point of honour that a boy should eat all that he had taken. Or again, you might climb the Law, where the whale's jawbone stood landmark in the buzzing wind, and behold the face of many counties, and the smoke and spires of many towns, and the sails of distant ships. You might bathe, now in the flaws of fine weather, that we pathetically call our summer, now in a gale of wind, with the sand scourging your bare hide, your clothes thrashing abroad from underneath their guardian stone, the froth of the great breakers casting you headlong ere it had drowned your knees. Or you might explore the tidal rocks, above all in the ebb of spring, when the very roots of the hills were for the nonce discovered; following my leader from one group to another, groping in slippery tangle for the wreck of ships, wading in pools after the abominable creatures of the sea, and ever with an eye cast backward on the march of the tide and the menaced line of your retreat. And then you might go Crusoeing, a word that covers all extempore eating in the open air: digging perhaps a house under the margin of the links, kindling a fire of the sea-ware, and cooking apples there—if they were truly apples, for I sometimes suppose the merchant must have played us off with some inferior and quite local fruit, capable of resolving, in the neighbourhood of fire, into mere sand and smoke and iodine; or perhaps pushing to Tantallon, you might lunch on sandwiches and visions in the grassy court, while the wind hummed in the crumbling turrets; or clambering along the coast, eat geans * (the worst, I must suppose, in Christendom) from an adventurous gean-tree that had taken root under a cliff, where it was shaken with an ague of east wind, and silvered after gales with salt, and grew so foreign among its bleak surroundings that to eat of its produce was an adventure in itself.

There are mingled some dismal memories with so many that were joyous. Of the fisher-wife, for instance, who had cut her throat at Canty Bay; and of how I ran with the other children to the top of the Quadrant, and beheld a posse of silent people escorting a cart, and on the cart, bound in a chair, her throat bandaged, and the bandage all bloody—horror!—the fisher-wife herself, who continued thenceforth to hag-ride my thoughts, and even to-day (as I recall the scene) darkens daylight.

* Wild cherries.

She was lodged in the little old jail in the chief street; but whether or no she died there, with a wise terror of the worst, I never inquired. She had been tippling; it was but a dingy tragedy; and it seems strange and hard that, after all these years, the poor crazy sinner should be still pilloried on her cart in the scrap-book of my memory. Nor shall I readily forget a certain house in the Quadrant where a visitor died, and a dark old woman continued to dwell alone with the dead body; nor how this old woman conceived a hatred to myself and one of my cousins, and in the dread hour of the dusk, as we were clambering on the garden-walls, opened a window in that house of mortality and cursed us in a shrill voice and with a marrowy choice of language. It was a pair of very colourless urchins that fled down the lane from this remarkable experience! But I recall with a more doubtful sentiment, compounded out of fear and exultation, the coil of equinoctial tempests; trumpeting squalls, scouring flaws of rain; the boats with their reefed lug-sails scudding for the harbour mouth, where danger lay, for it was hard to make when the wind had any east in it; the wives clustered with blowing shawls at the pierhead, where (if fate was against them) they might see boat and husband and sons—their whole wealth and their whole family—engulfed under their eyes; and (what I saw but once) a troop of neighbours forcing such an unfortunate homeward, and she squalling and battling in their midst, a figure scarcely human, a tragic Mænad.

These are things that I recall with interest; but what my memory dwells upon the most I have been all this while withholding. It was a sport peculiar to the place, and indeed to a week or so of our two months' holiday there. Maybe it still flourishes in its native spot; for boys and their pastimes are swayed by periodic forces inscrutable to man; so that tops and marbles reappear in their due season, regular like the sun and moon; and the harmless art of knucklebones has seen the fall of the Roman Empire and the rise of the United States. It may still flourish in its native spot, but nowhere else, I am persuaded; for I tried myself to introduce it on Tweedside, and was defeated lamentably; its charm being quite local, like a country wine that cannot be exported.

The idle manner of it was this:—

Toward the end of September, when school-time was drawing near and the nights were already black, we would begin to sally from our respective villas, each equipped with a tin bull's-eye lantern. The thing was so well known that it had worn a rut in the commerce of Great Britain; and the grocers, about the due time, began to garnish their windows with our particular brand of luminary. We wore them buckled to the waist upon a cricket belt, and over them, such was the rigour of the game, a buttoned top-coat. They smelled noisomely of blistered tin; they never burned aright, though they would always burn our fingers; their use was naught; the pleasure of them merely fanciful; and yet a boy with a bull's-eye under his top-coat asked for nothing more. The fishermen used lanterns about their boats, and it was from them, I suppose, that we had got the hint; but theirs were not bull's-eyes, nor did we ever play at being fishermen. The police carried them at their belts, and we had plainly copied them in that; yet we did not pretend to be policemen. Burglars, indeed, we may have had some haunting thoughts of; and we had certainly an eye to past ages when lanterns were more common, and to certain story-books in which we had found them to figure very largely. But take it for all in all, the pleasure of the thing was substantive; and to be a boy with a bull's-eye under his top-coat was good enough for us.

When two of these asses met, there would be an anxious " Have you got your lantern? " and a gratified " Yes! " That was the shibboleth, and very needful too; for, as it was the rule to keep our glory contained, none could recognise a lantern-bearer, unless (like the pole-cat) by the smell. Four or five would sometimes climb into the belly of a ten-man lugger, with nothing but the thwarts above them—for the cabin was usually locked; or choose out some hollow of the links where the wind might whistle overhead. There the coats would be unbuttoned and the bull's-eye discovered; and in the chequering glimmer, under the huge windy hall of the night, and cheered by a rich steam of toasting tin-ware, these fortunate young gentlemen would crouch together in the cold sand of the links or on the scaly bilges of the fishing-boat, and delight themselves with inappropriate talk. Woe is me that I may not give some specimens—some of their foresights of life, or deep inquiries into the rudiments of man and nature, these were so fiery and so innocent, they were so richly silly, so romantically young. But the talk, at any rate, was but a condiment; and these gatherings themselves only accidents in the career of the lantern-bearer. The essence of this bliss was to walk by yourself in the black night; the slide shut, the top-coat buttoned; not a ray escaping, whether to conduct your footsteps or to make your glory public; a mere pillar of darkness in the dark; and all the while, deep down in the privacy of your fool's heart, to know you had a bull's-eye at your belt, and to exult and sing over the knowledge.

II

It is said that a poet has died young in the breast of the most stolid. It may be contended, rather, that this (somewhat minor) bard in almost every case survives, and is the spice of life to his possessor. Justice is not done to the versatility and the unplumbed childishness of man's imagination. His life from without may seem but a rude mound of mud; there will be some golden chamber at the heart of it, in which he dwells delighted; and for as dark as his pathway seems to the observer, he will have some kind of a bull's-eye at his belt.

It would be hard to pick out a career more cheerless than that of Dancer, the miser, as he figures in the " Old Bailey Reports," a prey to the most sordid persecutions, the butt of his neighbourhood, betrayed by his hired man, his house beleaguered by the impish school-boy, and he himself grinding and fuming and impotently fleeing to the law against these pin-pricks. You marvel at first that anyone should willingly prolong a life so destitute of charm and dignity; and then you call to memory that had he chosen, had he ceased to be a miser, he could have been freed at once from these trials, and might have built himself a castle and gone escorted by a squadron. For the love of more recondite joys, which we cannot estimate, which, it may be, we should envy, the man had willingly forgone both comfort and con- sideration. " His mind to him a kingdom was "; and sure enough, digging into that mind, which seems at first a dust-heap, we unearth some priceless jewels. For Dancer must have had the love of power and the disdain of using it, a noble character in itself; disdain of many pleasures, a chief part of what is commonly called wis- dom; disdain of the inevitable end, that finest trait of mankind; scorn of men's opinions, another element of virtue; and at the back of all, a conscience just like yours and mine, whining like a cur, swindling like a thimble-rigger, but still pointing (there or thereabout) to some conventional standard. Here were a cabinet portrait to which Hawthorne perhaps had done justice; and yet not Hawthorne either, for he was mildly minded, and it lay not in him to create for us that throb of the miser's pulse, his fretful energy of gusto, his vast arms of ambition clutching in he knows not what: in- satiable, insane, a god with a muck-rake. Thus, at least, looking in the bosom of the miser, consideration detects the poet in the full tide of life, with more, in- deed, of the poetic fire than usually goes to epics; and tracing that mean man about his cold hearth, and to and fro in his discomfortable house, spies within him a blazing bonfire of delight. And so with others, who do not live by bread alone, but by some cherished and perhaps fantastic pleasure; who are meat salesmen to the external eye, and possibly to themselves are Shakespeares, Napoleons, or Beethovens; who have not one virtue to rub against another in the field of active life, and yet perhaps, in the life of contemplation, sit with the saints. We see them on the street, and we can count their buttons; but Heaven knows in what they pride themselves! Heaven knows where they have set their treasure!

There is one fable that touches very near the quick of life; the fable of the monk who passed into the woods, heard a bird break into song, hearkened for a trill or two, and found himself on his return a stranger at his convent gates; for he had been absent fifty years, and of all his comrades there survived but one to recognise him. It is not only in the woods that this enchanter carols, though perhaps he is native there. He sings in the most dolcful places. The miser hears him and chuckles, and the days are moments. With no more apparatus than an ill-smelling lantern I have evoked him on the naked links. All life that is not merely mechanical is spun out of two strands: seeking for that bird and hearing him. And it is just this that makes life so hard to value, and the delight of each so incommunicable. And just a knowledge of this, and a remembrance of those fortunate hours in which the bird has sung to us, that fills us with such wonder when we turn the pages of the realist. There, to be sure, we find a picture of life in so far as it consists of mud and of old iron, cheap desires and cheap fears, that which we are ashamed to remember and that which we are careless whether we forget; but of the note of that time-devouring nightingale we hear no news.

The case of these writers of romance is most obscure. They have been boys and youths; they have lingered outside the window of the beloved, who was then most probably writing to someone else; they have sat before a sheet of paper, and felt themselves mere continents of congested poetry, not one line of which would flow; they have walked alone in the woods, they have walked in cities under the countless lamps; they have been to sea, they have hated, they have feared, they have longed to knife a man, and maybe done it; the wild taste of life has stung their palate. Or, if you deny them all the rest, one pleasure at least they have tasted to the full—their books are there to prove it—the keen pleasure of successful literary composition. And yet they fill the globe with volumes, whose cleverness inspires me with despairing admiration, and whose consistent falsity to all I care to call existence, with despairing wrath. If I had no better hope than to continue to revolve among the dreary and petty businesses, and to be moved by the paltry hopes and fears with which they surround and animate their heroes, I declare I would die now. But there has never an hour of mine gone quite so dully yet; if it were spent waiting at a railway junction, I would have some scattering thoughts, I could count some grains of memory, compared to which the whole of one of these romances seems but dross.

These writers would retort (if I take them properly) that this was very true; that it was the same with themselves and other persons of (what they call) the artistic temperament; that in this we were exceptional, and should apparently be ashamed of ourselves; but that our works must deal exclusively with (what they call) the average man, who was a prodigious dull fellow, and quite dead to all but the paltriest considerations. I accept the issue. We can only know others by ourselves. The artistic temperament (a plague on the expression!) does not make us different from our fellowmen, or it would make us incapable of writing novels; and the average man (a murrain on the word!) is just like you and me, or he would not be average. It was Whitman who stamped a kind of Birmingham sacredness upon the latter phrase; but Whitman knew very well, and showed very nobly, that the average man was

full of joys and full of poetry of his own. And this
harping on life's dulness and man's meanness is a loud
profession of incompetence; it is one of two things: the
cry of the blind eye, *I cannot see*, or the complaint of
the dumb tongue, *I cannot utter*. To draw a life without delights is to prove I have not realised it. To
picture a man without some sort of poetry—well, it goes
near to prove my case, for it shows an author may have
little enough. To see Dancer only as a dirty, old,
small-minded, impotently fuming man, in a dirty house,
besieged by Harrow boys, and probably beset by small
attorneys, is to show myself as keen an observer
as . . . the Harrow boys. But these young gentlemen
(with a more becoming modesty) were content to pluck
Dancer by the coat-tails; they did not suppose they
had surprised his secret or could put him living in a
book: and it is there my error would have lain. Or say
that in the same romance—I continue to call these
books romances, in the hope of giving pain—say that
in the same romance, which now begins really to take
shape, I should leave to speak of Dancer, and follow
instead the Harrow boys; and say that I came on some
such business as that of my lantern-bearers on the links,
and described the boys as very cold, spat upon by
flurries of rain, and drearily surrounded, all of which
they were; and their talk as silly and indecent, which it
certainly was. I might upon these lines, and had I
Zola's genius, turn out, in a page or so, a gem of literary
art, render the lantern-light with the touches of a
master, and lay on the indecency with the ungrudging
hand of love; and when all was done, what a triumph
would my picture be of shallowness and dulness! how it
would have missed the point! how it would have belied
the boys! To the ear of the stenographer, the talk is
merely silly and indecent; but ask the boys themselves,
and they are discussing (as it is highly proper they
should) the possibilities of existence. To the eye of the
observer they are wet and cold and drearily surrounded;
but ask themselves, and they are in the heaven of

recondite pleasure, the ground of which is an ill-smelling lantern.

III

For, to repeat, the ground of a man's joy is often hard to hit. It may hinge at times upon a mere accessory, like the lantern, it may reside, like Dancer's in the mysterious inwards of psychology. It may consist with perpetual failure, and find exercise in the continued chase. It has so little bond with externals (such as the observer scribbles in his note-book) that it may even touch them not; and the man's true life, for which he consents to live, lie altogether in the field of fancy. The clergyman, in his spare hours, may be winning battles, the farmer sailing ships, the banker reaping triumph in the arts: all leading another life, plying another trade from that they chose; like the poet's housebuilder, who, after all, is cased in stone,

> " By his fireside, as impotent fancy prompts,
>   Rebuilds it to his liking."

In such a case the poetry runs underground. The observer (poor soul, with his documents!) is all abroad. For to look at the man is but to court deception. We shall see the trunk from which he draws his nourishment; but he himself is above and abroad in the green dome of foliage, hummed through by winds and nested in by nightingales. And the true realism were that of the poets, to climb up after him like a squirrel, and catch some glimpse of the heaven for which he lives. And the true realism, always and everywhere, is that of the poets to find out where joy resides, and give it a voice far beyond singing.

For to miss the joy is to miss all. In the joy of the actors lies the sense of any action. That is the explanation, that the excuse. To one who has not the secret of the lanterns, the scene upon the links is meaningless. And hence the haunting and truly spectral unreality of realistic books. Hence, when we read the English realists, the incredulous wonder with which we observe the hero's constancy under the submerging tide of dulness, and how he bears up with his jibbing sweetheart, and endures the chatter of idiot girls, and stands by his whole unfeatured wilderness of an existence, instead of seeking relief in drink or foreign travel. Hence in the French, in that meat-market of middle-aged sensuality, the disgusted surprise with which we see the hero drift sidelong, and practically quite untempted, into every description of misconduct and dishonour. In each, we miss the personal poetry, the enchanted atmosphere, that rainbow work of fancy that clothes what is naked and seems to ennoble what is base; in each, life falls dead like dough, instead of soaring away like a balloon into the colours of the sunset; each is true, each inconceivable; for no man lives in the external truth, among salts and acids, but in the warm, phantasmagoric chamber of his brain, with the painted windows and the storied walls.

Of this falsity we have had a recent example from a man who knows far better—Tolstoi's *Powers of Darkness*. Here is a piece full of force and truth, yet quite untrue. For before Mikita was led into so dire a situation he was tempted, and temptations are beautiful at least in part; and a work which dwells on the ugliness of crime and gives no hint of any loveliness in the temptation, sins against the modesty of life, and even when a Tolstoi writes it, sinks to melodrama. The peasants are not understood; they saw their life in fairer colours; even the deaf girl was clothed in poetry for Mikita, or he had never fallen. And so, once again even an Old Bailey melodrama, without some brightness of poetry and lustre of existence, falls into the inconceivable and ranks with fairy tales.

IV

In nobler books we are moved with something like the
emotions of life; and this emotion is very variously
provoked. We are so moved when Levine labours in the
field, when André sinks beyond emotion, when Richard
Feverel and Lucy Desborough meet beside the river,
when Antony, "not cowardly, puts off his helmet,"
when Kent has infinite pity on the dying Lear, when, in
Dostoieffsky's *Despised and Rejected*, the uncomplain-
ing hero drains his cup of suffering and virtue. These
are notes that please the great heart of man. Not only
love, and the fields, and the bright face of danger, but
sacrifice and death and unmerited suffering humbly supported, touch in us the vein of the poetic. We love to
think of them, we long to try them, we are humbly
hopeful that we may prove heroes also.

We have heard, perhaps, too much of lesser matters.
Here is the door, here is the open air.

Itur in antiquam silvam.

III

BEGGARS

I

IN a pleasant, airy, uphill country, it was my fortune when I was young to make the acquaintance of a certain beggar. I call him beggar, though he usually allowed his coat and his shoes (which were open-mouthed, indeed) to beg for him. He was the wreck of an athletic man, tall, gaunt, and bronzed; far gone in consumption, with that disquieting smile of the mortally stricken on his face; but still active afoot, still with the brisk military carriage, the ready military salute. Three ways led through this piece of country; and as I was inconstant in my choice, I believe he must often have awaited me in vain. But often enough, he caught me; often enough, from some place of ambush by the roadside, he would spring suddenly forth in the regulation attitude, and launching at once into his inconsequential talk, fall into step with me upon my farther course. "A fine morning, sir, though perhaps a trifle inclining to rain. I hope I see you well, sir. Why no, sir, I don't feel as hearty myself as I could wish, but I am keeping about my ordinary. I am pleased to meet you on the road, sir. I assure you I quite look forward to one of our little conversations." He loved the sound of his own voice inordinately, and though (with something too off-hand to call servility) he would always hasten to agree with anything you said, yet he could never suffer you to say it to an end. By what transition he slid to his favourite subject I have no memory; but we had never been long together on the

way before he was dealing, in a very military manner,
with the English poets. "Shelley was a fine poet, sir,
though a trifle atheistical in his opinions. His Queen
Mab, sir, is quite an atheistical work. Scott, sir, is not
so poetical a writer. With the works of Shakespeare I
am not so well acquainted, but he was a fine poet.
Keats—John Keats, sir—he was a very fine poet."
With such references, such trivial criticism, such loving
parade of his own knowledge, he would beguile the road,
striding forward uphill, his staff now clapped to the
ribs of his deep, resonant chest, now swinging in the air
with the remembered jauntiness of the private soldier;
and all the while his toes looking out of his boots, and
his shirt looking out of his elbows, and death looking
out of his smile, and his big, crazy frame shaken by
accesses of cough.

He would often go the whole way home with me:
often to borrow a book, and that book always a poet.
Off he would march, to continue his mendicant rounds,
with the volume slipped into the pocket of his ragged
coat; and although he would sometimes keep it quite a
while, yet it came always back again at last, not much
the worse for its travels into beggardom. And in this
way, doubtless, his knowledge grew and his glib, random
criticism took a wider range. But my library was not
the first he had drawn upon: at our first encounter, he
was already brimful of Shelley and the atheistical Queen
Mab, and "Keats—John Keats, sir." And I have often
wondered how he came by these acquirements; just as
I often wondered how he fell to be a beggar. He had
served through the Mutiny—of which (like so many
people) he could tell practically nothing beyond the
names of places, and that it was "difficult work, sir,"
and very hot, or that so-and-so was "a very fine commander, sir." He was far too smart a man to have
remained a private; in the nature of things, he must
have won his stripes. And yet here he was without a
pension. When I touched on this problem, he would
content himself with diffidently offering me advice. "A

man should be very careful when he is young, sir. If you'll excuse me saying so, a spirited young gentleman like yourself, sir, should be very careful. I was perhaps a trifle inclined to atheistical opinions myself." For (perhaps with a deeper wisdom than we are inclined in these days to admit) he plainly bracketed agnosticism with beer and skittles.

Keats—John Keats, sir—and Shelley were his favourite bards. I cannot remember if I tried him with Rossetti; but I know his taste to a hair, and if ever I did, he must have doted on that author. What took him was a richness in the speech; he loved the exotic, the unexpected word; the moving cadence of a phrase; a vague sense of emotion (about nothing) in the very letters of the alphabet: the romance of language. His honest head was very nearly empty, his intellect like a child's; and when he read his favourite authors, he can almost never have understood what he was reading. Yet the taste was not only genuine, it was exclusive; I tried in vain to offer him novels; he would none of them; he cared for nothing but romantic language that he could not understand. The case may be commoner than we suppose. I am reminded of a lad who was laid in the next cot to a friend of mine in a public hospital, and who was no sooner installed than he sent out (perhaps with his last pence) for a cheap Shakespeare. My friend pricked up his ears; fell at once in talk with his new neighbour, and was ready, when the book arrived, to make a singular discovery. For this lover of great literature understood not one sentence out of twelve, and his favourite part was that of which he understood the least—the inimitable, mouth-filling rodomontade of the ghost in *Hamlet*. It was a bright day in hospital when my friend expounded the sense of this beloved jargon: a task for which I am willing to believe my friend was very fit, though I can never regard it as an easy one. I know indeed a point or two, on which I would gladly question Mr. Shakespeare, that lover of big words, could he revisit the glimpses of the moon, or

could I myself climb backward to the spacious days of
Elizabeth. But in the second case, I should most likely
pretermit these questionings, and take my place instead
in the pit at the Blackfriars, to hear the actor in his
favourite part, playing up to Mr. Burbage, and rolling
out—as I seem to hear him—with a ponderous gusto—

> " Unhousel'd, disappointed, unanel'd."

What a pleasant chance, if we could go there in a party!
and what a surprise for Mr. Burbage, when the ghost
received the honours of the evening!

As for my old soldier, like Mr. Burbage and Mr.
Shakespeare, he is long since dead; and now lies buried,
I suppose, and nameless and quite forgotten, in some
poor city graveyard.—But not for me, you brave heart,
have you been buried! For me, you are still afoot,
tasting the sun and air, and striding southward. By the
groves of Comiston and beside the Hermitage of Braid,
by the Hunters' Tryst, and where the curlews and
plovers cry around Fairmilehead, I see and hear you,
stalwartly carrying your deadly sickness, cheerfully
discoursing of uncomprehended poets.

II

The thought of the old soldier recalls that of another
tramp, his counterpart. This was a little, lean, and fiery
man, with the eyes of a dog and the face of a gipsy;
whom I found one morning encamped with his wife and
children and his grinder's wheel, beside the burn of
Kinnaird. To this beloved dell I went, at that time,
daily; and daily the knife-grinder and I (for as long as
his tent continued pleasantly to interrupt my little
wilderness) sat on two stones, and smoked, and plucked
grass, and talked to the tune of the brown water. His
children were mere whelps, they fought and bit among
the fern like vermin. His wife was a mere squaw; I saw
her gather brush and tend the kettle, but she never

ventured to address her lord while I was present. The
tent was a mere gipsy hovel, like a sty for pigs. But the
grinder himself had the fine self-sufficiency and grave
politeness of the hunter and the savage; he did me the
honours of this dell, which had been mine but the day
before, took me far into the secrets of his life, and used
me (I am proud to remember) as a friend.

Like my old soldier, he was far gone in the national
complaint. Unlike him, he had a vulgar taste in letters;
scarce flying higher than the story papers; probably
finding no difference, certainly seeking none, between
Tannahill and Burns; his noblest thoughts, whether of
poetry or music, adequately embodied in that somewhat
obvious ditty,

> " Will ye gang, lassie, gang
>   To the braes o' Balquhidder ":

—which is indeed apt to echo in the ears of Scottish
children, and to him, in view of his experience, must
have found a special directness of address. But if he
had no fine sense of poetry in letters, he felt with a deep
joy the poetry of life. You should have heard him
speak of what he loved; of the tent pitched beside the
talking water; of the stars overhead at night; of the
blest return of morning, the peep of day over the moors,
the awaking birds among the birches; how he abhorred
the long winter shut in cities; and with what delight,
at the return of the spring, he once more pitched his
camp in the living out-of-doors. But we were a pair of
tramps; and to you, who are doubtless sedentary and
a consistent first-class passenger in life, he would scarce
have laid himself so open;—to you, he might have been
content to tell his story of a ghost—that of a buccaneer
with his pistols as he lived—whom he had once encountered in a seaside cave near Buckie; and that would
have been enough, for that would have shown you the
mettle of the man. Here was a piece of experience
solidly and livingly built up in words, here was a story
created, *teres atque rotundus.*

And to think of the old soldier, that lover of the literary bards! He had visited stranger spots than any seaside cave; encountered men more terrible than any spirit; done and dared and suffered in that incredible, unsung epic of the Mutiny War; played his part with the field force of Delhi, beleaguering and beleaguered; shared in that enduring, savage anger and contempt of death and decency that, for long months together, bedevil'd and inspired the army; was hurled to and fro in the battle-smoke of the assault; was there, perhaps, where Nicholson fell; was there when the attacking column, with hell upon every side, found the soldier's enemy—strong drink, and the lives of tens of thousands trembled in the scale, and the fate of the flag of England staggered. And of all this he had no more to say than "hot work, sir," or "the army suffered a great deal, sir," or "I believe General Wilson, sir, was not very highly thought of in the papers." His life was naught to him, the vivid pages of experience quite blank: in words his pleasure lay—melodious, agitated words—printed words, about that which he had never seen and was connately incapable of comprehending. We have here two temperaments face to face; both untrained, unsophisticated, surprised (we may say) in the egg; both boldly charactered:—that of the artist, the lover and artificer of words; that of the maker, the seer, the lover and forger of experience. If the one had a daughter and the other had a son, and these married, might not some illustrious writer count descent from the beggar-soldier and the needy knife-grinder?

III

Every one lives by selling something, whatever be his right to it. The burglar sells at the same time his own skill and courage and my silver plate (the whole at the most moderate figure) to a Jew receiver. The bandit sells the traveller an article of prime necessity: that

traveller's life. And as for the old soldier, who stands
for central mark to my capricious figures of eight, he
dealt in a specialty; for he was the only beggar in the
world who ever gave me pleasure for my money. He
had learned a school of manners in the barracks and had
the sense to cling to it, accosting strangers with a regimental freedom, thanking patrons with a merely regimental difference, sparing you at once the tragedy of his
position and the embarrassment of yours. There was
not one hint about him of the beggar's emphasis, the
outburst of revolting gratitude, the rant and cant, the
" God bless you, Kind, Kind gentleman," which insults
the smallness of your alms by disproportionate vehe-
mence, which is so notably false, which would be so
unbearable if it were true. I am sometimes tempted to
suppose this reading of the beggar's part a survival of
the old days when Shakespeare was intoned upon the
stage and mourners keened beside the death-bed; to
think that we cannot now accept these strong emotions
unless they be uttered in the just note of life; nor (save
in the pulpit) endure these gross conventions. They
wound us, I am tempted to say, like mockery; the high
voice of keening (as it yet lingers on) strikes in the face
of sorrow like a buffet; and the rant and cant of the
staled beggar stirs in us a shudder of disgust. But the
fact disproves these amateur opinions. The beggar
lives by his knowledge of the average man. He knows
what he is about when he bandages his head, and hires
and drugs a babe, and poisons life with *Poor Mary Ann*
or *Long, long ago;* he knows what he is about when he
loads the critical ear and sickens the nice conscience
with intolerable thanks; they know what they are
about, he and his crew, when they pervade the slums
of cities, ghastly parodies of suffering, hateful parodies
of gratitude. This trade can scarce be called an imposi-
tion; it has been so blown upon with exposures; it
flaunts its fraudulence so nakedly. We pay them as
we pay those who show us, in huge exaggeration, the
monsters of our drinking-water; or those who daily

predict the fall of Britain. We pay them for the pain
they inflict, pay them, and wince, and hurry on. And
truly there is nothing that can shake the conscience like
a beggar's thanks; and that polity in which such protestations can be purchased for a shilling, seems no
scene for an honest man.

Are there, then, we may be asked, no genuine beggars? And the answer is, Not one. My old soldier was
a humbug like the rest; his ragged boots were, in the
stage phrase, properties; whole boots were given him
again and again, and always gladly accepted; and the
next day, there he was on the road as usual, with toes
exposed. His boots were his method; they were the
man's trade; without his boots he would have starved;
he did not live by charity, but by appealing to a gross
taste in the public, which loves the limelight on the
actor's face, and the toes out of the beggar's boots.
There is a true poverty, which no one sees: a false and
merely mimetic poverty, which usurps its place and
dress, and lives and above all drinks, on the fruits of
the usurpation. The true poverty does not go into the
streets; the banker may rest assured, he has never put a
penny in its hand. The self-respecting poor beg from
each other; never from the rich. To live in the frock-
coated ranks of life, to hear canting scenes of gratitude
rehearsed for two-pence, a man might suppose that
giving was a thing gone out of fashion; yet it goes forward on a scale so great as to fill me with surprise. In
the houses of the working-class, all day long there will
be a foot upon the stair; all day long there will be a
knocking at the doors; beggars come, beggars go, without stint, hardly with intermission, from morning till
night; and meanwhile, in the same city and but a few
streets off, the castles of the rich stand unsummoned.
Get the tale of any honest tramp, you will find it was
always the poor who helped him; get the truth from any
workman who has met misfortunes, it was always next
door that he would go for help, or only with such exceptions as are said to prove a rule; look at the course of

the mimetic beggar, it is through the poor quarters that he trails his passage, showing his bandages to every window, piercing even to the attics with his nasal song. Here is a remarkable state of things in our Christian commonwealths, that the poor only should be asked to give.

IV

There is a pleasant tale of some worthless, phrasing Frenchman, who was taxed with ingratitude: "*Il faut savoir garder l'indépendance du cœur,*" cried he. I own I feel with him. Gratitude without familiarity, gratitude otherwise than as a nameless element in a friendship, is a thing so near to hatred that I do not care to split the difference. Until I find a man who is pleased to receive obligations, I shall continue to question the tact of those who are eager to confer them. What an art it is, to give, even to our nearest friends! and what a test of manners to receive! How, upon either side, we smuggle away the obligation, blushing for each other; how bluff and dull we make the giver; how hasty, how falsely cheerful, the receiver! And yet an act of such difficulty and distress between near friends, it is supposed we can perform to a total stranger and leave the man transfixed with grateful emotions. The last thing you can do to a man is to burthen him with an obligation, and it is what we propose to begin with! But let us not be deceived: unless he is totally degraded to his trade, anger jars in his inside, and he grates his teeth at our gratuity.

We should wipe two words from our vocabulary: gratitude and charity. In real life, help is given out of friendship, or it is not valued; it is received from the hand of friendship, or it is resented. We are all too proud to take a naked gift: we must seem to pay it, if in nothing else, then with the delights of our society. Here, then, is the pitiful fix of the rich man; here is that needle's eye in which he stuck already in the days of Christ, and still sticks to-day, firmer, if possible, than ever: that he has the money and lacks the love which should make his money acceptable. Here and now, just as of old in Palestine, he has the rich to dinner, it is with the rich that he takes his pleasure: and when his turn comes to be charitable, he looks in vain for a recipient. His friends are not poor, they do not want; the poor are not his friends, they will not take. To whom is he to give? Where to find—note this phrase—the Deserving Poor? Charity is (what they call) centralised; offices are hired; societies founded, with secretaries paid or unpaid: the hunt of the Deserving Poor goes merrily forward. I think it will take more than a merely human secretary to disinter that character. What! a class that is to be in want from no fault of its own, and yet greedily eager to receive from strangers; and to be quite respectable, and at the same time quite devoid of self-respect; and play the most delicate part of friendship, and yet never be seen; and wear the form of man, and yet fly in the face of all the laws of human nature:—and all this, in the hope of getting a belly-god Burgess through a needle's eye! O, let him stick, by all means: and let his polity tumble in the dust; and let his epitaph and all his literature (of which my own works begin to form no inconsiderable part) be abolished even from the history of man! For a fool of this monstrosity of dulness, there can be no salvation: and the fool who looked for the elixir of life was an angel of reason to the fool who looks for the Deserving Poor!

v

And yet there is one course which the unfortunate gentleman may take. He may subscribe to pay the taxes. There were the true charity, impartial and impersonal, cumbering none with obligation, helping all. There were a destination for loveless gifts; there were the way to reach the pocket of the deserving poor, and yet save the time of secretaries! But, alas! there is no colour of romance in such a course; and people nowhere demand the picturesque so much as in their virtues.

PULVIS ET UMBRA

WE look for some reward of our endeavours and are disappointed; not success, not happiness, not even peace of conscience, crowns our ineffectual efforts to do well. Our frailties are invincible, our virtues barren; the battle goes sore against us to the going down of the sun. The canting moralist tells us of right and wrong; and we look abroad, even on the face of our small earth, and find them change with every climate, and no country where some action is not honoured for a virtue and none where it is not branded for a vice; and we look in our experience, and find no vital congruity in the wisest rules, but at the best a municipal fitness. It is not strange if we are tempted to despair of good. We ask too much. Our religions and moralities have been trimmed to flatter us, till they are all emasculate and sentimentalised, and only please and weaken. Truth is of a rougher strain. In the harsh face of life, faith can read a bracing gospel. The human race is a thing more ancient than the ten commandments; and the bones and revolutions of the Kosmos, in whose joints we are but moss and fungus, more ancient still.

I

Of the Kosmos in the last resort, science reports many doubtful things and all of them appalling. There seems no substance to this solid globe on which we stamp: nothing but symbols and ratios. Symbols and ratios carry us and bring us forth and beat us down; gravity

that swings the incommensurable suns and worlds
through space, is but a figment varying inversely as the
squares of distances; and the suns and worlds themselves, imponderable figures of abstraction, NH_3 and
H_2O. Consideration dares not dwell upon this view;
that way madness lies; science carries us into zones of
speculation, where there is no habitable city for the
mind of man.

But take the Kosmos with a grosser faith, as our
senses give it us. We behold space sown with rotatory
islands, suns and worlds and the shards and wrecks of
systems: some, like the sun, still blazing; some rotting,
like the earth; others, like the moon, stable in desola-
tion. All of these we take to be made of something we
call matter: a thing which no analysis can help us to
conceive; to whose incredible properties no familiarity
can reconcile our minds. This stuff, when not purified
by the lustration of fire, rots uncleanly into something
we call life; seized through all its atoms with a pedicu-
lous malady; swelling in tumours that become independent, sometimes even (by an abhorrent prodigy)
locomotory; one splitting into millions, millions coher-
ing into one, as the malady proceeds through varying
stages. This vital putrescence of the dust, used as we
are to it, yet strikes us with occasional disgust, and the
profusion of worms in a piece of ancient turf, or the air
of a marsh darkened with insects, will sometimes check
our breathing so that we aspire for cleaner places. But
none is clean: the moving sand is infected with lice;
the pure spring, where it bursts out of the mountain, is
a mere issue of worms; even in the hard rock the crystal
is forming.

In two main shapes this eruption covers the countenance of the earth: the animal and the vegetable: one
in some degree the inversion of the other: the second
rooted to the spot; the first coming detached out of its
natal mud, and scurrying abroad with the myriad feet
of insects or towering into the heavens on the wings of
birds: a thing so inconceivable that, if it be well

considered, the heart stops. To what passes with the anchored vermin, we have little clue: doubtless they have their joys and sorrows, their delights and killing agonies: it appears not how. But of the locomotory, to which we ourselves belong, we can tell more. These share with us a thousand miracles: the miracles of sight, of hearing, of the projection of sound, things that bridge space; the miracles of memory and reason, by which the present is conceived, and when it is gone, its image kept living in the brains of man and brute; the miracle of reproduction, with its imperious desires and staggering consequences. And to put the last touch upon this mountain mass of the revolting and the inconceivable, all these prey upon each other, lives tearing other lives in pieces, cramming them inside themselves, and by that summary process, growing fat: the vegetarian, the whale, perhaps the tree, not less than the lion of the desert; for the vegetarian is only the eater of the dumb.

Meanwhile our rotatory island loaded with predatory life, and more drenched with blood, both animal and vegetable, than ever mutinied ship, scuds through space with unimaginable speed, and turns alternate cheeks to the reverberation of a blazing world, ninety million miles away.

II

What a monstrous spectre is this man, the disease of the agglutinated dust, lifting alternate feet or lying drugged with slumber; killing, feeding, growing, bringing forth small copies of himself; grown upon with hair like grass, fitted with eyes that move and glitter in his face; a thing to set children screaming;—and yet looked at nearlier, known as his fellows know him, how surprising are his attributes! Poor soul, here for so little, cast among so many hardships, filled with desires so incommensurate and so inconsistent, savagely surrounded, savagely descended, irremediably condemned to prey upon his fellow lives: who should have blamed him had he been of a piece with his destiny and a being merely barbarous? And we look and behold him instead filled with imperfect virtues: infinitely childish, often admirably valiant, often touchingly kind; sitting down, amidst his momentary life, to debate of right and wrong and the attributes of the deity; rising up to do battle for an egg or die for an idea; singling out his friends and his mate with cordial affection; bringing forth in pain, rearing with long-suffering solicitude, his young. To touch the heart of his mystery, we find in him one thought, strange to the point of lunacy: the thought of duty; the thought of something owing to himself, to his neighbour, to his God: an ideal of decency, to which he would rise if it were possible; a limit of shame, below which, if it be possible, he will not stoop. The design in most men is one of conformity; here and there, in picked natures, it transcends itself and soars on the other side, arming martyrs with independence; but in all, in their degrees, it is a bosom thought:—Not in man alone, for we trace it in dogs and cats whom we know fairly well, and doubtless some similar point of honour sways the elephant, the oyster, and the louse, of whom we know so little:—But in man, at least, it sways with so complete an empire that merely selfish things come second, even with the selfish: that appetites are starved, fears are conquered, pains supported; that almost the dullest shrinks from the reproof of a glance, although it were a child's; and all but the most cowardly stand amid the risks of war; and the more noble, having strongly conceived an act as due to their ideal, affront and embrace death. Strange enough if, with their singular origin and perverted practice, they think they are to be rewarded in some future life: stranger still, if they are persuaded of the contrary, and think this blow, which they solicit, will strike them senseless for eternity. I shall be reminded what a tragedy of misconception and misconduct man at large presents: of organised injustice, cowardly violence, and treacherous crime; and of the damning imperfections of the best. They

cannot be too darkly drawn. Man is indeed marked for
failure in his efforts to do right. But where the best
consistently miscarry, how tenfold more remarkable
that all should continue to strive; and surely we should
find it both touching and inspiriting, that in a field from
which success is banished, our race should not cease to
labour.

If the first view of this creature, stalking in his rotatory isle, be a thing to shake the courage of the stoutest,
on this nearer sight, he startles us with an admiring
wonder. It matters not where we look, under what
climate we observe him, in what stage of society, in
what depth of ignorance, burthened with what erroneous
morality; by campfires in Assiniboia, the snow powder-
ing his shoulders, the wind plucking his blanket, as he
sits, passing the ceremonial calumet and uttering his
grave opinions like a Roman senator; in ships at sea, a
man inured to hardship and vile pleasures, his brightest
hope a fiddle in a tavern and a bedizened trull who sells
herself to rob him, and he for all that simple, innocent,
cheerful, kindly like a child, constant to toil, brave to
drown, for others; in the slums of cities, moving among
indifferent millions to mechanical employments, without hope of change in the future, with scarce a pleasure
in the present, and yet true to his virtues, honest up to
his lights, kind to his neighbours, tempted perhaps in
vain by the bright gin-palace, perhaps long-suffering
with the drunken wife that ruins him; in India (a
woman this time) kneeling with broken cries and
streaming tears, as she drowns her child in the sacred
river; in the brothel, the discard of society, living
mainly on strong drink fed with affronts, a fool, a thief,
the comrade of thieves, and even here keeping the point
of honour and the touch of pity, often repaying the
world's scorn with service, often standing firm upon a
scruple, and at a certain cost, rejecting riches:—everywhere some virtue cherished or affected, everywhere
some decency of thought and carriage, everywhere the
ensign of man's ineffectual goodness:—ah! if I could

show you this! if I could show you these men and women, all the world over, in every stage of history, under every abuse of error, under every circumstance of failure, without hope, without help, without thanks, still obscurely fighting the lost fight of virtue, still clinging, in the brothel or on the scaffold, to some rag of honour, the poor jewel of their souls! They may seek to escape, and yet they cannot; it is not alone their privilege and glory, but their doom; they are condemned to some nobility; all their lives long, the desire of good is at their heels, the implacable hunter.

Of all earth's meteors, here at least is the most strange and consoling: that this ennobled lemur, this hair-crowned bubble of the dust, this inheritor of a few years and sorrows, should yet deny himself his rare delights, and add to his frequent pains, and live for an ideal, however misconceived. Nor can we stop with man. A new doctrine, received with screams a little while ago by canting moralists, and still not properly worked into the body of our thoughts, lights us a step farther into the heart of this rough but noble universe. For nowadays the pride of man denies in vain his kinship with the original dust. He stands no longer like a thing apart. Close at his heels we see the dog, prince of another genus: and in him too, we see dumbly testified the same cultus of an unattainable ideal, the same constancy in failure. Does it stop with the dog? We look at our feet where the ground is blackened with the swarming ant: a creature so small, so far from us in the hierarchy of brutes, that we can scarce trace and scarce comprehend his doings; and here also, in his ordered polities and rigorous justice, we see confessed the law of duty and the fact of individual sin. Does it stop, then, with the ant? Rather this desire of well-doing and this doom of frailty run through all the grades of life: rather is this earth, from the frosty top of Everest to the next margin of the internal fire, one stage of ineffectual virtues and one temple of pious tears and perseverance. The whole creation groaneth and

travaileth together. It is the common and the godlike
law of life. The browsers, the biters, the barkers, the
hairy coats of field and forest, the squirrel in the oak,
the thousand-footed creeper in the dust, as they share
with us the gift of life, share with us the love of an
ideal: strive like us—like us are tempted to grow weary
of the struggle—to do well; like us receive at times
unmerited refreshment, visitings of support, returns of
courage; and are condemned like us to be crucified
between that double law of the members and the will.
Are they like us, I wonder, in the timid hope of some
reward, some sugar with the drug? do they, too, stand
aghast at unrewarded virtues, at the sufferings of those
whom, in our partiality, we take to be just, and the
prosperity of such as, in our blindness, we call wicked?
It may be, and yet God knows what they should look
for. Even while they look, even while they repent, the
foot of man treads them by thousands in the dust, the
yelping hounds burst upon their trail, the bullet speeds,
the knives are heating in the den of the vivisectionist;
or the dew falls, and the generation of a day is blotted
out. For these are creatures, compared with whom our
weakness is strength, our ignorance wisdom, our brief
span eternity.

And as we dwell, we living things, in our isle of
terror and under the imminent hand of death, God
forbid it should be man the erected, the reasoner, the
wise in his own eyes—God forbid it should be man that
wearies in well-doing, that despairs of unrewarded effort,
or utters the language of complaint. Let it be enough
for faith, that the whole creation groans in mortal
frailty, strives with unconquerable constancy: surely
not all in vain.

V

THE COAST OF FIFE

MANY writers have vigorously described the pains of the first day or the first night at school; to a boy of any enterprise, I believe, they are more often agreeably exciting. Misery—or at least misery unrelieved—is confined to another period, to the days of suspense and the " dreadful looking-for," of departure; when the old life is running to an end, and the new life, with its new interests, not yet begun; and to the pain of an imminent parting, there is added the unrest of a state of conscious pre-existence. The area-railings, the beloved shop-window, the smell of semi-suburban tanpits, the song of the church bells upon a Sunday, the thin, high voices of compatriot children in a playing-field —what a sudden, what an overpowering pathos breathes to him from each familiar circumstance! The assaults of sorrow come not from within, as it seems to him, but from without. I was proud and glad to go to school; had I been let alone, I could have borne up like any hero; but there was around me, in all my native town, a conspiracy of lamentation: " Poor little boy, he is going away—unkind little boy, he is going to leave us "; so the unspoken burthen followed me as I went, with yearning and reproach. And at length, one melancholy afternoon in the early autumn, and at a place where it seems to me, looking back, it must be always autumn and generally Sunday, there came suddenly upon the face of all I saw—the long empty road, the lines of the tall houses, the church upon the hill, the woody hillside garden—a look of such a piercing sadness that my heart died; and seating myself on a

door-step, I shed tears of miserable sympathy. A
benevolent cat cumbered me the while with consolations
—we two were alone in all that was visible of the
London Road: two poor waifs who had each tasted
sorrow—and she fawned upon the weeper, and gambolled for his entertainment, watching the effect, it
seemed, with motherly eyes.

For the sake of the cat, God bless her! I confessed
at home the story of my weakness; and so it comes
about that I owed a certain journey, and the reader
owes the present paper, to a cat in the London Road.
It was judged, if I had thus brimmed over on the
public highway, some change of scene was (in the medi-
cal sense) indicated; my father at the time was visiting
the harbour lights of Scotland; and it was decided he
should take me along with him around a portion of the
shores of Fife; my first professional tour, my first journey in the complete character of man, without the help
of petticoats.

The Kingdom of Fife (that royal province) may be
observed by the curious on the map, occupying a tongue
of land between the firths of Forth and Tay. It may be
continually seen from many parts of Edinburgh (among
the rest, from the windows of my father's house) dying
away into the distance and the easterly *haar* with one
smoky seaside town beyond another, or in winter print-
ing on the grey heaven some glittering hill-tops. It
has no beauty to recommend it, being a low, sea-salted,
wind-vexed promontory; trees very rare, except (as
common on the east coast) along the dens of rivers; the
fields well cultivated, I understand, but not lovely to
the eye. It is of the coast I speak: the interior may be
the garden of Eden. History broods over that part of
the world like the easterly *haar*. Even on the map, its
long row of Gaelic place-names bear testimony to an
old and settled race. Of these little towns, posted along
the shore as close as sedges, each with its bit of harbour,
its old weather-beaten church or public building, its
flavour of decayed prosperity and decaying fish, not

one but has its legend, quaint or tragic: Dunfermline, in whose royal towers the king may be still observed (in the ballad) drinking the blood-red wine; somnolent Inverkeithing, once the quarantine of Leith; Aberdour, hard by the monastic islet of Inchcolm, hard by Donibristle where the " bonny face was spoiled "; Burntisland, where, when Paul Jones was off the coast, the Reverend Mr. Shirra had a table carried between tidemarks, and publicly prayed against the rover at the pitch of his voice and his broad lowland dialect; Kinghorn, where Alexander " brak's neckbane " and left Scotland to the English wars; Kirkcaldy, where the witches once prevailed extremely and sank tall ships and honest mariners in the North Sea; Dysart, famous —well famous at least to me for the Dutch ships that lay in its harbour, painted like toys and with pots of flowers and cages of song birds in the cabin windows, and for one particular Dutch skipper who would sit all day in slippers on the break of the poop, smoking a long German pipe; Wemyss (pronounce Weems) with its bat-haunted caves, where the Chevalier Johnstone, on his flight from Culloden, passed a night of superstitious terror; Leven, a bald, quite modern place, sacred to summer visitors, whence there has gone but yesterday the tall figure and the white locks of the last Englishman in Delhi, my uncle Dr. Balfour, who was still walking his hospital rounds, while the troopers from Meerut clattered and cried " Deen, Deen " along the streets of the imperial city, and Willoughby mustered his handful of heroes at the magazine, and the nameless brave one in the telegraph office was perhaps already fingering his last despatch; and just a little beyond Leven, Largo Law and the smoke of Largo town mounting about its feet, the town of Alexander Selkirk, better known under the name of Robinson Crusoe. So on, the list might be pursued (only for private reasons, which the reader will shortly have an opportunity to guess) by St. Monans, and Pittenweem, and the two Anstruthers, and Cellardyke, and Crail, where Primate Sharpe was once a humble and innocent country minister: on to the heel of the land, to Fife Ness, overlooked by a seawood of matted elders, and the quaint old mansion of Balcomie, itself overlooking but the breach or the quiescence of the deep—the Carr Rock beacon rising close in front, and as night draws in, the star of the Inchcape reef springing up on the one hand, and the star of the May Island on the other, and farther off yet a third and a greater on the craggy foreland of St. Abb's. And but a little way round the corner of the land, imminent itself above the sea, stands the gem of the province and the light of mediæval Scotland, St. Andrews, where the great Cardinal Beaton held garrison against the world, and the second of the name and title perished (as you may read in Knox's jeering narrative) under the knives of true-blue Protestants, and to this day (after so many centuries) the current voice of the professor is not hushed.

Here it was that my first tour of inspection began, early on a bleak easterly morning. There was a crashing run of sea upon the shore, I recollect, and my father and the man of the harbour light must sometimes raise their voices to be audible. Perhaps it is from this circumstance, that I always imagine St. Andrews to be an ineffectual seat of learning, and the sound of the east wind and the bursting surf to linger in its drowsy class-rooms and confound the utterance of the professor, until teacher and taught are alike drowned in oblivion, and only the sea-gull beats on the windows and the draught of the sea-air rustles in the pages of the open lecture. But upon all this, and the romance of St. Andrews in general, the reader must consult the works of Mr. Andrew Lang; who has written of it but the other day in his dainty prose and with his incommunicable humour, and long ago in one of his best poems, with grace, and local truth and a note of unaffected pathos. Mr. Lang knows all about the romance, I say, and the educational advantages, but I doubt if he had turned his attention to the harbour

lights; and it may be news even to him, that in the year
1863 their case was pitiable. Hanging about with the
east wind humming in my teeth, and my hands (I make
no doubt) in my pockets, I looked for the first time
upon that tragi-comedy of the visiting engineer which
I have seen so often re-enacted on a more important
stage. Eighty years ago, I find my grandfather writing:
" It is the most painful thing that can occur to me to
have a correspondence of this kind with any of the
keepers, and when I come to the Light House, instead of
having the satisfaction to meet them with approbation
and welcome their Family, it is distressing when one is
obliged to put on a most angry countenance and demeanour." This painful obligation has been hereditary
in my race. I have myself, on a perfectly amateur and
unauthorised inspection of Turnberry Point, bent my
brows upon the keeper on the question of storm-panes;
and felt a keen pang of self-reproach, when we went
downstairs again and I found he was making a coffin
for his infant child; and then regained my equanimity
with the thought that I had done the man a service,
and when the proper inspector came he would be readier
with his panes. The human race is perhaps credited
with more duplicity than it deserves. The visitation of
a lighthouse at least is a business of the most transparent nature. As soon as the boat grates on the shore,
and the keepers step forward in their uniformed coats,
the very slouch of the fellows' shoulders tells their story,
and the engineer may begin at once to assume his
" angry countenance." Certainly the brass of the hand-
rail will be clouded; and if the brass be not immaculate,
certainly all will be to match—the reflectors scratched,
the spare lamp unready, the storm-panes in the store-
house. If a light is not rather more than middling
good, it will be radically bad. Mediocrity (except in
literature) appears to be unattainable by man. But of
course the unfortunate of St. Andrews was only an amateur, he was not in the Service, he had no uniform coat,
he was (I believe) a plumber by his trade and stood

(in the mediæval phase) quite out of the danger of my father; but he had a painful interview for all that, and perspired extremely.

From St. Andrews, we drove over Magus Muir. My father had announced we were " to post," and the phrase called up in my hopeful mind visions of top-boots and the pictures in Rowlandson's *Dance of Death;* but it was only a jingling cab that came to the inn door, such as I had driven in a thousand times at the low price of one shilling on the streets of Edinburgh. Beyond this disappointment, I remember nothing of that drive. It is a road I have often travelled, and of not one of these journeys do I remember any single trait. The fact has not been suffered to encroach on the truth of the imagination. I still see Magus Muir two hundred years ago; a desert place, quite unenclosed; in the midst, the primate's carriage fleeing at the gallop; the assassins loose-reined in pursuit, Burley Balfour, pistol in hand, among the first. No scene of history has ever written itself so deeply on my mind; not because Balfour, that questionable zealot, was an ancestral cousin of my own; not because of the pleadings of the victim and his daughter; not even because of the live bum-bee that flew out of Sharpe's 'bacco-box, thus clearly indicating his complicity with Satan; nor merely because, as it was after all a crime of a fine religious flavour, it figured in Sunday books and afforded a grateful relief from *Ministering Children* or the *Memoirs of Mrs. Katherine Winslowe.* The figure that always fixed my attention is that of Hackston of Rathillet, sitting in the saddle with his cloak about his mouth, and through all that long, bungling, vociferous hurly-burly, revolving privately a case of conscience. He would take no hand in the deed, because he had a private spite against the victim, and " that action " must be sullied with no suggestion of a worldly motive; on the other hand, " that action " in itself was highly justified, he had cast in his lot with " the actors," and he must stay there, inactive but publicly sharing the responsibility. " You are a gentleman—you will protect me!" cried the wounded old man, crawling towards him. "I will never lay a hand on you," said Hackston, and put his cloak about his mouth. It is an old temptation with me, to pluck away that cloak and see the face—to open that bosom and to read the heart. With incomplete romances about Hackston, the drawers of my youth were lumbered. I read him up in every printed book that I could lay my hands on. I even dug among the Wodrow manuscripts, sitting shamefaced in the very room where my hero had been tortured two centuries before, and keenly conscious of my youth in the midst of other and (as I fondly thought) more gifted students. All was vain: that he had passed a riotous nonage, that he was a zealot, that he twice displayed (compared with his grotesque companions) some tincture of soldierly resolution and even of military common-sense, and that he figured memorably in the scene of Magus Muir, so much and no more could I make out. But whenever I cast my eyes backward, it is to see him like a landmark on the plains of history, sitting with his cloak about his mouth, inscrutable. How small a thing creates an immortality! I do not think he can have been a man entirely commonplace; but had he not thrown his cloak about his mouth, or had the witnesses forgot to chronicle the action, he would not thus have haunted the imagination of my boyhood, and to-day he would scarce delay me for a paragraph. An incident, at once romantic and dramatic, which at once awakes the judgment and makes a picture for the eye, how little do we realise its perdurable power! Perhaps no one does so but the author, just as none but he appreciates the influence of jingling words; so that he looks on upon life, with something of a covert smile, seeing people led by what they fancy to be thoughts and what are really the accustomed artifices of his own trade, or roused by what they take to be principles and are really picturesque effects. In a pleasant book about a school-class club, Colonel Fergusson has recently told a little anecdote.

A " Philosophical Society " was formed by some Academy boys—among them, Colonel Fergusson himself, Fleeming Jenkin, and Andrew Wilson, the Christian Buddhist and author of *The Abode of Snow*. Before these learned pundits, one member laid the following ingenious problem: " What would be the result of putting a pound of potassium in a pot of porter? " " I should think there would be a number of interesting bi-products," said a smatterer at my elbow; but for me the tale itself was a bi-product, and stands as a type of much that is most human. For this inquirer who conceived himself to burn with a zeal entirely chemical, was really immersed in a design of a quite different nature; unconsciously to his own recently breeched intelligence, he was engaged in literature. Putting, pound, potassium, pot, porter; initial p, mediant t—that was his idea, poor little boy! So with politics and that which excites men in the present, so with history and that which rouses them in the past: there lie at the root of what appears most serious unsuspected elements. The triple town of Anstruther Wester, Anstruther Easter, and Cellardyke, all three Royal Burghs—or two Royal Burghs and a less distinguished suburb, I forget which—lies continuously along the sea-side, and boasts of either two or three separate parish churches, and either two or three separate harbours. These ambiguities are painful; but the fact is (although it argue me uncultured), I am but poorly posted upon Cellardyke. My business lay in the two Anstruthers. A tricklet of a stream divides them, spanned by a bridge; and over the bridge at the time of my knowledge, the celebrated Shell House stood outpost on the west. This had been the residence of an agreeable eccentric; during his fond tenancy, he had illustrated the outer walls, as high (if I remember rightly) as the roof, with elaborate patterns and pictures, and snatches of verse in the vein of *exegi monumentum;* shells and pebbles, artfully contrasted and conjoined, had been his medium; and I like to think of him standing back upon the bridge, when all was finished, drinking in the general effect and (like Gibbon) already lamenting his employment.

The same bridge saw another sight in the seventeenth century. Mr. Thomson, the " curat " of Anstruther Easter, was a man highly obnoxious to the devout: in the first place, because he was a " curat "; in the second place, because he was a person of irregular and scandalous life; and in the third place, because he was generally suspected of dealings with the Enemy of Man. These three disqualifications, in the popular literature of the time, go hand in hand; but the end of Mr. Thomson was a thing quite by itself, and in the proper phrase, a manifest judgment. He had been at a friend's house in Anstruther Wester, where (and elsewhere, I suspect), he had partaken of the bottle; indeed, to put the thing in our cold modern way, the reverend gentleman was on the brink of *delirium tremens*. It was a dark night, it seems; a little lassie came carrying a lantern to fetch the curate home; and away they went down the street of Anstruther Wester, the lantern swinging a bit in the child's hand, the barred lustre tossing up and down along the front of slumbering houses, and Mr. Thomson not altogether steady on his legs nor (to all appearance) easy in mind. The pair had reached the middle of the bridge when (as I conceive the scene) the poor tippler started in some baseless fear and looked behind him; the child, already shaken by the minister's strange behaviour, started also; in so doing, she would jerk the lantern; and for the space of a moment the lights and the shadows would be all confounded. Then it was that to the unhinged toper and the twittering child, a huge bulk of blackness seemed to sweep down, to pass them close by as they stood upon the bridge, and to vanish on the farther side in the general darkness of the night. "Plainly the devil came for Mr. Thomson! " thought the child. What Mr. Thomson thought himself, we have no ground of knowledge; but he fell upon his knees in the midst of the

bridge like a man praying. On the rest of the journey
to the manse, history is silent; but when they came to
the door, the poor caitiff, taking the lantern from the
child, looked upon her with so lost a countenance that
her little courage died within her, and she fled home
screaming to her parents. Not a soul would venture
out; all that night, the minister dwelt alone with his
terrors in the manse; and when the day dawned, and
men made bold to go about the streets, they found the
devil had come indeed for Mr. Thomson.

This manse of Anstruther Easter has another and a
more cheerful association. It was early in the morning, about a century before the days of Mr. Thomson,
that his predecessor was called out of bed to welcome a
Grandee of Spain, the Duke of Medina Sidonia, just
landed in the harbour underneath. But sure there was
never seen a more decayed grandee; sure there was
never a duke welcomed from a stranger place of exile.
Half-way between Orkney and Shetland, there lies a
certain isle; on the one hand the Atlantic, on the other
the North Sea, bombard its pillared cliffs; sore-eyed,
short-living, inbred fishers and their families herd in
its few huts; in the graveyard pieces of wreck-wood
stand for monuments; there is nowhere a more inhospitable spot. *Belle-Isle-en-Mer* — Fair-Isle-at-Sea —
that is a name that has always rung in my mind's ear
like music; but the only " Fair Isle " on which I ever
set my foot, was this unhomely, rugged turret-top of
submarine sierras. Here, when his ship was broken,
my lord Duke joyfully got ashore; here for long months
he and certain of his men were harboured; and it was
from this durance that he landed at last to be welcomed (as well as such a papist deserved, no doubt)
by the godly incumbent of Anstruther Easter; and after
the Fair Isle, what a fine city must that have appeared!
and after the island diet, what a hospitable spot the
minister's table! And yet he must have lived on
friendly terms with his outlandish hosts. For to this
day there still survives a relic of the long winter

evenings when the sailors of the great Armada crouched
about the hearths of the Fair-Islanders, the planks of
their own lost galleon perhaps lighting up the scene,
and the gale and the surf that beat about the coast
contributing their melancholy voices. All the folk of
the north isles are great artificers of knitting: the Fair-
Islanders alone dye their fabrics in the Spanish manner.
To this day, gloves and nightcaps, innocently decorated,
may be seen for sale in the Shetland warehouse at Edinburgh, or on the Fair Isle itself in the catechist's house;
and to this day, they tell the story of the Duke of
Medina Sidonia's adventure.

It would seem as if the Fair Isle had some attraction
for " persons of quality." When I landed there myself,
an elderly gentleman, unshaved, poorly attired, his
shoulders wrapped in a plaid, was seen walking to and
fro, with a book in his hand, upon the beach. He paid
no heed to our arrival, which we thought a strange thing
in itself; but when one of the officers of the *Pharos*,
passing narrowly by him, observed his book to be a
Greek Testament, our wonder and interest took a
higher flight. The catechist was cross-examined; he
said the gentleman had been put across some time before
in Mr. Bruce of Sumburgh's schooner, the only link
between the Fair Isle and the rest of the world,
and that he held services and was doing " good." So
much came glibly enough; but when pressed a little
further, the catechist displayed embarrassment. A
singular diffidence appeared upon his face: " They tell
me," said he, in low tones, " that he's a lord." And a
lord he was, a peer of the realm pacing that inhospitable
beach with his Greek Testament, and his plaid about
his shoulders, set upon doing good, as he understood it,
worthy man! And his grandson, a good-looking little
boy, much better dressed than the lordly evangelist,
and speaking with a silken English accent very foreign
to the scene, accompanied me for a while in my exploration of the island. I suppose this little fellow is
now my lord, and wonder how much he remembers of

the Fair Isle. Perhaps not much; for he seemed to accept very quietly his savage situation; and under such guidance, it is like that this was not his first nor yet his last adventure.

VI

THE EDUCATION OF AN ENGINEER

ANSTRUTHER is a place sacred to the Muse; she inspired (really to a considerable extent) Tennant's vernacular poem *Anster Fair;* and I have there waited upon her myself with much devotion. This was when I came as a young man to glean engineering experience from the building of the breakwater. What I gleaned, I am sure I do not know; but in deed I had already my own private determination to be an author; I loved the art of words and the appearances of life; and *travellers,* and *headers,* and *rubble,* and *polished ashlar,* and *pierres perdues,* and even the thrilling question of the *string-course,* interested me only (if they interested me at all) as properties for some possible romance or as words to add to my vocabulary. To grow a little catholic is the compensation of years; youth is one-eyed; and in those days, though I haunted the breakwater by day, and even loved the place for the sake of the sunshine, the thrilling seaside air, the wash of waves on the sea-face, the green glimmer of the divers' helmets far below, and the musical chinking of the masons, my one genuine preoccupation lay elsewhere, and my only industry was in the hours when I was not on duty. I lodged with a certain Bailie Brown, a carpenter by trade; and there, as soon as dinner was despatched, in a chamber scented with dry rose-leaves, drew in my chair to the table and proceeded to pour forth literature, at such a speed and with such intimations of early death and immortality, as I now look back upon with wonder. Then it was that I wrote *Voces Fidelium,* a series of dramatic monologues in verse;

218

then that I indited the bulk of a covenanting novel—
like so many others, never finished. Late I sat into the
night, toiling (as I thought) under the very dart of
death, toiling to leave a memory behind me. I feel
moved to thrust aside the curtain of the years, to hail
that poor feverish idiot, to bid him go to bed and clap
Voces Fidelium on the fire before he goes; so clear does
he appear before me, sitting there between his candles
in the rose-scented room and the late night; so ridiculous a picture (to my elderly wisdom) does the fool
present! But he was driven to his bed at last without
miraculous intervention; and the manner of his driving
sets the last touch upon this eminently youthful business. The weather was then so warm that I must keep
the windows open; the night without was populous with
moths. As the late darkness deepened, my literary
tapers beaconed forth more brightly; thicker and thicker
came the dusty night-fliers, to gyrate for one brilliant
instant round the flame and fall in agonies upon my
paper. Flesh and blood could not endure the spectacle;
to capture immortality was doubtless a noble enterprise,
but not to capture it at such a cost of suffering; and
out would go the candles, and off would I go to bed in
the darkness, raging to think that the blow might fall
on the morrow, and there was *Voces Fidelium* still
incomplete. Well, the moths are all gone, and *Voces
Fidelium* along with them; only the fool is still on hand
and practises new follies.

Only one thing in connection with the harbour
tempted me, and that was the diving, an experience I
burned to taste of. But this was not to be, at least in
Anstruther; and the subject involves a change of scene
to the subarctic town of Wick. You can never have
dwelt in a country more unsightly than that part of
Caithness, the land faintly swelling, faintly falling, not
a tree, not a hedgerow, the fields divided by single
slate stones set upon their edge, the wind always singing
in your ears and (down the long road that led nowhere) thrumming in the telegraph wires. Only as you

approached the coast was there anything to stir the
heart. The plateau broke down to the North Sea in formidable cliffs, the tall out-stacks rose like pillars ringed
about with surf, the coves were over-brimmed with
clamorous froth, the sea-birds screamed, the wind sang
in the thyme on the cliff's edge; here and there, small
ancient castles toppled on the brim; here and there, it
was possible to dip into a dell of shelter, where you
might lie and tell yourself you were a little warm, and
hear (near at hand) the whin-pods bursting in the afternoon sun and (farther off) the rumour of the turbulent
sea. As for Wick itself, it is one of the meanest of man's
towns, and situate certainly on the baldest of God's
bays. It lives for herring, and a strange sight it is to see
(of an afternoon) the heights of Pulteney blackened by
seaward-looking fishers, as when a city crowds to a review—or, as when bees have swarmed, the ground is
horrible with lumps and clusters; and a strange sight,
and a beautiful, to see the fleet put silently out against
a rising moon, the sea-line rough as a wood with sails,
and ever and again and one after another, a boat flitting
swiftly by the silver disk. This mass of fishers, this
great fleet of boats, is out of all proportion to the town
itself; and the oars are manned and the nets hauled
by immigrants from the Long Island (as we call the
outer Hebrides), who come for that season only, and
depart again, if "the take" be poor, leaving debts
behind them. In a bad year, the end of the herring
fishery is therefore an exciting time; fights are common,
riots often possible; an apple knocked from a child's
hand was once the signal for something like a war;
and even when I was there, a gunboat lay in the bay
to assist the authorities. To contrary interests, it
should be observed, the curse of Babel is here added:
the Lews men are Gaelic speakers, those of Caithness
have adopted English; an odd circumstance, if you
reflect that both must be largely Norsemen by descent.
I remember seeing one of the strongest instances of this
division: a thing like a Punch-and-Judy box erected

on the flat grave-stones of the churchyard; from the
hutch or proscenium—I know not what to call it—an
eldritch-looking preacher laying down the law in Gaelic
about some one of the name of *Powl*, whom I at last
divined to be the apostle to the Gentiles; a large congregation of the Lews men very devoutly listening; and on
the outskirts of the crowd, some of the town's children
(to whom the whole affair was Greek and Hebrew) pro-
fanely playing tigg. The same descent, the same country, the same narrow sect of the same religion, and all
these bonds made very largely nugatory by an acci-
dental difference of dialect.

Into the bay of Wick stretched the dark length of the
unfinished breakwater, in its cage of open staging; the
travellers (like frames of churches) over-plumbing all;
and away at the extreme end, the divers toiling unseen
on the foundation. On a platform of loose planks, the
assistants turned their air-mills; a stone might be
swinging between wind and water; underneath the
swell ran gaily; and from time to time, a mailed
dragon with a window-glass snout came dripping up
the ladder. Youth is a blessed season after all; my
stay at Wick was in the year of *Voces Fidelium* and
the rose-leaf room at Bailie Brown's; and already I
did not care two straws for literary glory. Posthumous
ambition perhaps requires an atmosphere of roses; and
the more rugged excitant of Wick east winds had made
another boy of me. To go down in the diving-dress,
that was my absorbing fancy; and with the countenance of a certain handsome scamp of a diver, Bob
Bain by name, I gratified the whim.

It was grey, harsh, easterly weather, the swell ran
pretty high, and out in the open there were " skipper's
daughters," when I found myself at last on the diver's
platform, twenty pounds of lead upon each foot and
my whole person swollen with ply and ply of woollen
underclothing. One moment, the salt wind was whistling
round my night-capped head; the next, I was crushed
almost double under the weight of the helmet. As that

intolerable burthen was laid upon me, I could have found it in my heart (only for shame's sake) to cry off from the whole enterprise. But it was too late. The attendants began to turn the hurdy-gurdy, and the air to whistle through the tube; some one screwed in the barred window of the vizor; and I was cut off in a moment from my fellow-men; standing there in their midst, but quite divorced from intercourse: a creature deaf and dumb, pathetically looking forth upon them from a climate of his own. Except that I could move and feel, I was like a man fallen in a catalepsy. But time was scarce given me to realise my isolation; the weights were hung upon my back and breast, the signal-rope was thrust into my unresisting hand; and setting a twenty-pound foot upon the ladder, I began ponderously to descend.

Some twenty rounds below the platform, twilight fell. Looking up, I saw a low green heaven mottled with vanishing bells of white; looking around, except for the weedy spokes and shafts of the ladder, nothing but a green gloaming, somewhat opaque but very restful and delicious. Thirty rounds lower, I stepped off on the *pierres perdues* of the foundation; a dumb helmeted figure took me by the hand, and made a gesture (as I read it) of encouragement; and looking in at the creature's window, I beheld the face of Bain. There we were, hand to hand and (when it pleased us) eye to eye; and either might have burst himself with shouting, and not a whisper come to his companion's hearing. Each, in his own little world of air, stood incommunicably separate.

Bob had told me ere this a little tale, a five minutes' drama at the bottom of the sea, which at that moment possibly shot across my mind. He was down with another, settling a stone of the sea-wall. They had it well adjusted, Bob gave the signal, the scissors were slipped, the stone set home; and it was time to turn to something else. But still his companion remained bowed over the block like a mourner on a tomb, or only raised himself to make absurd contortions and mysterious signs unknown to the vocabulary of the diver. There, then, these two stood for a while, like the dead and the living; till there flashed a fortunate thought into Bob's mind, and he stooped, peered through the window of that other world, and beheld the face of its inhabitant wet with streaming tears. Ah! the man was in pain! And Bob, glancing downward, saw what was the trouble: the block had been lowered on the foot of that unfortunate—he was caught alive at the bottom of the sea under fifteen tons of rock.

That two men should handle a stone so heavy, even swinging in the scissors, may appear strange to the inexpert. These must bear in mind the great density of the water of the sea, and the surprising results of transplantation to that medium. To understand a little what these are, and how a man's weight, so far from being an encumbrance, is the very ground of his agility, was the chief lesson of my submarine experience. The knowledge came upon me by degrees. As I began to go forward with the hand of my estranged companion, a world of tumbled stones was visible, pillared with the weedy uprights of the staging: overhead, a flat roof of green: a little in front, the sea-wall, like an unfinished rampart. And presently in our upward progress, Bob motioned me to leap upon a stone. I looked to see if he were possibly in earnest, and he only signed to me the more imperiously. Now the block stood six feet high; it would have been quite a leap to me unencumbered; with the breast and back weights, and the twenty pounds upon each foot, and the staggering load of the helmet, the thing was out of reason. I laughed aloud in my tomb; and to prove to Bob how far he was astray, I gave a little impulse from my toes. Up I soared like a bird, my companion soaring at my side. As high as to the stone, and then higher, I pursued my impotent and empty flight. Even when the strong arm of Bob had checked my shoulders, my heels continued their ascent; so that I blew out sideways like an autumn leaf, and must be hauled in, hand over hand, as sailors haul in the slack of a sail, and propped upon my feet again like an intoxicated sparrow. Yet a little higher on the foundation, and we began to be affected by the bottom of the swell, running there like a strong breeze of wind. Or so I must suppose; for, safe in my cushion of air, I was conscious of no impact; only swayed idly like a weed, and was now borne helplessly abroad, and now swiftly—and yet with dream-like gentleness—impelled against my guide. So does a child's balloon divagate upon the currents of the air, and touch and slide off again from every obstacle. So must have ineffectually swung, so resented their inefficiency, those light crowds that followed the Star of Hades, and uttered exiguous voices in the land beyond Cocytus.

There was something strangely exasperating, as well as strangely wearying, in these uncommanded evolutions. It is bitter to return to infancy, to be supported, and directed, and perpetually set upon your feet, by the hand of someone else. The air besides, as it is supplied to you by the busy millers on the platform, closes the eustachian tubes and keeps the neophyte perpetually swallowing, till his throat is grown so dry that he can swallow no longer. And for all these reasons—although I had a fine, dizzy, muddle-headed joy in my surroundings, and longed, and tried, and always failed, to lay hands on the fish that darted here and there about me, swift as humming-birds—yet I fancy I was rather relieved than otherwise when Bain brought me back to the ladder and signed to me to mount. And there was one more experience before me even then. Of a sudden, my ascending head passed into the trough of a swell. Out of the green, I shot at once into a glory of rosy, almost of sanguine light—the multitudinous seas incarnadined, the heaven above a vault of crimson. And then the glory faded into the hard, ugly daylight of a Caithness autumn, with a low sky, a grey sea, and a whistling wind.

Bob Bain had five shillings for his trouble, and I had done what I desired. It was one of the best things I got from my education as an engineer: of which however, as a way of life, I wish to speak with sympathy. It takes a man into the open air; it keeps him hanging about harbour-sides, which is the richest form of idling; it carries him to wild islands; it gives him a taste of the genial dangers of the sea; it supplies him with dexterities to exercise; it makes demands upon his ingenuity; it will go far to cure him of any taste (if ever he had one) for the miserable life of cities. And when it has done so it carries him back and shuts him in an office! From the roaring skerry and the wet thwart of the tossing boat, he passes to the stool and desk; and with a memory full of ships, and seas, and perilous headlands, and the shining pharos, he must apply his long-sighted eyes to the petty niceties of drawing, or measure his inaccurate mind with several pages of consecutive figures. He is a wise youth, to be sure, who can balance one part of genuine life against two parts of drudgery between four walls, and for the sake of the one, manfully accept the other.

Wick was scarce an eligible place of stay. But how much better it was to hang in the cold wind upon the pier, to go down with Bob Bain among the roots of the staging, to be all day in a boat coiling a wet rope and shouting orders—not always very wise—than to be warm and dry, and dull and dead-alive, in the most comfortable office. And Wick itself had in those days a note of originality. It may have still, but I misdoubt it much. The old minister of Keiss would not preach, in these degenerate times, for an hour and a half upon the clock. The gipsies must be gone from their caverns; where you might see, from the mouth, the women tending their fire, like Meg Merrilies, and the men sleeping off their coarse potations; and where in winter gales, the surf would beleaguer them closely, bursting in their very door. A traveller to-day upon the Thurso coach would scarce observe a little cloud of smoke among the moorlands, and be told, quite openly, it marked a private still. He would not indeed make that journey, for there is now no Thurso coach. And even if he could, one little thing that happened to me could never happen to him, or not with the same trenchancy of contrast.

We had been upon the road all evening; the coach-top was crowded with Lews fishers going home, scarce anything but Gaelic had sounded in my ears; and our way had lain throughout over a moorish country very modern to behold. Latish at night, though it was still broad day in our sub-arctic latitude, we came down upon the shores of the roaring Pentland Firth, that grave of mariners; on one hand, the cliffs of Dunnet Head ran seaward; in front was the little bare, white town of Castleton, its streets full of blowing sand; nothing beyond, but the North Islands, the great deep, and the perennial ice-fields of the Pole. And here, in the last imaginable place, there sprang up young outlandish voices and a chatter of some foreign speech; and I saw, pursuing the coach with its load of Hebridean fishers—as they had pursued *vetturini* up the passes of the Apennines or perhaps along the grotto under Virgil's tomb—two little dark-eyed, white-toothed Italian vagabonds, of twelve to fourteen years of age, one with a hurdy-gurdy, the other with a cage of white mice. The coach passed on, and their small Italian chatter died in the distance; and I was left to marvel how they had wandered into that country, and how they fared in it, and what they thought of it, and when (if ever) they should see again the silver wind-breaks run among the olives, and the stone-pine stand guard upon Etruscan sepulchres.

Upon any American, the strangeness of this incident is somewhat lost. For as far back as he goes in his own land, he will find some alien camping there; the Cornish miner, the French or Mexican half-blood, the negro in the south, these are deep in the woods and far among the mountains. But in an old, cold, and rugged country such as mine, the days of immigration are long at an end; and away up there, which was at that time far beyond the northernmost extreme of railways, hard upon the shore of that ill-omened strait of whirlpools, in a land of moors where no stranger came, unless it should be a sportsman to shoot grouse or an antiquary to decipher runes, the presence of these small pedestrians struck the mind as though a bird of paradise had risen from the heather or an albatross come fishing in the bay of Wick. They were as strange to their surroundings as my lordly evangelist or the old Spanish grandee on the Fair Isle.

VII

A CHRISTMAS SERMON

BY the time this paper appears, I shall have been talking for twelve months; and it is thought I should take my leave in a formal and seasonable manner. Valedictory eloquence is rare, and death-bed sayings have not often hit the mark of the occasion. Charles Second, wit and sceptic, a man whose life had been one long lesson in human incredulity, an easy-going comrade, a manœuvring king—remembered and embodied all his wit and scepticism along with more than his usual good-humour in the famous " I am afraid, gentlemen, I am an unconscionable time a-dying."

I

An unconscionable time a-dying—there is the picture (" I am afraid, gentlemen,") of your life and of mine. The sands run out, and the hours are " numbered and imputed," and the days go by; and when the last of these finds us, we have been a long time dying, and what else? The very length is something, if we reach that hour of separation undishonoured; and to have lived at all is doubtless (in the soldierly expression) to have served. There is a tale in Tacitus of how the veterans mutinied in the German wilderness; of how they mobbed Germanicus, clamouring to go home; and of how, seizing their general's hand, these old war-worn exiles passed his finger along their toothless gums. *Sunt lacrymæ rerum:* this was the most eloquent of the songs of Simeon. And when a man has lived to a fair age, he bears his marks of service. He may have

never been remarked upon the breach at the head of
the army; at least he shall have lost his teeth on the
camp bread.

The idealism of serious people in this age of ours
is of a noble character. It never seems to them that
they have served enough; they have a fine impatience
of their virtues. It were perhaps more modest to be
singly thankful that we are no worse. It is not only our
enemies, those desperate characters—it is we ourselves
who know not what we do;—thence springs the glim-
mering hope that perhaps we do better than we think:
that to scramble through this random business with
hands reasonably clean, to have played the part of a
man or woman with some reasonable fulness, to have
often resisted the diabolic, and at the end to be still
resisting it, is for the poor human soldier to have done
right well. To ask to see some fruit of our endeavour
is but a transcendental way of serving for reward; and
what we take to be contempt of self is only greed of
hire.

And again if we require so much of ourselves, shall
we not require much of others? If we do not genially
judge our own deficiencies, is it not to be feared we
shall be even stern to the trespasses of others? And he
who (looking back upon his own life) can see no more
than that he has been unconscionably long a-dying, will
he not be tempted to think his neighbour unconscionably long of getting hanged? It is probable that nearly
all who think of conduct at all, think of it too much;
it is certain we all think too much of sin. We are not
damned for doing wrong, but for not doing right;
Christ would never hear of negative morality; *thou
shalt* was ever his word, with which he superseded *thou
shalt not*. To make our idea of morality centre on
forbidden acts is to defile the imagination and to introduce into our judgments of our fellow-men a secret element of gusto. If a thing is wrong for us, we should
not dwell upon the thought of it; or we shall soon dwell
upon it with inverted pleasure. If we cannot drive it

from our minds—one thing of two: either our creed is in
the wrong and we must more indulgently remodel it; or
else, if our morality be in the right, we are criminal
lunatics and should place our persons in restraint. A
mark of such unwholesomely divided minds is the passion for interference with others: the Fox without the
Tail was of this breed, but had (if his biographer is to
be trusted) a certain antique civility now out of date.
A man may have a flaw, a weakness, that unfits him for
the duties of life, that spoils his temper, that threatens
his integrity, or that betrays him into cruelty. It has
to be conquered; but it must never be suffered to engross
his thoughts. The true duties lie all upon the farther
side, and must be attended to with a whole mind so soon
as this preliminary clearing of the decks has been
effected. In order that he may be kind and honest,
it may be needful he should become a total abstainer;
let him become so then, and the next day let him forget
the circumstance. Trying to be kind and honest will
require all his thoughts; a mortified appetite is never a
wise companion; in so far as he has had to mortify an
appetite, he will still be the worse man; and of such an
one a great deal of cheerfulness will be required in
judging life, and a great deal of humility in judging
others.

It may be argued again that dissatisfaction with our
life's endeavour springs in some degree from dulness.
We require higher tasks, because we do not recognise
the height of those we have. Trying to be kind and
honest seems an affair too simple and too inconsequential for gentlemen of our heroic mould; we had
rather set ourselves to something bold, arduous, and
conclusive; we had rather found a schism or suppress a
heresy, cut off a hand or mortify an appetite. But the
task before us, which is to co-endure with our existence,
is rather one of microscopic fineness, and the heroism
required is that of patience. There is no cutting of the
Gordian knots of life; each must be smilingly un-
ravelled.

To be honest, to be kind—to earn a little and to spend a little less, to make upon the whole a family happier for his presence, to renounce when that shall be necessary and not be embittered, to keep a few friends but these without capitulation—above all, on the same grim condition, to keep friends with himself—here is a task for all that a man has of fortitude and delicacy. He has an ambitious soul who would ask more; he has a hopeful spirit who should look in such an enterprise to be successful. There is indeed one element in human destiny that not blindness itself can controvert: whatever else we are intended to do, we are not intended to succeed; failure is the fate allotted. It is so in every art and study; it is so above all in the continent art of living well. Here is a pleasant thought for the year's end or for the end of life: Only self-deception will be satisfied, and there need be no despair for the despairer.

II

But Christmas is not only the mile-mark of another year, moving us to thoughts of self-examination: it is a season, from all its associations, whether domestic or religious, suggesting thoughts of joy. A man dissatisfied with his endeavours is a man tempted to sadness. And in the midst of the winter, when his life runs lowest and he is reminded of the empty chairs of his beloved, it is well he should be condemned to this fashion of the smiling face. Noble disappointment, noble self-denial are not to be admired, not even to be pardoned, if they bring bitterness. It is one thing to enter the kingdom of heaven maim; another to maim yourself and stay without. And the kingdom of heaven is of the childlike, of those who are easy to please, who love and who give pleasure. Mighty men of their hands, the smiters and the builders and the judges, have lived long and done sternly and yet preserved this lovely character; and among our carpet interests and twopenny concerns, the shame were indelible if *we*

should lose it. Gentleness and cheerfulness, these come
before all morality; they are the perfect duties. And it
is the trouble with moral men that they have neither
one nor other. It was the moral man, the Pharisee,
whom Christ could not away with. If your morals
make you dreary, depend upon it they are wrong. I do
not say " give them up," for they may be all you have;
but conceal them like a vice, lest they should spoil the
lives of better and simpler people.

A strange temptation attends upon man: to keep his
eye on pleasures, even when he will not share in them;
to aim all his morals against them. This very year a
lady (singular iconoclast!) proclaimed a crusade against
dolls; and the racy sermon against lust is a feature of
the age. I venture to call such moralists insincere. At
any excess or perversion of a natural appetite, their
lyre sounds of itself with relishing denunciations; but
for all displays of the truly diabolic—envy, malice,
the mean lie, the mean silence, the calumnious truth, the
backbiter, the petty tyrant, the peevish poisoner of
family life—their standard is quite different. These are
wrong, they will admit, yet somehow not so wrong;
there is no zeal in their assault on them, no secret element of gusto warms up the sermon; it is for things not
wrong in themselves that they reserve the choicest of
their indignation. A man may naturally disclaim all
moral kinship with the Reverend Mr. Zola or the hob-
goblin old lady of the dolls; for these are gross and
naked instances. And yet in each of us some similar
element resides. The sight of a pleasure in which we
cannot or else will not share moves us to a particular
impatience. It may be because we are envious, or because we are sad, or because we dislike noise and romp-
ing—being so refined, or because—being so philosophic
—we have an overweighing sense of life's gravity: at
least, as we go on in years, we are all tempted to frown
upon our neighbour's pleasures. People are nowadays
so fond of resisting temptations; here is one to be
resisted. They are fond of self-denial; here is a

propensity that cannot be too peremptorily denied. There is an idea abroad among moral people that they should make their neighbours good. One person I have to make good: myself. But my duty to my neighbour is much more nearly expressed by saying that I have to make him happy—if I may.

III

Happiness and goodness, according to canting moralists, stand in the relation of effect and cause. There was never anything less proved or less probable: our happiness is never in our own hands; we inherit our constitution; we stand buffet among friends and enemies; we may be so built as to feel a sneer or an aspersion with unusual keenness, and so circumstanced as to be unusually exposed to them; we may have nerves very sensitive to pain, and be afflicted with a disease very painful. Virtue will not help us, and it is not meant to help us. It is not even its own reward, except for the self-centred and—I had almost said—the unamiable. No man can pacify his conscience; if quiet be what he want, he shall do better to let that organ perish from disuse. And to avoid the penalties of the law, and the minor *capitis diminutio* of social ostracism, is an affair of wisdom—of cunning, if you will—and not of virtue.

In his own life, then, a man is not to expect happiness, only to profit by it gladly when it shall arise; he is on duty here; he knows not how or why, and does not need to know; he knows not for what hire, and must not ask. Somehow or other, though he does not know what goodness is, he must try to be good; somehow or other, though he cannot tell what will do it, he must try to give happiness to others. And no doubt there comes in here a frequent clash of duties. How far is he to make his neighbour happy? How far must he respect that smiling face, so easy to cloud, so hard to brighten again? And how far, on the other side, is he bound to be his brother's keeper and the prophet of his own morality? How far must he resent evil?

The difficulty is that we have little guidance; Christ's sayings on the point being hard to reconcile with each other, and (the most of them) hard to accept. But the truth of his teaching would seem to be this: in our own person and fortune, we should be ready to accept and to pardon all; it is *our* cheek we are to turn, *our* coat that we are to give away to the man who has taken *our* cloak. But when another's face is buffeted, perhaps a little of the lion will become us best. That we are to suffer others to be injured, and stand by, is not conceivable and surely not desirable. Revenge, says Bacon, is a kind of wild justice; its judgments at least are delivered by an insane judge; and in our own quarrel we can see nothing truly and do nothing wisely. But in the quarrel of our neighbour, let us be more bold. One person's happiness is as sacred as another's; when we cannot defend both, let us defend one with a stout heart. It is only in so far as we are doing this, that we have any right to interfere: the defence of B is our only ground of action against A. A has as good a right to go to the devil, as we to go to glory; and neither knows what he does.

The truth is that all these interventions and denunciations and militant mongerings of moral half-truths, though they be sometimes needful, though they are often enjoyable, do yet belong to an inferior grade of duties. Ill-temper and envy and revenge find here an arsenal of pious disguises; this is the playground of inverted lusts. With a little more patience and a little less temper, a gentler and wiser method might be found in almost every case; and the knot that we cut by some fine heady quarrel-scene in private life, or, in public affairs, by some denunciatory act against what we are pleased to call our neighbour's vices, might yet have been unwoven by the hand of sympathy.

IV

To look back upon the past year, and see how little
we have striven and to what small purpose; and how
often we have been cowardly and hung back, or tem-
erarious and rushed unwisely in; and how every day
and all day long we have transgressed the law of kindness:—it may seem a paradox, but in the bitterness of
these discoveries, a certain consolation resides. Life is
not designed to minister to a man's vanity. He goes
upon his long business most of the time with a hanging
head, and all the time like a blind child. Full of rewards and pleasures as it is—so that to see the day
break or the moon rise, or to meet a friend, or to hear
the dinner-call when he is hungry, fills him with surprising joys—this world is yet for him no abiding city.
Friendships fall through, health fails, weariness assails
him; year after year, he must thumb the hardly varying
record of his own weakness and folly. It is a friendly
process of detachment. When the time comes that he
should go, there need be few illusions left about himself.
Here lies one who meant well, tried a little, failed much:
—surely that may be his epitaph, of which he need not
be ashamed. Nor will he complain at the summons
which calls a defeated soldier from the field: defeated,
ay, if he were Paul or Marcus Aurelius!—but if there is
still one inch of fight in his old spirit, undishonoured.
The faith which sustained him in his life-long blindness
and life-long disappointment will scarce even be required in this last formality of laying down his arms.
Give him a march with his old bones; there, out of the
glorious sun-coloured earth, out of the day and the dust
and the ecstasy—there goes another Faithful Failure!

From a recent book of verse, where there is more
than one such beautiful and manly poem, I take this
memorial piece: it says better than I can, what I love
to think; let it be our parting word:—

"A late lark twitters from the quiet skies;
And from the west,
Where the sun, his day's work ended,
Lingers as in content,
There falls on the old, grey city
An influence luminous and serene,
A shining peace.

"The smoke ascends
In a rosy-and-golden haze. The spires
Shine, and are changed. In the valley
Shadows rise. The lark sings on. The sun,
Closing his benediction,
Sinks, and the darkening air
Thrills with a sense of the triumphing night—
Night, with her train of stars
And her great gift of sleep.

"So be my passing!
My task accomplished and the long day done,
My wages taken, and in my heart
Some late lark singing,
Let me be gathered to the quiet west,
The sundown splendid and serene,
Death." *

* From *A Book of Verses,* by William Ernest Henley. D. Nutt, 1888.

VIII

ROSA QUO LOCORUM

I

THROUGH what little channels, by what hints and premonitions, the consciousness of the man's art dawns first upon the child, it should be not only interesting but instructive to inquire. A matter of curiosity to-day, it will become the ground of science to-morrow. From the mind of childhood there is more history and more philosophy to be fished up than from all the printed volumes in a library. The child is conscious of an interest, not in literature, but in life. A taste for the precise, the adroit, or the comely in the use of words, comes late; but long before that he has enjoyed in books a delightful dress-rehearsal of experience. He is first conscious of this material—I had almost said this practical—preoccupation; it does not follow that it really came the first. I have some old fogged negatives in my collection that would seem to imply a prior stage. "The Lord is gone up with a shout, and God with the sound of a trumpet"—memorial version, I know not where to find the text—rings still in my ear from my first childhood, and perhaps with something of my nurse's accent. There was possibly some sort of image written in my mind by these loud words, but I believe the words themselves were what I cherished. I had about the same time, and under the same influence—that of my dear nurse—a favourite author: it is possible the reader has not heard of him—the Rev. Robert Murray M'Cheyne. My nurse and I admired his name exceedingly, so that I must have been taught

the love of beautiful sounds before I was breeched; and
I remember two specimens of his muse until this day:

> "Behind the hills of Naphtali
> The sun went slowly down,
> Leaving on mountain, tower, and tree,
> A tinge of golden brown."

There is imagery here, and I set it on one side. The
other—it is but a verse—not only contains no image,
but is quite unintelligible even to my comparatively
instructed mind, and I know not even how to spell the
outlandish vocable that charmed me in my childhood:

> "Jehovah Tschidkenu is nothing to her"; *

I may say, without flippancy, that He was nothing to
me either, since I had no ray of a guess of what He
was about; yet the verse, from then to now, a longer
interval than the life of a generation, has continued to
haunt me.

I have said that I should set a passage distinguished
by obvious and pleasing imagery, however faint; for
the child thinks much in images, words are very live to
him, phrases that imply a picture eloquent beyond their
value. Rummaging in the dusty pigeonholes of memory, I came once upon a graphic version of the famous
psalm, "The Lord is my shepherd": and from the
places employed in its illustration, which are all in the
immediate neighbourhood of a house then occupied by
my father, I am able to date it before the seventh
year of my age, although it was probably earlier in fact.
The "pastures green" were represented by a certain
suburban stubble-field, where I had once walked with
my nurse, under an autumnal sunset, on the banks of
the Water of Leith: the place is long ago built up; no
pastures now, no stubble-fields; only a maze of little
streets and smoking chimneys and shrill children. Here,
in the fleecy person of a sheep, I seemed to myself

---

* "Jehovah Tsidkenu," translated in the Authorised Version
as "The Lord our Righteousness" (Jeremiah xxiii. 6 and xxxiii.
16).

to follow something unseen, unrealised, and yet benignant; and close by the sheep in which I was incarnated
—as if for greater security—rustled the skirts of my
nurse. "Death's dark vale" was a certain archway
in the Warriston Cemetery: a formidable yet beloved
spot, for children love to be afraid—in measure as they
love all experience of vitality. Here I beheld myself
some paces ahead (seeing myself, I mean, from behind),
utterly alone in that uncanny passage: on the one side
of me a rude, knobby shepherd's staff, such as cheers
the heart of the cockney tourist, on the other a rod like
a billiard-cue appeared to accompany my progress: the
staff sturdily upright, the billiard-cue inclined confidentially, like one whispering, towards my ear. I was
aware—I will never tell you how—that the presence of
these articles afforded me encouragement. The third
and last of my pictures illustrated the words:

> "My table Thou hast furnishèd
> In presence of my foes:
> My head Thou dost with oil anoint,
> And my cup overflows":

and this was perhaps the most interesting of the series.
I saw myself seated in a kind of open stone summer-house at table; over my shoulder a hairy, bearded, and
robed presence anointed me from an authentic shoe-horn; the summer-house was part of the green court
of a ruin, and from the far side of the court black and
white imps discharged against me ineffectual arrows.
The picture appears arbitrary, but I can trace every
detail to its source, as Mr. Brock analysed the dream of
Alan Armadale. The summer-house and court were
muddled together out of Billing's *Antiquities of Scotland;* the imps conveyed from Bagster's *Pilgrim's
Progress;* the bearded and robed figure from any one of
a thousand Bible pictures; and the shoe-horn was
plagiarised from an old illustrated Bible, where it figured in the hand of Samuel anointing Saul, and had
been pointed out to me as a jest by my father. It was

shown me for a jest, remark; but the serious spirit of infancy adopted it in earnest. Children are all classics; a bottle would have seemed an intermediary too trivial —that divine refreshment of whose meaning I had no guess; and I seized on the idea of that mystic shoe-horn with delight, even as, a little later, I should have written flagon, chalice, hanaper, beaker, or any word that might have appealed to me at the moment as least contaminate with mean associations. In this string of pictures I believe the gist of the psalm to have consisted; I believe it had no more to say to me; and the result was consolatory. I would go to sleep dwelling with restfulness upon these images; they passed before me, besides, to an appropriate music; for I had already singled out from that rude psalm the one lovely verse which dwells in the minds of all, not growing old, not disgraced by its association with long Sunday tasks, a scarce conscious joy in childhood, in age a companion thought:

> "In pastures green Thou leadest me,
> The quiet waters by."

The remainder of my childish recollections are all of the matter of what was read to me, and not of any manner in the words. If these pleased me, it was unconsciously; I listened for news of the great vacant world upon whose edge I stood; I listened for delightful plots that I might re-enact in play, and romantic scenes and circumstances that I might call up before me, with closed eyes, when I was tired of Scotland and home, and that weary prison of the sick-chamber in which I lay so long in durance. *Robinson Crusoe;* some of the books of that cheerful, ingenious, romantic soul, Mayne Reid; and a work (rather gruesome and bloody for a child, but very picturesque) called *Paul Blake;* these are the three strongest impressions I remember: *The Swiss Family Robinson* came next, *longo intervallo.* At these I played, conjured up their scenes, and delighted to hear them rehearsed unto seventy times seven.

I am not sure but what *Paul Blake* came after I could read. It seems connected with a visit to the country, and an experience unforgettable. The day had been warm; H—— and I had played together charmingly all day in a sandy wilderness across the road; then came the evening with a great flash of colour and a heavenly sweetness in the air. Somehow my playmate had vanished, or is out of the story, as the sagas say, but I was sent into the village on an errand; and, taking a book of fairy tales, went down alone through a fir-wood, reading as I walked. How often since then it has befallen me to be happy even so; but that was the first time: the shock of that pleasure I have never since forgot, and if my mind serves me to the last, I never shall; for it was then that I knew I loved reading.

II

To pass from hearing literature to reading it is to take a great and dangerous step. With not a few, I think a large proportion of their pleasure then comes to an end; "the malady of not marking" overtakes them; they read thenceforward by the eye alone and hear never again the chime of fair words or the march of the stately period. *Non ragioniam* of these. But to all the step is dangerous; it involves coming of age; it is even a kind of second weaning. In the past all was at the choice of others; they chose, they digested, they read aloud for us and sang to their own tune the books of childhood. In the future we are to approach the silent, inexpressive type alone, like pioneers; and the choice of what we are to read is in our own hands thenceforward. For instance, in the passages already adduced, I detect and applaud the ear of my old nurse; they were of her choice, and she imposed them on my infancy, reading the works of others as a poet would scarce dare to read his own; gloating on the rhythm, dwelling with delight on assonances and alliterations. I know very well my mother must have been all the while trying to educate my taste upon more secular authors; but the vigour and the continual opportunities of my nurse triumphed, and after a long search, I can find in these earliest volumes of my autobiography no mention of anything but nursery rhymes, the Bible, and Mr. M'Cheyne.

I suppose all children agree in looking back with delight on their school Readers. We might not now find so much pathos in "Bingen on the Rhine," "A Soldier of the Legion lay dying in Algiers," or in "The Soldier's Funeral," in the declaration of which I was held to have surpassed myself. "Robert's voice," said the master on this memorable occasion, "is not strong, but impressive": an opinion which I was fool enough to carry home to my father; who roasted me for years in consequence. I am sure one should not be so deliciously tickled by the humorous pieces:

"What, crusty? cries Will, in a taking,
    Who would not be crusty with half a year's baking?"

I think this quip would leave us cold. The "Isles of Greece" seems rather tawdry too; but on the "Address to the Ocean," or on "The Dying Gladiator," "time has writ no wrinkle."

"'T is the morn, but dim and dark;
    Whither flies the silent lark?"——

does the reader recall the moment when his eye first fell upon these lines in the Fourth Reader; and "surprised with joy, impatient as the wind," he plunged into the sequel? And there was another piece, this time in prose, which none can have forgotten; many like me must have searched Dickens with zeal to find it again, and in its proper context, and have perhaps been conscious of some inconsiderable measure of disappointment, that it was only Tom Pinch who drove, in such a pomp of poetry, to London.

But in the Reader we are still under guides. What a boy turns out for himself, as he rummages in the bookshelves, is the real test and pleasure. My father's

library was a spot of some austerity: the proceedings
of learned societies, some Latin divinity, cyclopædias,
physical science, and, above all, optics, held the chief
place upon the shelves, and it was only in holes and
corners that anything really legible existed as by accident. The *Parent's Assistant, Rob Roy, Waverley,* and
Guy Mannering, the *Voyages of Captain Woods Rogers,*
Fuller's and Bunyan's *Holy Wars, The Reflections of
Robinson Crusoe, The Female Bluebeard,* G. Sand's
Mare au Diable (how came it in that grave assembly!),
Ainsworth's *Tower of London,* and four old volumes of
Punch—these were the chief exceptions. In these latter,
which made for years the chief of my diet, I very early
fell in love (almost as soon as I could spell) with the
Snob Papers. I knew them almost by heart, particularly the visit to the Pontos; and I remember my surprise when I found, long afterwards, that they were
famous, and signed with a famous name; to me, as I
read and admired them, they were the works of Mr.
Punch. Time and again I tried to read *Rob Roy,* with
whom of course I was acquainted from the *Tales of a
Grandfather;* time and again the early part, with Rashleigh and (think of it!) the adorable Diana, choked me
off; and I shall never forget the pleasure and surprise
with which, lying on the floor one summer evening, I
struck of a sudden into the first scene with Andrew
Fairservice. "The worthy Dr. Lightfoot"—"mis-
trysted with a bogle"—"a wheen green trash"—
"Jenny, lass, I think I ha'e her": from that day to this
the phrases have been unforgotten. I read on, I need
scarce say; I came to Glasgow, I bided tryst on Glasgow
Bridge, I met Rob Roy and the Bailie in the Tolbooth,
all with transporting pleasure; and then the clouds
gathered once more about my path; and I dozed and
skipped until I stumbled half-asleep into the clachan of
Aberfoyle, and the voices of Iverach and Galbraith recalled me to myself. With that scene and the defeat
of Captain Thornton the book concluded; Helen and
her sons shocked even the little schoolboy of nine or ten

with their unreality; I read no more, or I did not grasp
what I was reading; and years elapsed before I consciously met Diana and her father among the hills, or
saw Rashleigh dying in the chair. When I think of
that novel and that evening, I am impatient with all
others; they seem but shadows and impostors; they cannot satisfy the appetite which this awakened; and I
dare be known to think it the best of Sir Walter's by
nearly as much as Sir Walter is the best of novelists.
Perhaps Mr. Lang is right, and our first friends in the
land of fiction are always the most real. And yet I had
read before this *Guy Mannering*, and some of *Waverley*,
with no such delighted sense of truth and humour, and I
read immediately after the greater part of the Waverley
Novels, and was never moved again in the same way
or to the same degree. One circumstance is suspicious:
my critical estimate of the Waverley Novels has scarce
changed at all since I was ten. *Rob Roy, Guy Mannering,* and *Redgauntlet* first; then, a little lower, *The For-
tunes of Nigel;* then, after a huge gulf, *Ivanhoe* and
Anne of Geierstein; the rest nowhere; such was the
verdict of the boy. Since then *The Antiquary, St.
Roman's Well, Kenilworth,* and *The Heart of Mid-
lothian* have gone up in the scale; perhaps *Ivanhoe* and
Anne of Geierstein have gone a trifle down; Diana
Vernon has been added to my admirations in that enchanted world of *Rob Roy;* I think more of the letters
in *Redgauntlet,* and Peter Peebles, that dreadful piece
of realism, I can now read about with equanimity, interest, and I had almost said pleasure, while to the
childish critic he often caused unmixed distress. But
the rest is the same; I could not finish *The Pirate* when
I was a child, I have never finished it yet; *Peveril of
the Peak* dropped half-way through from my schoolboy
hands, and though I have since waded to an end in a
kind of wager with myself, the exercise was quite
without enjoyment. There is something disquieting in
these considerations. I still think the visit to Ponto's
the best part of the *Book of Snobs:* does that mean

that I was right when I was a child; or does it mean that I have never grown since then, that the child is not the man's father, but the man? and that I came into the world with all my faculties complete, and have only learned sinsyne to be more tolerant of boredom? . . .

FONTAINEBLEAU

THIS essay first appeared in *The Magazine of Art*, May and June, 1884.

FONTAINEBLEAU

VILLAGE COMMUNITIES OF PAINTERS

I

THE charm of Fontainebleau is a thing apart. It is
a place that people love even more than they admire. The vigorous forest air, the silence, the majestic
avenues of highway, the wilderness of tumbled boulders, the great age and dignity of certain groves—these
are but ingredients, they are not the secret of the philtre.
The place is sanative; the air, the light, the perfumes,
and the shapes of things concord in happy harmony.
The artist may be idle and not fear the " blues." He
may dally with his life. Mirth, lyric mirth, and a
vivacious classical contentment are of the very essence
of the better kind of art; and these, in that most smiling
forest, he has the chance to learn or to remember. Even
on the plain of Bière, where the Angelus of Millet still
tolls upon the ear of fancy, a larger air, a higher heaven,
something ancient and healthy in the face of nature,
purify the mind alike from dulness and hysteria. There
is no place where the young are more gladly conscious
of their youth, or the old better contented with their
age.

The fact of its great and special beauty further rec-
ommends this country to the artist. The field was
chosen by men in whose blood there still raced some
of the gleeful or solemn exultation of great art—Millet
who loved dignity like Michelangelo, Rousseau whose
modern brush was dipped in the glamour of the ancients.
It was chosen before the day of that strange turn in
the history of art, of which we now perceive the

culmination in impressionistic tales and pictures—that
voluntary aversion of the eye from all speciously strong
and beautiful effects—that disinterested love of dulness
which has set so many Peter Bells to paint the riverside primrose. It was then chosen for its proximity to
Paris. And for the same cause, and by the force of
tradition, the painter of to-day continues to inhabit
and to paint it. There is in France scenery incomparable for romance and harmony. Provence, and the
valley of the Rhone from Vienne to Tarascon, are one
succession of masterpieces waiting for the brush. The
beauty is not merely beauty; it tells, besides, a tale to
the imagination, and surprises while it charms. Here
you shall see castellated towns that would befit the
scenery of dreamland; streets that glow with colour like
cathedral windows; hills of the most exquisite proportions; flowers of every precious colour, growing thick
like grass. All these, by the grace of railway travel, are
brought to the very door of the modern painter; yet
he does not seek them; he remains faithful to Fontainebleau, to the eternal bridge of Gretz, to the watering-
pot cascade in Cernay valley. Even Fontainebleau was
chosen for him; even in Fontainebleau he shrinks from
what is sharply charactered. But one thing, at least,
is certain, whatever he may choose to paint and in
whatever manner, it is good for the artist to dwell
among graceful shapes. Fontainebleau, if it be but
quiet scenery, is classically graceful; and though the
student may look for different qualities, this quality,
silently present, will educate his hand and eye.

But, before all its other advantages—charm, loveliness, or proximity to Paris—comes the great fact that it
is already colonised. The institution of a painters'
colony is a work of time and tact. The population must
be conquered. The innkeeper has to be taught, and he
soon learns, the lesson of unlimited credit; he must be
taught to welcome as a favoured guest a young gentleman in a very greasy coat, and with little baggage beyond a box of colours and a canvas; and he must learn

to preserve his faith in customers who will eat heartily
and drink of the best, borrow money to buy tobacco,
and perhaps not pay a stiver for a year. A colour merchant has next to be attracted. A certain vogue must
be given to the place, lest the painter, most gregarious
of animals, should find himself alone. And no sooner
are these first difficulties overcome, than fresh perils
spring up upon the other side; and the bourgeois and
the tourist are knocking at the gate. This is the crucial
moment for the colony. If these intruders gain a footing, they not only banish freedom and amenity; pretty
soon, by means of their long purses, they will have
undone the education of the innkeeper; prices will rise
and credit shorten; and the poor painter must fare
farther on and find another hamlet. "Not here, O
Apollo!" will become his song. Thus Trouville and,
the other day, St. Raphael were lost to the arts. Curious
and not always edifying are the shifts that the French
student uses to defend his lair; like the cuttlefish, he
must sometimes blacken the waters of his chosen pool;
but at such a time and for so practical a purpose Mrs.
Grundy must allow him license. Where his own purse
and credit are not threatened, he will do the honours of
his village generously. Any artist is made welcome,
through whatever medium he may seek expression;
science is respected; even the idler, if he prove, as he
so rarely does, a gentleman, will soon begin to find himself at home. And when that essentially modern
creature, the English or American girl-student, began
to walk calmly into his favourite inns as if into a
drawing-room at home, the French painter owned
himself defenceless; he submitted or he fled. His
French respectability, quite as precise as ours, though
covering different provinces of life, recoiled aghast
before the innovation. But the girls were painters;
there was nothing to be done; and Barbizon, when
I last saw it and for the time at least, was practically ceded to the fair invader. Paterfamilias, on
the other hand, the common tourist, the holiday shop-

man, and the cheap young gentleman upon the spree, he hounded from his villages with every circumstance of contumely.

This purely artistic society is excellent for the young artist. The lads are mostly fools; they hold the latest orthodoxy in its crudeness; they are at that stage of education, for the most part, when a man is too much occupied with style to be aware of the necessity for any matter; and this, above all for the Englishman, is excellent. To work grossly at the trade, to forget sentiment, to think of his material and nothing else, is, for a while at least, the king's highway of progress. Here, in England, too many painters and writers dwell dispersed, unshielded, among the intelligent bourgeois. These, when they are not merely indifferent, prate to him about the lofty aims and moral influence of art. And this is the lad's ruin. For art is, first of all and last of all, a trade. The love of words and not a desire to publish new discoveries, the love of form and not a novel reading of historical events, mark the vocation of the writer and the painter. The arabesque, properly speaking, and even in literature, is the first fancy of the artist; he first plays with his material as a child plays with a kaleidoscope; and he is already in a second stage when he begins to use his pretty counters for the end of representation. In that, he must pause long and toil faithfully; that is his apprenticeship; and it is only the few who will really grow beyond it, and go forward, fully equipped, to do the business of real art—to give life to abstractions and significance and charm to facts. In the meanwhile, let him dwell much among his fellowcraftsmen. They alone can take a serious interest in the childish tasks and pitiful successes of these years. They alone can behold with equanimity this fingering of the dumb keyboard, this polishing of empty sentences, this dull and literal painting of dull and insignificant subjects. Outsiders will spur him on. They will say, "Why do you not write a great book? paint a great picture?" If his guardian angel fail him, they may even persuade him to the attempt, and, ten to one, his hand is coarsened and his style falsified for life.

And this brings me to a warning. The life of the apprentice to any art is both unstrained and pleasing; it is strewn with small successes in the midst of a career of failure, patiently supported; the heaviest scholar is conscious of a certain progress; and if he come not appreciably nearer to the art of Shakespeare, grows letter-perfect in the domain of A-B, ab. But the time comes when a man should cease prelusory gymnastic, stand up, put a violence upon his will, and for better or worse, begin the business of creation. This evil day there is a tendency continually to postpone: above all with painters. They have made so many studies that it has become a habit; they make more, the walls of exhibitions blush with them; and death finds these aged students still busy with their hornbook. This class of man finds a congenial home in artist villages; in the slang of the English colony at Barbizon we used to call them " Snoozers." Continual returns to the city, the society of men farther advanced, the study of great works, a sense of humour or, if such a thing is to be had, a little religion or philosophy, are the means of treatment. It will be time enough to think of curing the malady after it has been caught; for to catch it is the very thing for which you seek that dreamland of the painters' village. " Snoozing " is a part of the artistic education; and the rudiments must be learned stupidly, all else being forgotten, as if they were an object in themselves.

Lastly, there is something, or there seems to be something, in the very air of France that communicates the love of style. Precision, clarity, the cleanly and crafty employment of material, a grace in the handling, apart from any value in the thought, seem to be acquired by the mere residence; or if not acquired, become at least the more appreciated. The air of Paris is alive with this technical inspiration. And to leave that airy city and awake next day upon the borders of the forest is but to change externals. The same spirit of dexterity and finish breathes from the long alleys and the lofty groves, from the wildernesses that are still pretty in their confusion, and the great plain that contrives to be decorative in its emptiness.

II

In spite of its really considerable extent, the forest of Fontainebleau is hardly anywhere tedious. I know the whole western side of it with what, I suppose, I may call thoroughness; well enough at least to testify that there is no square mile without some special character and charm. Such quarters, for instance, as the Long Rocher, the Bas-Bréau, and the Reine Blanche, might be a hundred miles apart; they have scarce a point in common beyond the silence of the birds. The two last are really conterminous; and in both are tall and ancient trees that have outlived a thousand political vicissitudes. But in the one the great oaks prosper placidly upon an even floor; they be-shadow a great field; and the air and the light are very free below their stretching boughs. In the other the trees find difficult footing; castles of white rock lie tumbled one upon another, the foot slips, the crooked viper slumbers, the moss clings in the crevice; and above it all the great beech goes spiring and casting forth her arms, and, with a grace beyond church architecture, canopies this rugged chaos. Meanwhile, dividing the two cantons, the broad white causeway of the Paris road runs in an avenue: a road conceived for pageantry and for triumphal marches, an avenue for an army; but, its days of glory over, it now lies grilling in the sun between cool groves, and only at intervals the vehicle of the cruising tourist is seen far away and faintly audible along its ample sweep. A little upon one side, and you find a district of sand and birch and boulder; a little upon the other lies the valley of Apremont, all juniper and heather; and close beyond that you may walk into

a zone of pine-trees. So artfully are the ingredients
mingled. Nor must it be forgotten that, in all this part,
you come continually forth upon a hill-top, and behold
the plain, northward and westward, like an unrefulgent
sea; nor that all day long the shadows keep changing;
and at last, to the red fires of sunset, night succeeds,
and with the night a new forest, full of whisper, gloom,
and fragrance. There are few things more renovating
than to leave Paris, the lamplit arches of the Carrousel,
and the long alignment of the glittering streets, and
to bathe the senses in this fragrant darkness of the
wood.

In this continual variety the mind is kept vividly
alive. It is a changeful place to paint, a stirring place
to live in. As fast as your foot carries you, you pass
from scene to scene, each vigorously painted in the
colours of the sun, each endeared by that hereditary
spell of forests on the mind of man who still remembers
and salutes the ancient refuge of his race.

And yet the forest has been civilized throughout. The
most savage corners bear a name, and have been cherished like antiquities; in the most remote, Nature has
prepared and balanced her effects as if with conscious
art; and man, with his guiding arrows of blue paint,
has countersigned the picture. After your farthest wandering, you are never surprised to come forth upon the
vast avenue of highway, to strike the centre point of
branching alleys, or to find the aqueduct trailing,
thousand-footed, through the brush. It is not a wilderness; it is rather a preserve. And, fitly enough, the
centre of the maze is not a hermit's cavern. In the
midst a little mirthful town lies sunlit, humming with
the business of pleasure; and the palace, breathing distinction and peopled by historic names, stands smoke-
less among gardens.

Perhaps the last attempt at savage life was that of
the harmless humbug who called himself the hermit. In
a great tree, close by the high road, he had built himself
a little cabin after the manner of the Swiss Family

Robinson; thither he mounted at night, by the romantic aid of a rope ladder, and if dirt be any proof of sincerity, the man was savage as a Sioux. I had the pleasure of his acquaintance; he appeared grossly stupid, not in his perfect wits, and interested in nothing but small change; for that he had a great avidity. In the course of time he proved to be a chicken-stealer, and vanished from his perch; and perhaps from the first he was no true votary of forest freedom, but an ingenious, theatrically-minded beggar, and his cabin in the tree was only stock-in-trade to beg withal. The choice of his position would seem to indicate so much; for if in the forest there are no places still to be discovered, there are many that have been forgotten and that lie unvisited. There, to be sure, are the blue arrows waiting to reconduct you, now blazed upon a tree, now posted in the corner of a rock. But your security from interruption is complete; you might camp for weeks, if there were only water, and not a soul suspect your presence; and if I may suppose the reader to have committed some great crime and come to me for aid, I think I could still find my way to a small cavern, fitted with a hearth and chimney, where he might lie perfectly concealed. A confederate landscape-painter might daily supply him with food; for water, he would have to make a nightly tramp as far as to the nearest pond; and at last, when the hue and cry began to blow over, he might get gently on the train at some side station, work round by a series of junctions, and be quietly captured at the frontier.

Thus Fontainebleau, although it is truly but a pleasure-ground, and although, in favourable weather, and in the more celebrated quarters, it literally buzzes with the tourist, yet has some of the immunities and offers some of the repose of natural forests. And the solitary, although he must return at night to his frequented inn, may yet pass the day with his own thoughts in the companionable silence of the trees. The demands of the imagination vary; some can be alone in a back

garden looked upon by windows; others, like the ostrich,
are content with a solitude that meets the eye; and
others, again, expand in fancy to the very borders of
their desert, and are irritably conscious of a hunter's
camp in an adjacent county. To these last, of course,
Fontainebleau will seem but an extended tea-garden: a
Rosherville on a by-day. But to the plain man it offers
solitude: an excellent thing in itself, and a good whet
for company.

III

I was for some time a consistent Barbizonian; *et ego
in Arcadia vixi*, it was a pleasant season; and that
noiseless hamlet lying close among the borders of the
wood is for me, as for so many others, a green spot
in memory. The great Millet was just dead, the green
shutters of his modest house were closed; his daughters
were in mourning. The date of my first visit was thus
an epoch in the history of art: in a lesser way, it was
an epoch in the history of the Latin Quarter. The *Petit
Cénacle* was dead and buried; Mürger and his crew of
sponging vagabonds were all at rest from their expedients; the tradition of their real life was nearly lost,
and the petrified legend of the *Vie de Bohème* had become a sort of gospel, and still gave the cue to zealous
imitators. But if the book be written in rose-water,
the imitation was still further expurgated; honesty was
the rule; the innkeepers gave, as I have said, almost
unlimited credit; they suffered the seediest painter to
depart, to take all his belongings, and to leave his bill
unpaid; and if they sometimes lost, it was by English
and Americans alone. At the same time, the great
influx of Anglo-Saxons had begun to affect the life of
the studious. There had been disputes; and, in one
instance at least, the English and the Americans had
made common cause to prevent a cruel pleasantry. It
would be well if nations and races could communicate
their qualities; but in practice when they look upon

each other, they have an eye to nothing but defects. The Anglo-Saxon is essentially dishonest; the French is devoid by nature of the principle that we call "Fair Play." The Frenchman marvelled at the scruples of his guest, and, when the defender of innocence retired overseas and left his bills unpaid, he marvelled once again; the good and evil were, in his eyes, part and parcel of the same eccentricity; a shrug expressed his judgment upon both.

At Barbizon there was no master, no pontiff in the arts. Palizzi bore rule at Gretz—urbane, superior rule —his memory rich in anecdotes of the great men of yore, his mind fertile in theories; sceptical, composed, and venerable to the eye; and yet beneath these outworks, all twittering with Italian superstition, his eye scouting for omens, and the whole fabric of his manners giving way on the appearance of a hunchback. Cernay had Pelouse, the admirable, placid Pelouse, smilingly critical of youth, who, when a full-blown commercial traveller, suddenly threw down his samples, bought a colour-box, and became the master whom we have all admired. Marlotte, for a central figure, boasted Olivier de Penne. Only Barbizon, since the death of Millet, was a headless commonwealth. Even its secondary lights, and those who in my day made the stranger welcome, have since deserted it. The good Lachèvre has departed, carrying his household gods; and long before that Gaston Lafenestre was taken from our midst by an untimely death. He died before he had deserved success; it may be, he would never have deserved it; but his kind, comely, modest countenance still haunts the memory of all who knew him. Another—whom I will not name—has moved farther on, pursuing the strange Odyssey of his decadence. His days of royal favour had departed even then; but he still retained, in his narrower life at Barbizon, a certain stamp of conscious importance, hearty, friendly, filling the room, the occupant of several chairs; nor had he yet ceased his losing battle, still labouring upon great canvases that none would buy, still waiting the return of fortune. But these days also were too good to last; and the former favourite of two sovereigns fled, if I heard the truth, by night. There was a time when he was counted a great man, and Millet but a dauber; behold, how the whirligig of time brings in his revenge! To pity Millet is a piece of arrogance; if life be hard for such resolute and pious spirits, it is harder still for us, had we the wit to understand it; but we may pity his unhappier rival, who, for no apparent merit, was raised to opulence and momentary fame, and, through no apparent fault, was suffered step by step to sink again to nothing. No misfortune can exceed the bitterness of such back foremost progress, even bravely supported as it was; but to those also who were taken early from the easel, a regret is due. From all the young men of this period, one stood out by the vigour of his promise; he was in the age of fermentation, enamoured of eccentricities. " Il faut faire de la peinture nouvelle," was his watchword; but if time and experience had continued his education, if he had been granted health to return from these excursions to the steady and the central, I must believe that the name of Hills had become famous.

Siron's inn, that excellent artists' barrack, was managed upon easy principles. At any hour of the night, when you returned from wandering in the forest, you went to the billiard-room and helped yourself to liquors, or descended to the cellar and returned laden with beer or wine. The Sirons were all locked in slumber; there was none to check your inroads; only at the week's end a computation was made, the gross sum was divided, and a varying share set down to every lodger's name under the rubric: *estrats*. Upon the more long-suffering the larger tax was levied; and your bill lengthened in a direct proportion to the easiness of your disposition. At any hour of the morning, again, you could get your coffee or cold milk, and set forth into the forest. The doves had perhaps wakened you, fluttering into your chamber; and on the threshold of the inn you were met by the aroma of the forest. Close by were the great aisles, the mossy boulders, the interminable field of forest shadow. There you were free to dream and wander. And at noon, and again at six o'clock, a good meal awaited you on Siron's table. The whole of your accommodation, set aside that varying item of the *estrats,* cost you five francs a day; your bill was never offered you until you asked it; and if you were out of luck's way, you might depart for where you pleased and leave it pending.

IV

Theoretically, the house was open to all comers; practically, it was a kind of club. The guests protected themselves, and, in so doing, they protected Siron. Formal manners being laid aside, essential courtesy was the more rigidly exacted; the new arrival had to feel the pulse of the society; and a breach of its undefined observances was promptly punished. A man might be as plain, as dull, as slovenly, as free of speech as he desired; but to a touch of presumption or a word of hectoring these free Barbizonians were as sensitive as a tea-party of maiden ladies. I have seen people driven forth from Barbizon; it would be difficult to say in words what they had done, but they deserved their fate. They had shown themselves unworthy to enjoy these corporate freedoms; they had pushed themselves; they had " made their head "; they wanted tact to appreciate the " fine shades " of Barbizonian etiquette. And once they were condemned, the process of extrusion was ruthless in its cruelty; after one evening with the formidable Bodmer, the Baily of our commonwealth, the erring stranger was beheld no more; he rose exceedingly early the next day, and the first coach conveyed him from the scene of his discomfiture. These sentences of banishment were never, in my knowledge, delivered against an artist; such would, I believe, have been illegal; but the odd and pleasant fact is this, that they were never needed. Painters, sculptors, writers, singers, I have seen all of these in Barbizon; and some were sulky and some blatant and inane; but one and all entered at once into the spirit of the association. This singular society is purely French, a creature of French virtues, and possibly of French defects. It cannot be imitated by the English. The roughness, the impatience, the more obvious selfishness, and even the more ardent friendship of the Anglo-Saxon, speedily dismember such a commonwealth. But this random gathering of young French painters, with neither apparatus nor parade of government, yet kept the life of the place upon a certain footing, insensibly imposed their etiquette upon the docile, and by caustic speech enforced their edicts against the unwelcome. To think of it is to wonder the more at the strange failure of their race upon the larger theatre. This inbred civility —to use the word in its completest meaning—this natural and facile adjustment of contending liberties, seems all that is required to make a governable nation and a just and prosperous country.

Our society, thus purged and guarded, was full of high spirits, of laughter, and of the initiative of youth. The few elder men who joined us were still young at heart, and took the key from their companions. We returned from long stations in the fortifying air, our blood renewed by the sunshine, our spirits refreshed by the silence of the forest; the Babel of loud voices sounded good; we fell to eat and play like the natural man; and in the high inn chamber, panelled with indifferent pictures and lit by candles guttering in the night air, the talk and laughter sounded far into the night. It was a good place and a good life for any naturally-minded youth; better yet for the student of painting, and perhaps best of all for the student of letters. He, too, was saturated in this atmosphere of style; he was shut out from the disturbing currents of the world, he might forget that there existed other and more pressing interests than that of art. But, in such

a place, it was hardly possible to write; he could not
drug his conscience, like the painter, by the production
of listless studies; he saw himself idle among many who
were apparently, and some who were really, employed;
and what with the impulse of increasing health and the
continual provocation of romantic scenes, he became
tormented with the desire to work. He enjoyed a strenuous idleness full of visions, hearty meals, long, swelter-
ing walks, mirth among companions; and still floating
like music through his brain, foresights of great works
that Shakespeare might be proud to have conceived,
headless epics, glorious torsos of dramas, and words
that were alive with import. So in youth, like Moses
from the mountain, we have sights of that House Beautiful of art which we shall never enter. They are
dreams and unsubstantial; visions of style that repose
upon no base of human meaning; the last heart-throbs
of that excited amateur who has to die in all of us
before the artist can be born. But they come to us
in such a rainbow of glory that all subsequent achievement appears dull and earthly in comparison. We were
all artists; almost all in the age of illusion, cultivating
an imaginary genius, and walking to the strains of
some deceiving Ariel; small wonder, indeed, if we were
happy! But art, of whatever nature, is a kind mistress;
and though these dreams of youth fall by their own
baselessness, others succeed, graver and more substan-
tial; the symptoms change, the amiable malady endures; and still, at an equal distance, the House Beautiful shines upon its hill-top.

V

Gretz lies out of the forest, down by the bright river.
It boasts a mill, an ancient church, a castle, and a
bridge of many sterlings. And the bridge is a piece
of public property; anonymously famous; beaming on
the incurious dilettante from the walls of a hundred exhibitions. I have seen it in the Salon; I have seen it in

the Academy; I have seen it in the last French Exposition, excellently done by Bloomer; in a black-and-white, by Mr. A. Henley, it once adorned this essay in the pages of the *Magazine of Art*. Long-suffering bridge! And if you visit Gretz to-morrow, you shall find another generation camped at the bottom of Chevillon's garden under their white umbrellas, and doggedly painting it again.

The bridge taken for granted, Gretz is a less inspiring place than Barbizon. I give it the palm over Cernay. There is something ghastly in the great empty village square of Cernay, with the inn tables standing in one corner, as though the stage were set for rustic opera, and in the early morning all the painters breaking their fast upon white wine under the windows of the villagers. It is vastly different to awake in Gretz, to go down the green inn-garden, to find the river streaming through the bridge, and to see the dawn begin across the poplared level. The meals are laid in the cool arbour, under fluttering leaves. The splash of oars and bathers, the bathing costumes out to dry, the trim canoes beside the jetty, tell of a society that has an eye to pleasure. There is " something to do " at Gretz. Perhaps, for that very reason, I can recall no such enduring ardours, no such glories of exhilaration, as among the solemn groves and uneventful hours of Barbizon. This " something to do " is a great enemy to joy; it is a way out of it; you wreak your high spirits on some cut-and-dry employment, and behold them gone! But Gretz is a merry place after its kind: pretty to see, merry to inhabit. The course of its pellucid river, whether up or down, is full of gentle attractions for the navigator: islanded reed-mazes where, in autumn, the red berries cluster; the mirrored and inverted images of trees; lilies, and mills, and the foam and thunder of weirs. And of all noble sweeps of roadway, none is nobler, on a windy dusk, than the high road to Nemours between its lines of talking poplar.

But even Gretz is changed. The old inn, long shored

and trussed and buttressed, fell at length under the mere weight of years, and the place as it was is but a fading image in the memory of former guests. They, indeed, recall the ancient wooden stair; they recall the rainy evening, the wide hearth, the blaze of the twig fire, and the company that gathered round the pillar in the kitchen. But the material fabric is now dust; soon, with the last of its inhabitants, its very memory shall follow; and they, in their turn, shall suffer the same law, and, both in name and lineament, vanish from the world of men. " For remembrance of the old house's sake," as Pepys once quaintly put it, let me tell one story. When the tide of invasion swept over France, two foreign painters were left stranded and penniless in Gretz; and there, until the war was over, the Chevillons ungrudgingly harboured them. It was difficult to obtain supplies; but the two waifs were still welcome to the best, sat down daily with the family to table, and at the due intervals were supplied with clean napkins, which they scrupled to employ. Madame Chevillon observed the fact and reprimanded them. But they stood firm; eat they must, but having no money they would soil no napkins.

VI

Nemours and Moret, for all they are so picturesque, have been little visited by painters. They are, indeed, too populous; they have manners of their own, and might resist the drastic process of colonisation. Montigny has been somewhat strangely neglected; I never knew it inhabited but once, when Will H. Low installed himself there with a barrel of *piquette*, and entertained his friends in a leafy trellis above the weir, in sight of the green country and to the music of the falling water. It was a most airy, quaint, and pleasant place of residence, just too rustic to be stagey; and from my memories of the place in general, and that garden trellis in particular—at morning, visited by birds, or at night, when the dew fell and the stars were of the party—I am inclined to think perhaps too favourably of the future of Montigny. Chailly-en-Bière has outlived all things, and lies dustily slumbering in the plain—the cemetery of itself. The great road remains to testify of its former bustle of postillions and carriage bells; and, like memorial tablets, there still hang in the inn room the paintings of a former generation, dead or decorated long ago. In my time, one man only, greatly daring, dwelt there. From time to time he would walk over to Barbizon, like a shade revisiting the glimpses of the moon, and after some communication with flesh and blood return to his austere hermitage. But even he, when I last revisited the forest, had come to Barbizon for good, and closed the roll of Chaillyites. It may revive—but I much doubt it. Achères and Recloses still wait a pioneer; Bourron is out of the question, being merely Gretz over again, without the river, the bridge, or the beauty; and of all the possible places on the western side, Marlotte alone remains to be discussed. I scarcely know Marlotte, and, very likely for that reason, am not much in love with it. It seems a glaring and unsightly hamlet. The inn of Mother Antonie is unattractive; and its more reputable rival, though comfortable enough, is commonplace. Marlotte has a name; it is famous; if I were the young painter I would leave it alone in its glory.

VII

These are the words of an old stager; and though time is a good conservative in forest places, much may be untrue to-day. Many of us have passed Arcadian days there and moved on, but yet left a portion of our souls behind us buried in the woods. I would not dig for these reliquiæ; they are incommunicable treasures that will not enrich the finder; and yet there may lie, interred below great oaks or scattered along forest paths, stores of youth's dynamite and dear remembrances. And as one generation passes on and renovates the field of tillage for the next, I entertain a fancy that when the young men of to-day go forth into the forest, they shall find the air still vitalised by the spirits of their predecessors, and, like those "unheard melodies" that are the sweetest of all, the memory of our laughter shall still haunt the field of trees. Those merry voices that in woods call the wanderer farther, those thrilling silences and whispers of the groves, surely in Fontaine-bleau they must be vocal of me and my companions? We are not content to pass away entirely from the scenes of our delight; we would leave, if but in gratitude, a pillar and a legend.

One generation after another fall like honey-bees upon this memorable forest, rifle its sweets, pack themselves with vital memories, and when the theft is consummated depart again into life richer, but poorer also. The forest, indeed, they have possessed, from that day forward it is theirs indissolubly, and they will return to walk in it at night in the fondest of their dreams, and use it for ever in their books and pictures. Yet when they make their packets, and put up their notes and sketches, something, it should seem, had been forgotten. A projection of themselves shall appear to haunt unfriended these scenes of happiness, a natural child of fancy, begotten and forgotten unawares. Over the whole field of our wanderings such fetches are still travelling like indefatigable bagmen; but the imps of Fontainebleau, as of all beloved spots, are very long of life, and memory is piously unwilling to forget their orphanage. If anywhere about that wood you meet my airy bantling, greet him with tenderness. He was a pleasant lad, though now abandoned. And when it comes to your own turn to quit the forest may you leave behind you such another; no Antony or Werther, let us hope, no tearful whipster, but, as becomes this not uncheerful and most active age in which we figure, the child of happy hours.

No art, it may be said, was ever perfect, and not many noble, that has not been mirthfully conceived.

And no man, it may be added, was ever anything but a wet blanket and a cross to his companions who boasted not a copious spirit of enjoyment. Whether as man or artist, let the youth make haste to Fontainebleau, and once there let him address himself to the spirit of the place; he will learn more from exercise than from studies, although both are necessary; and if he can get into his heart the gaiety and inspiration of the woods he will have gone far to undo the evil of his sketches. A spirit once well strung up to the concert-pitch of the primeval out-of-doors will hardly dare to finish a study and magniloquently ticket it a picture. The incommunicable thrill of things, that is the tuning-fork by which we test the flatness of our art. Here it is that Nature teaches and condemns, and still spurs up to further effort and new failure. Thus it is that she sets us blushing at our ignorant and tepid works; and the more we find of these inspiring shocks the less shall we be apt to love the literal in our productions. In all sciences and senses the letter kills; and to-day, when cackling human geese express their ignorant condemnation of all studio pictures, it is a lesson most useful to be learnt. Let the young painter go to Fontainebleau, and while he stupefies himself with studies that teach him the mechanical side of his trade, let him walk in the great air, and be a servant of mirth, and not pick and botanise, but wait upon the moods of nature. So he will learn—or learn not to forget—the poetry of life and earth, which, when he has acquired his frock, will save him from joyless reproduction.

MEMOIRS OF HIMSELF

BY

ROBERT LOUIS STEVENSON

BOOK I—CHILDHOOD

GIVEN TO ISOBEL STEWART STRONG

THE AMANUENSIS

FOR FUTURE USE WHEN THE UNDER-

WRITER IS DEAD

WITH LOVE

ROBERT LOUIS STEVENSON

Memoirs of Himself was printed for the first time in the Vailima Edition.

MEMOIRS OF HIMSELF

By Robert Louis Stevenson

I HAVE the more interest in beginning these memoirs where and how I do, because I am living absolutely alone in San Francisco, and because from two years of anxiety and, according to the doctors, a touch of malaria, I may say I am altogether changed into another character. After weeks in this city, I know only a few neighbouring streets; I seem to be cured of all my adventurous whims and even of human curiosity; and am content to sit here by the fire and await the course of fortune. Indeed I know myself no longer; and as I am changed in heart, I hope I have the more chance to look back impartially on all that has come and gone heretofore.

There is, after all, no truer sort of writing than what is to be found in autobiographies, and certainly none more entertaining. Or if any, it is in fiction of the higher class which is the quintessence and last word both of veracity and entertainment. A man is perhaps not very sure of his taste in matters that concern him so nearly as the facts of his own career; he is not perhaps in a position to expand or broider; but where can he have so fine an opportunity of condensation? I shall try here to be very dense and only to touch on what concerns me very deeply; for, as I am after all a man, that must be to some degree the concern of mankind.

It has been a question with me whether it could ever be worth while to write the lives of any that were not heroic; but a recollection of my own youth has sufficiently laid the scruple. This life of ours is at best so mixed a business, that between good and evil, between sense and folly, between the selfish and the generous impulse, we must always be glad to find ourselves countenanced and, as it were, brothered by a fellow-man; and where a life, low as it may be, has any upward tendency and does not progressively condescend with the baser parts of nature, if it be truly told, it may not only console but encourage others. Even where there is no human dignity, there will be some human pathos; even when no great right has been done, and the being under review has merely struggled along the borderland of good and evil with conspicuous lapses, that struggle itself is something holy. I suppose I am in agreement with the very best of men, when I say that I should wish, if I could live again, to change at least three-quarters of my thoughts and actions; and still, in company with the worst, I have moments in my experience upon which I can look back with unmingled satisfaction.

Jan: '79.

[Note in his mother's autograph.]
This must have been Jan. '80, he did not go to America till autumn 1879.
M. I. S. 1894.

BOOK I—CHILDHOOD

I was born in Edinburgh, in 1850, the 13th of November, my father Thomas Stevenson, my mother Margaret Isabella Balfour. My mother's family, the Balfours of Pilrig, is a good provincial stock; for near three centuries before my appearance, these Balfours had been judges, advocates, and ministers of the Gospel, and I believe them related to many of the so-called good families of Scotland. The present laird, John Balfour, has made out the family tree, but I have never had the curiosity to see it. It concerns me much more that John Balfour of Kinlock, the covenanting fanatic, was an ancestral cousin; and that Dr. Smith of Galston— "Smith opens out his cauld harangues"—was my mother's maternal grandfather. Thus I may call myself connected both with Scott and Burns.*

My father's family is much more remarkable; this much at least may be said for it, that its history is unparalleled. My father heard a tradition that the first of his race came from France as Barber-chirurgeon to Cardinal Beaton; but there is small reason to doubt that we Stevensons are of Scandinavian descent. I wish I could prove we were related to old John Stevenson, author of the "Rare soul-strengthening and comforting Cordial"; † and at least, so dark is the family history, I am at liberty to tell myself it may have been so. We rose out of obscurity in a clap. My father and Uncle David made the third generation, one Smith and two Stevensons, of direct descendants who had been engineers to the Board of Northern Lights; there is scarce a deep sea light from the Isle of Man north about to Berwick, but one of my blood designed it; and I have often thought that to find a family to compare with ours in the promise of immortal memory, we must go back to the Egyptian Pharaohs:—upon so many reefs and forelands that not very elegant name of Stevenson is engraved with a pen of iron upon granite. My name is as well known as that of the Duke of Argyle among the fishers, the skippers, the seamen, and the masons of my native land. Whenever I smell salt water, I know I am not far from one of the works of my ancestors. The Bell Rock stands monument for my grandfather; the Skerry Vohr for my Uncle Alan; and when the lights come out at sundown along the shores of Scotland, I am proud to think they burn more brightly for the genius of my father.

* Old Robert Wodrow too, of the inimitable *Analecta,* is my relation through the Balfours.
† Celtic, my dear?

I was an only child and, it may be in consequence, both intelligent and sickly. I have three powerful impressions of my childhood: my sufferings when I was sick, my delights in convalescence at my grandfather's manse of Colinton, near Edinburgh, and the unnatural activity of my mind after I was in bed at night. As to the first, I suppose it generally granted that none suffer like children from physical distress. We learn, as we grow older, a sort of courage under pain which marvellously lightens the endurance; we have made up our mind to its existence as a part of life; but the spirit of the child is filled with dismay and indignation, and these pangs of the mind are often little less intolerable than the physical distress that caused them. My recollection of the long nights when I was kept awake by coughing are only relieved by the thought of the tenderness of my nurse and second mother (for my first will not be jealous) Alison Cunningham. She was more patient than I can suppose of an angel; hours together she would help console me in my paroxysms; and I remember with particular distinctness how she would lift me out of bed, and take me, rolled in blankets, to the window, whence I might look forth into the blue night starred with street-lamps, and see where the gas still burned behind the windows of other sickrooms. These were feverish, melancholy times; I cannot remember to have raised my head or seen the moon or any of the heavenly bodies; my eyes were turned downward to the broad lamplit streets, and to where the trees of the garden rustled together all night in undecipherable blackness; yet the sight of the outer world refreshed and cheered me; and the whole sorrow and burden of the night was at an end with the arrival of the first of that long string of country carts that, in the dark hours of the morning with the neighing of horses, the cracking of whips, the shouts of drivers and a hundred other wholesome noises, creaked, rolled, and pounded past my window.

I suffered, at other times, from the most hideous

nightmares, which would wake me screaming and in the extremest frenzy of terror. On such occasions, none could pacify my nerves but my good father, who would rise from his own bed and sit by mine, full of childish talk and reproducing aimless conversations with the guard or the driver of a mail coach, until he had my mind disengaged from the causes of my panic. These were sometimes very strange; one that I remember seemed to indicate a considerable force of imagination: I dreamed I was to swallow the world: and the terror of the fancy arose from the complete conception I had of the hugeness and populousness of our sphere. Disproportion and a peculiar shade of brown, something like that of sealskin, haunted me particularly during these visitations.

I have not space to tell of my pleasures at the manse. I have been happier since; for I think most people exaggerate the capacity for happiness of a child; but I have never again been happy in the same way. For indeed, it was scarce a happiness of this world, as we conceive it when we are grown up, and was more akin to that of an animal than to that of a man. The sense of sunshine, of green leaves, and of the singing of birds, seems never to have been so strong in me as in that place. The deodar upon the lawn, the laurel thickets, the mills, the river, the church bell, the sight of people ploughing, the Indian curiosities with which my uncles had stocked the house, the sharp contrast between this place and the city where I spent the other portion of my time, all these took hold of me, and still remain upon my memory, with a peculiar sparkle and sensuous excitement. I have somewhere part of a long paper * on my solitary pleasures about the manse and garden; but I could write volumes and never be done; so clear, telling, and memorable were my impressions.

It is odd, after so long an interval, to recall those incidents that struck me deepest. Once as I lay,

* *Memories and Portraits,* 1887. *The Manse,* p. 59. Is this the paper referred to?

playing hunter, hid in a thick laurel, and with a toy gun upon my arm, I worked myself so hotly into the spirit of my play, that I think I can still see the herd of antelope come sweeping down the lawn and round the deodar; it was almost a vision. Again, one warm summer evening on the front green, my aunt showed me the wing-bone of an albatross, told me of its largeness and how it slept upon the wing above the vast Pacific, and quoted from the "Ancient Mariner":

> "With my cross bow,
> I shot the Albatross."

I do not believe anything so profoundly affected my imagination; and to this day, I am still faithful to the Albatross, as the most romantic creature of fable (or nature, I know not which), and the one, besides, that has the noblest name. I remember in particular, a view I had from the attic window, suddenly beholding with delighted wonder, my ordinary playgrounds at my feet; and another outlook, when I climbed a hawthorn near the gate, and saw over the wall upon the snuff-mill garden, thick with flowers and bright with sunshine, a paradise not hitherto suspected.

My grandfather, the noblest looking old man I have ever seen, was one of the last, I suppose, to speak broad Scots and be a gentleman; he did not, however, do so in his sermons; which were in English and pretty dry, I fancy. I remember showing him my soldiers one day after dinner, as he sat over his daily nuts and port; he told me to play at the battle of Coburg, which gave me a great sense of his antiquity, as I had never heard of that engagement. I chanced to be in the house when he was taken with his last sickness, and was packed home again to be out of the way. He was up, and trying to write letters, an hour or so before he died; so that I think we may say he died young, although he was eighty.* I shall never forget my last sight of him,

* In the manuscript the word "three" has been inserted after "eighty" in a different hand, making his grandfather eighty-three when he died.

the morning ere I left. He was pale and his eyes were, to me, somewhat appallingly blood-shot. He had a dose of Gregory's mixture administered and then a barley sugar drop to take the taste away; but when my aunt wished to give one of the drops to me, the rigid old gentleman interfered. No Gregory's mixture, no barley sugar, said he. I feel with a pang, that it is better he is dead for my sake; if he still see me, it is out of a clearer place than any earthly situation, whence he may make allowances and consider both sides. But had he lived in the flesh, he would have suffered perhaps as much from what I think my virtues as from what I acknowledge to be my faults. Thus we may be reconciled to the passing away of the aged, that it leaves a field for youth.

I have mentioned my aunt. In her youth she was a wit and a beauty, very imperious, managing, and self-sufficient. But as she grew up she began to suffice for all the family as well. An accident on horseback, she says, but I have heard it was a natural cause, made her nearly deaf and blind, and suddenly transformed this wilful empress into the most serviceable and amiable of women and the family maid of all work. There were thirteen of the Balfours, as (oddly enough) there were of the Stevensons also; and the children of the family came home to her to be nursed, to be educated, to be mothered, from the infanticidal climate of India. There must sometimes have been half a score of us children about the manse; and all were born a second time from Aunt Jane's tenderness. It was strange when a new party of these sallow young folk came home, perhaps with an Indian ayah. This little country manse was a centre of the world: and Aunt Jane represented Charity. The text, my mother says, must have been written for her and Aunt Jane: more are the children of the barren than the children of the married wife.

We children had naturally many plays together; I usually insisted on the lead, and was invariably exhausted to death by evening. One day of such happy excitement was often followed by two or three in bed with a fever—*furia scozzese.*

But the time when my mind displayed most activity was after I was put to bed and before I fell asleep. I remember these periods more distinctly and I believe further back than any other part of my childhood. I would lie awake declaiming aloud to myself my views of the universe in something that I called singing although I have no ear and in a measure of my own although at that time I can have known nothing of verse. One of these *Songstries,* for so I named my evening exercises, was taken down by my father from behind the door, and I have seen it within the last few years. It dealt summarily with the Fall of Man, taking a view most inimical to Satan; but what is truly odd, it fell into a loose, irregular measure with a tendency toward the ten-syllable heroic line. This, as I am sure I can then have heard little or nothing but hymn metres, seems to show a leaning in the very constitution of the language to that form of verse; or was it but a trick of the ear, inherited from eighteenth century ancestors? It was certainly marked when taken in connection with my high-strung religious ecstasies and terrors. It is to my nurse that I owe these last: my mother was shocked when, in days long after, she heard what I had suffered. I would not only lie awake to weep for Jesus, which I have done many a time, but I would fear to trust myself to slumber lest I was not accepted and should slip, ere I awoke, into eternal ruin. I remember repeatedly, although this was later on, and in the new house, waking from a dream of Hell, clinging to the horizontal bar of the bed, with my knees and chin together, my soul shaken, my body convulsed with agony. It is not a pleasant subject. I piped and snivelled over the Bible, with an earnestness that had been talked into me. I would say nothing without adding " If I am spared," as though to disarm fate by a show of submission; and some of this feeling still remains upon me in my thirtieth year.* I shook my numskull over the spiritual welfare of my parents, because they gave dinner parties and played cards, things contemned in the religious biographies on which my mind was fed; and once, for a crowning point, I turned the tables on my nurse herself. She was reading aloud to me from *Cassell's Family Paper* a story called *The Soldier of Fortune*.† It was about the Crimean War, then lately ended; and from some superfluity of love affairs, Cummy (so I called my nurse), had expressed some fear lest it should turn out " a regular novel." That night I had a pain in my side which frightened me: I began to see Hell pretty clear, and cast about for any sin of which this might be punishment, and *The Soldier of Fortune* occurred to me as my leading " worldliness " of the moment. I forswore it then and there; and next morning announced and uprightly held to my vow. So instead of something healthy about battles, I continued to have my mind defiled with Brainerd, M'Cheyne, and Mrs. Winslow, and a whole crowd of dismal and morbid devotees. I speak with measure; knowing these were admirable people. But I have never wished to be good in their way; nor, if that were the way of the majority, can I suppose that this world would be either good or kind or pleasant; and for a child, their utterances are truly poisonous. The life of Brainerd, for instance, my mother had the sense to forbid, when we were some way through it. God help the poor little hearts who are thus early plunged among the breakers of the spirit! They should dwell by shallow, sunny waters, plucking the lilies of optimism; but to go down into the great deep is not for these unused and trembling sailors.

When at night my mind was disengaged from either

* This I think proves Mrs. Stevenson's statement that the paper was written in 1880 and not 1879, as Stevenson has dated the Introduction.

† This story by the author of *Stanfield Hall* appeared in 1855. Chapter i. is in the issue of April 14th, and Chapter lxxix. (the last) in that of December 29th.

of these extremes, and there was no high wind, for I
always hated and do still bitterly hate the noise of a
storm about a house, I told myself romances in which
I played the hero. Now and then the subject would be
the animation of my playthings; but usually these fan-
tasies embraced the adventures of a lifetime, full of
far journeys and Homeric battles. I note these pe-
culiarities. They had no reference to religion; although
that filled my mind so greatly at other moments, I was
pure old pagan when I came to practice. Secondly, for
as far back as I can remember, they bore always some
relation to women, and Eros and Anteros must have
almost equally divided my allegiance. And lastly they
would be concluded always with a heroic, and sometimes with a cruel, death. I never left myself till I
was dead.

When I was five years of age, my cousin, Robert
Alan Stevenson, came to stay at my father's house;
he was three years older than I, an imaginative child
who had lived in a dream with his sisters, his parents,
and the *Arabian Nights*, and more unfitted for the
world, as was shown in the event, than an angel fresh
from heaven. I shall speak of him some day more at
length on his own account; but just now I have to do
with myself and only mention others as they touched
and moulded my character. We lived together in a
purely visionary state. We had countries; his was
Nosingtonia, mine Encyclopædia; where we ruled and
made wars and inventions, and of which we were perpetually drawing maps. His was shaped a little like
Ireland; mine lay diagonally across the paper like a
large tip-cat. We were never weary of dressing up.
We drew, we coloured our pictures; we painted and cut
out the figures for a pasteboard theatre; this last one of
the dearest pleasures of my childhood, and one I was
so loath to relinquish, that I followed it in secret till I
must have been fifteen. This visit of Bob's was altogether a great holiday in my life.

Incidentally, too, I was then introduced to literature.

My uncle, David Stevenson, offered a prize of £1 for the best *History of Moses* from any of us Stevenson cousins. My history was, of course, dictated; and from that day forth, I would always be dictating whenever I could command a pen. The *History of Moses* was copiously illustrated by the author in a very free style. In these pictures, each Israelite was represented with a pipe in his mouth, cheering the desert miles. I was, indeed, always drawing; but it was from a purely imitative and literary impulse. I never drew from nature, nor even from a copy; but broidered away at my fancies in a spirit the reverse of the artistic. It is told of me that I came once to my mother with these words: "Mamma, I have drawn a man's body; shall I draw his soul now?" And this shows how early I was at it, and how I merely used it as a language with no thought of exact form or plastic beauty. Not so much a quickness to draw, as an intensity of looking, should mark the youth of the true painter.

I learned to read when I was seven, looking over the pictures in illustrated papers while recovering from a gastric fever. It was thus done at a blow; all previous efforts to teach me having been defeated by my active idleness and remarkable inconsequence of mind. The same fever is remarkable to me for another reason: one of my little cousins (D. A. S.) having sent me a letter every day. This was a kindness I shall never forget till the day of my death; though I see little of him now, and cannot think he much affects me, I have an incredible, smothered warmth of affection towards him in my heart. As he will probably outlive me, I hope he may see these words and take the thanks I have been always too shy to renew to him in person.

On the whole I have not much joy in remembering these early years. I was as much an egotist as I have ever been; I had a feverish desire of consideration; I was ready to lie, although more often wrongly accused of it, or rather wrongfully punished for it, having lied unconsciously; I was sentimental, snivelling, goody, morbidly religious. I hope and do believe I am a better man than I was a child. With my respects to Wordsworth.

I was lovingly, but not always wisely treated, the great fault being Cummy's overhaste to make me a religious pattern. I have touched already on the cruelty of bringing a child among the awful shadows of man's life; but it must not be forgotten, it is also unwise, and a good way to defeat the educator's purpose. The idea of sin, attached to particular actions absolutely, far from repelling, soon exerts an attraction on young minds. Probably few over-pious children have not been tempted, sometime or other and by way of dire experiment, to deny God in set terms. The horror of the act, performed in solitude, under the blue sky; the smallness of the voice uttered in the stillness of noon; the panic flight from the scene of the bravado: all these will not have been forgotten. But the worst consequence is the romance conferred on doubtful actions; until the child grows to think nothing more glorious, than to be struck dead in the very act of some surprising wickedness. I can never again take so much interest in anything, as I took, in childhood, in doing for its own sake what I believed to be sinful. And generally, the principal effect of this false, common doctrine of sin, is to put a point on lust. The true doctrine has a very different influence, but had best be taught to children in particular instances, and under the general routine of kindness and unkindness.

Had I died in these years, I fancy I might perhaps have figured in a tract. I have been sometimes led to wonder if all the young saints of whom I have read and meditated with enthusiasm in my early periods, suffered from their biographers the same sort of kindly violence, or had idealised themselves by the same simply necessary suppressions, that would have fitted myself and my career for that gallery of worthies. In the case of the infantile saint, the devil's advocate is silence. The aspirations have not yet been brought to the touch of practice; the personal is still potential; saint and prig and coward are still not to be distinguished. Yet, in my case and with all my evil on my head, it is yet true there was something of the saintly. Not because I wept over the Saviour's agony; not because I could repeat, with some appropriate inflections, a psalm or two or the story of Shunamite's son; but because I had a great fund of simplicity, believed all things and the good rather than the evil, was very prone to love and inaccessible to hatred, and never failed in gratitude for any benefit I had the wit to understand. The sight of deformed persons and above all of hideous old women moved in me a sort of panic horror; yet I can well recall with what natural courtesy I strove to conceal my disaffection. Fairy, the hunchback druggist of Bridge of Allan, was a terror to me by day and haunted my dreams at night, but my pity was stronger than my distaste; and I made it a point to command myself and speak to him with a child's friendliness, whenever the poor vain man, little understanding what was in my heart, condescended to address me. There was an old woman, Annie Torrence, who helped at the washing, I believe; an inhuman, bearded spectre, with a human heart in spite of all; who made it her business to be kind to me and show off before me, singing, " It's all round my hat for a twelve month and a day " with witchlike steps and gestures, backing to and fro before me, the horrified and fascinated child. Out of my dreams, I have never feared so cordially any other phenomenon as this of Annie Torrence and her song; for I thought the song to be hers and to commemorate some romance of her so-long departed youth. Yet I know I was ever consciously busy in my own small and troubled soul, to bear a good face before this dismal entertainment and conceal from the old woman the disastrous effect she was producing. I think I was born with a sense of what is due to age; for the more I interrogate my recollections the more traces do I find of that respect struggling with the dislike of what is old and then seemed to me to be ugly. Of all the cruel things in life, the cruellest, it may be, is the departure of all beauty from those who have been the desired mothers and mistresses of men in a former generation. Pagans like Horace, devils like Villon— and yet he was a devil with a dash of the angelic, were it only in his wings—and simple crass vulgarians, like Gilbert, so much worse than the worst of the devilish— take an opportunity for some cheap effect of art from these distressing changes. I thank God, when I was a child I knew a higher decency. A man should have never been suckled at a woman's breast, he should never have slept in a woman's embrace, he should never have known, in the most passing manner, the pleasures of a woman's affection or the support of a woman's tenderness, so far to forget what is honourable in sentiment, what is essential in gratitude, or what is tolerable by other men.

To finish this matter, I must tell a story which illustrates the best of me and is, at the same time, pitifully comical. In Howe Street, round the corner from our house, I often saw a lame boy of rather a rough and poor appearance. He had one leg much shorter than the other, and wallowed in his walk, in consequence, like a ship in a seaway. I had read more than enough, in tracts and goody story books, of the isolation of the infirm; and after many days of bashfulness and hours of consideration, I finally accosted him, sheepishly enough I dare say, in these words: " Would you like to play with me? " I remember the expression which sounds exactly like a speech from one of the goody books that had nerved me to the venture. But the answer was not the one I had anticipated, for it was a blast of oaths. I need not say how fast I fled. This incident was the more to my credit as I had, when I was young, a desperate aversion to addressing strangers, though when once we had got into talk I was pretty certain to assume the lead. The last particular may still be recognised. About four years ago, I saw my lame lad, and knew him again at once. He was then a man of great strength, rolling along, with an inch of cutty in his mouth and a butcher's basket on his arm. Our meeting had been nothing to him, but it was a great affair to me.

I have long given up all idea of autobiographical writing. Truly this is not for lack of trial; again and again have I embarked upon that business, and again and again with results that I can only describe as revolting. I do not know if my mother would have known me in these presentments; I certainly should never have known myself. But if a man cannot write common sense and common honesty about himself, he may very well attain to sense and honesty about his neighbours. His neighbours, besides, are not unlikely more interesting upon their own account. And the man may thus gratify his own desire to babble about things directly connected about his past; leave something which may make a little honest profit for his heirs; and at the same time, run a decent chance of entertaining the reader.

This reader, whom I suppose to be not yet born, is advised upon the threshold that the present lines are being dictated under every conceivable circumstance of disadvantage. The intolerable clatter of a type-writer removes from me all that makes it valuable to be man; and the pace at which I and my amanuensis advance is precisely too slow to admit the ordinary flow of conversation, and just too fast to attain the merits of considered composition. I shall trust, for the comfort of the reader and the pecuniary advantage of my heirs, that as time goes on I may grow used to this cumbersome process; and in the meanwhile, for the sake of the practice, if with no great hope of attaining any valuable results, I shall continue, even as I have begun, in a condition closely bordering on that of the sleepwalker, and hypnotised by the sound of the accursed instrument, to pour forth words. These words are intended to convey my impressions and reminiscences of various distinguished men, chiefly literary, whom it has been my fortune to encounter. But this I feel to be still on the lap of the gods; and whether, to the accompaniment of the typewriter and under the unwonted strain and publicity of the act of dictation, I shall be able to say any one thing that I should wish to say, is a matter still beyond my forecast.

The first author whom it was my destiny to meet was Mr. Robert Michael Ballantyne. I dare say the reader is unacquainted with his works; they scarce seem to me designed for immortality; but they were exceedingly popular in my day with the whole world of children. Of these works I was myself an earnest student; and when Mr. Ballantyne decided to write a work in which my own grandfather was to play the part of something not unlike the hero, when he went to the Bell Rock on purpose to prepare himself for this important task, and when I myself was in consequence invited to meet him to dinner at my uncle's, my elation will be readily understood. Mr. Ballantyne proved to be an exceedingly good-looking, dark, full-bearded man; he sketched and displayed his sketches; he played on the piano, at that time quite a rare accomplishment with men; and he sang songs in which my cousins and I were expected to bear chorus. My cousins could, I could not; my cousins, perhaps because they did not admire Mr. Ballantyne so wholly as myself, were able to bear a part and, as it appeared to me, to shine in the conversation; I sat tongue-tied, I never told my love. I left my uncle's house, really sick of thwarted adoration; feeling that I was the true Codlins and my cousins usurping Shorts. I have forgotten to say that Mr. Ballantyne, in the course of conversation, brought forward a new claim to our esteem: he had been studying, with a view to yet another of his deciduous works, the life of firemen, had recently assisted at a fire, and if I have the story right, had with his own hands saved a life. Altogether, as a cheerful, good-looking, active, melodious, and courageous human creature (whatever I

may now think of his works) this sight of Mr. Ballantyne greatly strengthened an inborn partiality for
authors. For many a long day after, the story I told
myself at bed-time turned upon that superior being; I
met him again, I had peculiar opportunities to shine, I
distinguished myself by acts of daring, I was suddenly
endowed with musical powers of a high order; and my
ideal, turning to me with that black-bearded, white-
toothed smile I had so much admired when it was addressed to others, recognised at last my superiority to
my fallacious cousins.

It was many a long day before I came across another
celebrity. It is true I had the benefit of the acquaintance of a certain number of the French masters of
Edinburgh, one of whom came near celebrity and another succeeded in gaining the highest point of notoriety.
The best of the lot, my good friend M. Victor Richon,
had no particular claim to distinction. He was simply,
in the old phrase, a scholar and a gentleman; loved
letters well, understood them not ill; and was in every
word and work, both a pleasant and an improving comrade. It was in the house of Richon that I met that big,
gross, fat, black, hyperbolical, and entirely good-hu-
moured adventurer, Van Laun. I should think he
never harmed any one except those whom he induced to
drink with him. My last sight of him, when he had
quite given up school-mastering, and I myself had
entered mildly upon the career of letters, it entertains
me a good deal to recall. For upon that occasion,
seated in an elaborately mounted study and surrounded
with appliances which might have sufficed for a Voltaire
or a Goethe, he calmly proposed to me to make the
favourable reviewing of his own works the chief feature
of my industry. What I was to receive in return, I
never distinctly gathered; and for this reason, if for no
other, the scheme was not pursued. Seemingly my fat
acquaintance failed to find a substitute, for I have seen
his works rather roughly handled; and indeed I suppose
he has long since gone, where most of his old friends

had preceded him, to the paradise of drinkers. There he will find his former afternoon society complete; poor Sam Bough, poor Edmonstone the publisher, poor Mackay the jeweller, all victims to the kindly jar. There too, if he chooses to recognise him, he may meet the third of my French acquaintances, Chantrelle the murderer.

I should say, looking back from the unfair superior ground of subsequent knowledge, that Chantrelle bore upon his brow the most open marks of criminality; or rather, I should say so if I had not met another man who was his exact counterpart in looks, and who was yet, by all that I could learn of him, a model of kindness and good conduct. I seem to come across nothing but dark men: Chantrelle was coal-black in hair, coal-black of eye, and of a sallow leathery skin. Ill-nature, a painfully acute temper, a quivering, black sensibility of nerves, were written on every line of his face and confessed in every movement of his body. When I knew him, he seemed never happy except when he was drunk; and even then there was something uncomfortable in his mirth, something feverish and wild, such as I have seen represented by Herr Formes in the first act of *Freischütz*. There was good cause for this had I only known. He had left France because of murder; he had left England because of a murder; already, since he was in Edinburgh, more than one—as I was told by the Procurator-Fiscal, more than four or five—had fallen a victim to his little supper parties and his favourite dish of toasted cheese and opium. And with all this expense of life, he was only clinging to solvency by his eyelids, he was being forced daily nearer to that last mismanaged crime that was to bring him to the gallows. I saw something of the expedients to which he was reduced, something of the wild hopes that buoyed him; and in seeing this, something also of his quite remarkable powers. One evening he met me on the street; asked me if I had seen Van Laun's translation of Molière; and when I told him I had and confessed that I could see no merit in that piece of work, his eyes blazed with hope, he had me to a public house; and bidding me name any passage in Molière with which I was well acquainted, offered to improvise without book a better version than Van Laun's. I accepted the challenge; and he, as far as I was in a position to judge, did well what he professed. But of course I was like himself without book; and I told him I was in no position to judge fairly, and that he must give me a written specimen before I could, as he desired, approach a publisher on his behalf. Well, I heard no more of it; the spark of hope, I must suppose, died out; he fell back on " the simpler plan " of killing other people; and when next I saw the translator of Molière, he was hearing, with singular and painful changes of countenance, the evidence on his own trial for murder. I do not think murder can be a good profession; Chantrelle had talents to succeed in any trade, honest or dishonest; and though it may be said that he did for a while succeed in that grisly one he had selected, it never brought him even decent means of livelihood, and to judge from his face, can have contributed little to his peace of mind.

I am not going to say anything of local or legal celebrities. I stick as close as I can by letters, which have been my trade and my chief pleasure. So that I must pass on direct to a certain very fortunate visit which I paid to England in the summer of the year 1873. I was at that time, as I had always been, firmly decided upon the career of letters. I was exceedingly well read and up in the last humours and fashions of the day. My text-book, or perhaps I should rather say my organ, was the *Fortnightly Review*, where I had the satisfaction of finding something like my own views, it still seems to me, exceptionally well expressed, and enjoying the ripe work of John Morley and his contributors. About that time the *Review* embraced some small-type pages of critical notices, signed by what I supposed to be the agreeable pseudonym of Sidney Colvin, and conceived in a style which I then thought little short of perfect; although nowadays I believe both Colvin and myself regard it as the last word of affectation. My visit to England was to a country rectory, the house of a cousin of mine and of her husband, the delightful Churchill Babington; I knew what I had to expect, croquet parties, the parsons' wives, the ecclesiastical celebrations; that I should there meet with the flesh-and-blood Colvin of the *Fortnightly Review*, was a thing beyond the bound of my extremest hopes.

Yet so it fell out. Nor only that, but I was brought under his notice, by a lady whose generous pleasure— perhaps I might almost say, whose weakness—it was to discover youthful genius. With a little goodwill and a little friendship, genius is mighty easily supplied. Mrs. Sitwell found it or supplied it in my case, and announced the discovery or the attribution to Colvin. So it came about that when I went down to Cockfield Station, I was not only in a state of great agitation myself at the notion of meeting one of my great men, but the great man was prepared to notice me with favour. These preparations go a long way in life. I do not know, I do not think, that Colvin would have taken to me by nature; I am doubtful whether I should be taken to him. Meeting as we did, I the ready wor-shipper, he the ready patron, we had not got up the hill to the rectory before we had begun to make friends.

Sidney Colvin came of a stock of Indo-Scots. The most of his immediate ancestors and many of his col-laterals had been men in high places in the Government of Hindostan. From this descent and these relations, he had acquired something arbitrary, something a little official, in manner and character, which was not a little increased by his experience as a Cambridge Don. He always had the air of a man accustomed to obedience; I do not know which was effect or which was cause, but he was very generally obeyed; I have pretty generally obeyed him myself, and I am not subordinate by nature. A great shrewdness, a great simplicity of character, were conjoined in him; I do not know that I have ever found them dissociated: an almost childish simplicity seems the head-mark of the true reader of his neighbours. Certainly in Colvin the two were to be found in extreme, there is no man whose trenchant insight I more fear, none at whose childishness I have more often smiled. I conceive of him mostly as of a soldier or a public servant thrown away. As a man of letters, the weakness of his health, which was little fitted for the prolonged unhealthy strain of that trade, and the extreme, almost morbid morosity of his taste, have smitten him with something near to impotence. The little he has done has been accomplished at a great cost of labour to himself, a cost of money to his publishers, and of time and temper to the unhappy printer, that would be hard to parallel. Balzac was a current writer when compared to Sidney Colvin. It is very hard for me, even if I were merely addressing the unborn, to say what I owe to and what I think of this most trusty and noble-minded man. If I am what I am and where I am, if I have done anything at all or done anything well, his is the credit. It was he who paved my way in letters; it was he who set before me, kept before me, and still, as I write, keeps before me, a difficult standard of achievement; and it was to him and to Fleeming Jenkin that I owed my safety at the most difficult periods of my life. A friend of one's own age is too easily pleased or too easily silenced to be of much corrective use; a friend who is much our senior is too often a taskmaster whom we serve with counterfeits and please with falsehoods. These two had the tact and wisdom to suffer me to be very much myself; to accept and cherish what was good in me; to condone much of what was evil; and whilst still holding before me a standard to which I could never quite attain, neither to damp nor to disgust me of the trial. In the change of our relative ages, my dear Colvin has become so easy for me to live with, that I have a difficulty in recalling how it was at first. Doubtless the *Fortnightly*

Review would always have filled me with some awe.
But it was far from being that alone; it was rather the
certainty of his relations, the strong and restful impression of his courage, his unselfishness in all great matters
(where alone, as I am sometimes tempted to think, unselfishness is graceful) that began in me the somewhat
awful respect with which I at first regarded him.

On that first summer of our acquaintance, he had me
to stay with him at his house and to dine with him
more than once at the old Savile Club, afterwards and
so long my own headquarters. At the Savile I saw,
just saw, Walter Pater; at Norwood, I dined with King-
don Clifford, and was then, as always afterwards,
principally impressed by his irresponsible boyishness of
mind and manner. Clifford was then in the hot fit
of the most noisy atheism, the stage in which I believe
he died. It was indeed the fashion of the hour; even
to the fastidious Colvin, the humblest pleasantry was
welcome if it were winged against God Almighty or the
Christian Church. It was my own proficiency in such
remarks that gained me most credit; and my great
social success of the period, not now to be sniffed at,
was gained by outdoing poor Clifford in a contest of
schoolboy blasphemy. I thought the more of this when
I heard afterwards through Tait of some of Clifford's
former vagaries of opinion, and of the mark of the cross
with which he used to hallow his examination papers
at Cambridge. He was a very brilliant fellow and he
never grew up. I remember when he agreed to manage
the scientific part of the *Academy* for Appleton: nothing, as I was told, could ever induce him to be up to
time with his work; arrears gathered in the scientific
department up to monstrosity; Appleton himself, it is
like enough, would be a little to leeward with the financ-
ing department; and one way or another at least, the
whole affair blew up. Clifford was the most to blame,
so I heard, and so, knowing Appleton's delightful temper, I am well prepared to believe; but the scientific
Ariel had not the least idea he was in fault: and his

talk at the time consisted almost entirely of humorous proposals for revenge upon poor Appleton. He used to plan at dinner time how to decoy the editor of the *Academy* to a desert island, or to wall him up in the safe where Henriot kept his explosives; and whether or not Appleton lost in money, I am sure that Clifford gained a vast deal of enjoyment from the quarrel. The last time I saw him, the hand of death was visibly upon him; not long after John Collier and his wife carried him to Madeira to die, in about the thirtieth year of his age and surely not more than the fifteenth of his character. Clifford on this occasion I saw; Swinburne I was to have seen. But this was in that somewhat stormy period of the bard's existence, when those who loved him best were sometimes tempted to desire his absence; and after consulting a common friend, it was judged unwise to send an invitation. I regret this the more, as Swinburne also, like the rest of us, was on the high seas of blasphemy; so that had I met him then, I might have had a chance of shining; and much of what he has since done and become, induces me to think I should value his esteem. I could tell a lot of funny stories of the days when he was partial to the bottle, and I had rather not. Some other gentleman will probably preserve them.

SELECTIONS FROM HIS
NOTE BOOK

THESE notes were printed for the first time in the Vailima Edition.

SELECTIONS FROM HIS NOTE BOOK

THE council are at a loss to understand why government money should be employed to buy out the efforts of individual societies. They are fully alive to the utility of grants for scientific purposes; but they must be allowed to hold such grants as merely supplementary to private enterprise; and when they are put into competition one with another, when government money is employed to interfere with voluntary and gratuitous exertions in the same direction, the council beg to suggest to your Lordships that such an application is directly hurtful to the cause of Science.

Prostitution tends by a certain negative natural selection, to reduce the tendency of the race to propagate; the men of most violent sexual passions are, by prostitution, prevented to a large extent from having children, and so the race is left to be continued by the more sober and continent, among whom chastity is the precursor of matrimony. The early marriages of the Irish prevent the action of this adjustment.

Heine's vocabulary I know very well, and can therefore read him with ease; Holzmann's I find myself rapidly learning. In our own language we do not have this paucity of choice in writers thrust upon our notice. Goethe, I find, remains always equally hard to me; I do not learn his trick as I do with other writers: this shows him (I suppose) one of those few great men who can speak a whole language, and not merely a dialect. Shakespeare must be just such another: I remember hearing that he uses in his few plays an enormously greater number of words than Scott uses in all his regiment of volumes.

———

" One of the effective conditions " is perhaps a better expression than " a cause "; but it is merely a substitution of misconception—all conditions are effective and equally effective; that is, if you change any one, you change the whole gross result. We are not confused when we say that it was the match which caused the town to blow up, and understand thoroughly that that little match was merely a *visible link* in a vast chain of coexistences; now, what we call causes are to their effects, precisely what the match is to the explosion.

———

The harm of prostitution lies not in itself, but in the disastrous moral influence of ostracism. This *decivilisation*, this rejection of individuals or classes from the social commonwealth, would have its own natural result, whosoever was the individual or the class upon which it was brought to bear. Hunted religionists become cruel and inhuman, just as ostracised harlots do; only the different other conditions produce cruelty and inhumanity in different shapes. It must be remembered, however, that prostitution is quite beyond parallel in this particular circumstance, that the pariah is obliged to homologate the justice of the *capitis deminutio* to which she is condemned. A Jew, a Christian, a Mormon, or a Thug were proud of the reproach, and wear the byeword as a distinction; while you may make many a prostitute cry by merely naming her trade to her. If you think seriously of all the depressing, demoralising, decivilising influences brought to bear upon her, I think you will find it matter for wonder not that she is so fallen, but that she is still (and that in so many instances) as honest, kind, and decent as she is.

Civilisation consists in the making of citizens (*cives*); and that is, in the selection of persons adapted to co-exist with the greatest number of their fellows, and in their continual readaptation and improvement for such coexistence. The moment that this obvious truth is recognised, a large number of moral principles receive authoritative sanction.

It becomes immediately obvious, for example, that uniformity is precisely what was to be avoided. Absolute uniformity of tastes in a large number of human beings is precisely the worst possible condition for peaceable coexistence: Jack Sprat and his wife in the nursery rhyme, offer an ideal example of adaptation for coexistence.

It is very hard to think that we must cease and not continue to see the wonderful game of the universe played before us, into all eternity, to watch the grand procession of sequences, to have worlds and systems and civilisations formed and deformed under our eyes for ever; but D. S. G. His will be done.

A good example of a false correlation in Sociology is that which connected the Roman Catholic religion with uncleanly habits. See Hazlitt's *Plain Speaker*.

The ordinary criterion of beauty is congruity with certain established artistic conventions.

Goethe mentioned to Crabbe Robinson that he had written his Roman Carnival by sitting on a balcony and noting in pencil whatever he saw pass him: this is just like Walt Whitman's process; only the principle of grouping is different. Goethe's was an *artistic synthesis;* Walt Whitman's is an *ethical synthesis.* Goethe used his details to make a poem with; Walt Whitman, to enforce a lesson.

Christ's strange doctrine about blame was shirked by the apostles and by every one after them: Walt Whitman is the first person who has taken it up and broadly restated it.

———

Faith means holding the same opinions as the person employing the word. It is faith to agree with Dr. Orthodoxy; but it is unbelief to believe in the persistence of force.

———

Unity may be defined as a ratio of equality: zero and infinity as the two terms in the ratio of greatest possible inequality.

———

Scientific language like most other language is extremely unsatisfactory. As being a series of *petitiones principii*—as being *committed* from beginning to end to former and less perfect theories. Look at the degraded terminology of mechanics—the very name being a misnomer with its so-called mechanical powers and other misleading and incorrect expressions. Any attempt again to talk scientifically of heat or the variations of temperature involves, on the now proved dynamical hypothesis, a series of misstatements—a string of verbal confusions. When we compare this with metaphysical terminology and its perfect adaptation to the various theories it has to express, we cannot help being painfully conscious of the incapacity of scientific men to deal with this really most important of all subjects.

When I say that terminology is the most important of all subjects, I believe I am perfectly justified by the facts. Any advance in thinking must be followed by advanced powers of expressions; the measure of the definiteness and specificality of language; for all thought that transcends existing means of expression, and thus fails to become communicable and practical, may be regarded as non-existent; just as the idea of gravitation may be regarded as non-existent in savage minds, although all the involved facts and, to a certain extent, the general conception are present in a latent and unformulated shape. What we call thinking is, indeed, only the formulation of thought; and I do not believe that any one who has ever tried to write upon abstract or ill-understood topics, can object to such a definition.

———

Scientific men, who imagine that their science affords an answer to the problems of existence, are perhaps the most to be pitied of mankind; and *contemned*.

———

The name of materialist is now become a misnomer. To the persons upon whom this byeword is principally exercised, matter like force or cause, is merely a *word* put in to supply a gap in knowledge—a hypothetical vinculum, substratum, or nexus is required by our habits of speech, and, in all three cases, is supplied by a vague and practically meaningless word. Unityarians (not unitarians) is probably the most expressive designation for this much-maltreated community of thinkers.

———

When, by the Act of 1736, the sale of spirits was made practically illegal, an amount of smuggling, violence, and crime was immediately called into being, so enormous as to oblige the withdrawal of the measure after it had been only two years in operation. This is just the same case as that of the prostitutes—a class, rejected from the commonwealth, immediately decivilising.

In a great measure our power of thinking is limited by our knowledge of words; indeed, there are very few minds capable of anything more worthy of the name of thought than the mere ordering and conjoining of their parrot-learned word-symbols; while our powers of exchanging thought are entirely and absolutely bounded by the number and definiteness of our words. Most men think and speak in a manner abstractly algebraic; they know well enough how to shift and arrange and rearrange their x's and z's; they are sometimes ingenious to a fault in dealing with all possible combinations of such unknown terms; but they never dream of carrying their operations a step farther and finding out what these x's and z's originally represented. For example, if I were to enter with you, just now, into an elaborate discussion as to whether sacrilege were irreverent (and equally vain subjects have been debated before now), it would perhaps be easy enough for me to prove the affirmative of the proposition; but how? I should indeed have proved x to z; but only because it was a postulate of my method, that z is equal to x. Such word-juggling, such logical legerdemain, is the great danger of all abstract thought. We can never argue on anything beyond the relations between certain words; and if you and I understand by our words a different substrate of thought—if we have different values for the same symbols and yet have no means of mutually explaining this disagreement—we cannot wonder that we reach different solutions and mutually regard that difference as the result of dishonesty. We may see the difficulty in its highest terms, when a missionary asks a savage if he believes it is the virtuous who are to be happiest in a future state and receives an affirmative reply: the good man is much pleased with such incipient orthodoxy; while all the time they have been juggling it with each other with misunderstood symbols. The missionary had Christian virtue in his mind; while the Tupinamba means by the virtuous " those who have well revenged themselves and eaten many of their enemies"; while the Virginian understands by the same term, simply those of his own tribe, and by the wicked, those of any other not at peace with them. (Tzlai's Prin. Cult. II. 79.)

It is astonishing how often there is no definite conception whatever, at the back of the most definite sounding words; and how often language is the cloak with which a man conceals, not his thought, but his want of thought. If we remember how we acquired our words, it may help us to understand the curiously stupid attitude in which we stand with regard to them. As long, of course, as purely concrete ideas are in question, the acquisition is pretty easy and definite; and we tell the child that this is a stool and that such a thing is black, to his perfect enlightenment: that is to say, he will know in future by what vocal symbol he is to refer to certain articles and certain attributes. But the process with regard to abstractions is widely different. A child is told that, if it lie, it is not good; that if it be disobedient, it is not good; that if it make a noise at family worship, it is not good; that Mr. So-and-So is not good, because he does not go to church, and the whole course of education is a simple addition of one such fact to another, a gradual accumulation of actions which are to be represented by the symbol "good" and others which are to be represented by the opposite symbol "bad." We have no guarantee that a person, so educated, has any abstract notion of what he means by "Goodness" or what he means by "God." He has probably made no synthesis of the different ideas that he recognises as coming under either; it is ten to one that he has never set them side by side, never thought abstractly of why they were thus to be commonly designated, of what principle of congruity had brought them thus loosely together in his mind; and hence, when people reject an act as being incompatible with their ideas of goodness or an attribute as being inconsistent with their beliefs regarding God, it is generally, not because they have any real conception of either abstraction, but because such act or such attribute has never before been presented to them duly ticketed as " good " or " divine."

Let me try an illustration. If you or I were asked to describe a scene which we had seen only yesterday or only this morning, our description would partake largely of the nature of a simple inventory; certain phenomena, certain colours, certain forms, a certain distribution of observed objects would all be chronicled; but we should in reality have no conception of the scene ourselves, and present none to our readers. Now, if Dickens had been there or Wordsworth, the locality would have been synthesised, some salient unity among all the details would have presented itself to their minds and would be found impressed on their description. This is a fair parallel to men's attitude with regard to abstract ideas; and the majority of them remain in the inventory stage and quite dead to any principle of colligation.

Let us apply this to the common argument for Christianity, based on an appeal to our sense of right and wrong. The different categories of actions, pointed out to us during childhood as respectively good or bad, coincide more or less exactly with similar divisions in the New Testament; it has been the object of our parents to call those things right which Christ (or perhaps St. Paul) would have called right, and those things wrong which he would have called wrong; consequently, in the vague, floating congeries of distinguished actions which we have learned from dictation, most, or perhaps all, are actions mentioned and similarly distinguished in the Christian Ethics. Now, let me ask any one if he had ever deduced from these cases a definite ruling principle, or had born in him some regulative belief by which he has checked these decisions and found them right. I suspect that very few could answer in the affirmative. There may have been a certain approximation to generalising from the particular instances; there may be, on the other hand, some recollection of an early sense of justice and injustice—strongest when he had his bottom thrashed, a case in which he has since been led to understand that it had led him wrong; but, beyond these, there is nothing; and the main fact is that he has been taught the New Testament and has become a sort of case-lawyer in the Christian Ethics. What then does this great test amount to, with the generality of men? Merely to the old juggle of x and z: does the teaching of Christ coincide with what you have been taught in childhood; that is, with the teaching of Christ?

The recurrence in Walt Whitman of the inventory school of poetry, which has been extinct in England since Chaucer and Gower, is a fair promise of literary renovation. It is only when a man sees the world " as a little child," fresh and unhackneyed, from some quite new literary standpoint, that such bald capitulation of objects will ever be written—far more, read.

I do not admit immortality, but I can not believe in death: that is to say, in my own death. I can easily enough understand the death of others; they pass out of my field of vision, they cease to perform their respective antics before me: but how can you destroy that field of vision? how do you expect me to conceive myself as no longer existent? Cease to live I may; but not cease to be: it can only be a change of function.

People say we are conscious of no compulsion on our wills; but consciousness will not bear testimony to compulsion in the physical world, any more than in the mental world. When a child overbalances himself and falls to the ground he has no consciousness of compulsion, he has never heard of gravity, the whole fact for him is that he has overbalanced himself and is *therefore* fallen to the ground. The notion of compulsion is quite a late one.

———

The presently orthodox have a nasty way of using the word *theory*. They talk of the theory of necessity; apparently oblivious of the fact that freewill, too, is only a theory and, in some people's opinion, a very untenable one. Mr. Darwin is a theoriser; very well, but what are those that adhere so stoutly to the contrary view? merely theorisers also. This sounds very trivial; but it is a great truth for all that, and a much neglected truth into the bargain.

Immutable laws? I recognise no such immutability; I know no such laws. All that we can learn is the action of laws; and that action is continually changing and passing into higher and more complex states of combination and reaction. As in Babbage's calculating machine, the basis changes at a certain number; so have we had changes of basis in our observed orders of facts—after many back-looking races, whose motion tended to dissipate as they advanced, we have come suddenly upon a forward-looking Aryan race. I believe in immutable laws; but I do not know any.

———

Nothing so thoroughly brings back to us the unthinkable moralities of the past, as the story of Abraham and Isaac. It is strange enough that this grown man should have consented to follow his father on such a fool's errand and, when he learned at last the object of the journey, should have meekly suffered himself to be bound for the sacrifice; but it is far stranger to think that, while we have plenty of praise of Abraham's faith, we hear not a syllable of comment on Isaac's obedience, that the whole of his conduct in the matter was too much *matter of course* for commendation. This comparison gives us an *aperçu* at the same time into the contemporaneous theology. A man was evidently expected to do much more for his parents than for his God; and this is natural enough; for there was a large choice of deities out of which a man could make his selection, but he never could have another father. All through the earlier part of the Old Testament there are incidents and expressions that can only be understood in the light of this *competition of Godheads*.

The chaptering of the Bible has been much condemned; but some of it is extremely politic. The break between the twentieth and the twenty-first chapter of Genesis, for example, is evidently introduced to divert the reader's attention from some suggestive facts that might have thrown a doubt upon the legitimacy of Isaac.

I think the paradox about multiplying by nothing, was the first thing that overset and disgusted me in Algebra. It is simple enough if laboriously explained in words; as thus: Multiplication by one means taking a number (call it x) *once* and using it in your question; Multiplication by two, means taking x, and then x again, and using both in your question; and so forth. The paradox arises from not quite grasping that simple idea. A person who has not quite grasped it reasons thus: if I multiply x by nothing, it is the same thing as not multiplying x by anything, and consequently I shall have x remaining unchanged, to be used by me in my question. Now the true statement (in terms of the plain definition of multiplication) runs thus: if I multiply x by nothing, it means simply that I do not take x at all, that I do not introduce x into my question, consequently that I introduce nothing into my question; and so we define x multiplied by nothing, as being equal to nothing. It results from this that whenever we use a number in our work at all, we mean that we *have taken* that number to use in our question—that is, that we have *taken it once,* because we have taken it neither twice, nor thrice, nor no times—that is, whenever we use a number at all, we use *that number multiplied by one.* Hence, briefly:

(1) *multiplied by one* means that a number is present in the question in hand:

(2) *multiplied by two* means that this number and another number equal to it are both present in the question in hand; while

(3) *multiplied by nothing* means simply that the number is absent.

The notion of unity that a child picks up either from general conversation or from school teaching, is extremely bewildering and paralysing to his mind. He gets the notion connected in his mind with that of zero; instead of with that of a mere datum; he thinks of our arbitrary *one* as an absolute *one;* and hence it is that to not a few men and, till within the last few years, to the great majority of women, a fraction remained unthinkable. A certain step, of course, is made —a certain hint, at least, is given to any one who thinks—when he hears that our Fahrenheit zero is not the zero of heat.

The multiplication question becomes paradoxical as we saw, merely from an indistinct idea of multiplication. This indistinctness starts with the very first introduction of the four rules. If it were always steadily kept before the scholar that multiplication is simply the addition of like numbers—that to add x multiplied by two to a question, is merely to add x first and then a number equal to x or to add x twice; and that to add x multiplied by one, is to add simply x or x once; he would have no difficulty in completing the series, and seeing that to add x multiplied by nothing is to add x no times, or not to add x.

There is only one rule, addition; or perhaps we may say two, for the sake of beginners, addition and subtraction. To make separate rules of multiplication and division, which are merely quick methods of adding and subtracting equal numbers, is hopelessly to confuse the scholar's head at the outset. Yet I have never seen the thing fairly set before the children in any school. What, for example, would be simpler than to make them occasionally check their multiplication and division sums by going through the whole process of addition or subtraction. This would surely keep the idea before their minds.

Chinese civilisation can be very justly compared to Bee civilisation. Both present the same advanced position with the same absolute incapacity to advance further. In both, too, we see the curious correlation of perfection of delicate imitative handicraft, with a state of political and intellectual equilibrium—a correlation which is perfectly comprehensible.

The old notion of offerings to the dead—of the necessity for a son to each man's body—of the Hindoo name for a son—a deliverer out of hell—of the old Hebrew practice of marrying a brother's widow in order to raise up seed to him—and the like, when taken all together and regarded as a universal, or almost universal, phase of human civilisation, may account for the first genesis of the messianic idea. The notion becoming gradually more and more abstract, as is the case with all such notions—being gradually put back and back, and generalised from the family to the nation, and again from the nation to the whole human race, might easily enough result in some abstract and refined dogmas as that of the Jewish Messiah, and in its further development into that of the world-saviour, Christ. This is no fanciful course for a doctrine to follow; all religious

dogma, without exception, tending finally to become
ever more sublimated and more generalised, until like
a circle in the waters, it dissipates itself into a non-
existence. Hence we have as parallels: the progress, on
the one hand, of a power of nature into a special Godhead and then into a more general Godhead for a more
general division; and then, once again into a perfectly
general Godhead for all nature whatsoever; and the
progress, on the other hand, of a son to work salvation
first for each family, then for a nation and then for the
whole world. Equally in both cases, too, do we find the
last degree of generality; when we find God gradually
withdrawn from all nature to a mere residual mystery,
and the Saviour sublimated out of a personality, into
a mere type of self-suffering and thus self-redeeming
mankind.

————

The conduct of Unionists to " Free-lances " offers a
curious parallel to the conduct of all organised societies
towards the persons variously termed criminals, or out-
laws, or lapsed-masses, or what not. The free-lance
will not see that the provisions of the Union are for the
benefit of the industrial community; or does recognise
this and yet prefers his own freedom, his full earnings,
his selfish indulgence to all co-operation in the good
work; and hence the unionist takes the strong hand,
and suppresses him. Society has done the same thing
to all who have failed to recognise the excellence and
humanity of its arrangements or who have preferred
their own pagan gratifications; the Church, too; and the
nation. Why then blame the unionist?

————

I never know whether to be more surprised at Darwin
himself for making so much of Natural Selection, or at
his opponents for making so little of it. One would
have thought that its action was on the face of things;
but on the other hand, one would have thought that the

presence of other modificative and co-modificative principles in all the phenomena to be explained, was equally patent and unmistakable. And accordingly Darwin is reminding us every page that he postulates " spontaneous variations " or " compensations of growth " or " correlated variations " or something of the kind, as the material which his selection is to weigh in the balance and keep and cast away as useless; in other words, that all spontaneity, all inception, is independent of his own special doctrine. Hence, the battle is going on at present on a wrong field; both sides are fighting for a position that is really neutral; and the tug of war can only arrive when they have recognised this fact and turn against each other's strongholds.

National character will not really account for anything. It used to be set down to some national characteristic of the Greeks, that they should have first entered into that age of discussion, curiosity, and innovation that has extended, almost uninterrupted, down to our times. But where was this national characteristic before they began to discuss and to innovate, while they were still conforming and consolidating? or, if it was there latent all the time, what made it begin suddenly to act at a certain period? The Chinese, too, must have had their period of curiosity, discussion, innovation, of philosophical and scientific activity; indeed, they were a far more wonderful people than even the Greeks, a people, as it seemed, with a livelier principle of progress in them, with more promise of strong, continuous advance; what, then, has become of their national characteristic? Hence, when Renan tries to explain the Jewish monotheism, by some hypothetical bias in the Semitic mind and certain congruous external circumstances; and when his opponent, Holzmann, combats this explanation by mentioning the case of Arabs and others of the same family and subject to much the same conditions of life, whose religious ideas remained undeveloped; both sides, as it seems to me, have missed their way. The Semitic bias, perhaps, and certainly the influence of their surroundings, had an effect upon these views; but, besides those, there was the influence of the Egyptians, the ambition and genius of Moses, and who shall say how many thousand causes, small or great, congruous or contrary, all tending together to transform and mould and modify. We are as yet utterly incapable of weighing causes in Sociology; the privative side, for example, seems to confuse the question hopelessly. Let us take one case of a cause and a hopelessly distant and incongruous effect. Because people were made to fast by the R. C. Church and because fish could be eaten on fast days, the monks encouraged the formation of ponds in la Brenne; the ponds accordingly multiplied out of measure; and in the issue, a fertile district was changed into an unhealthy morass. I wonder what national characteristic had to do here; as an immediate cause, evidently nothing; but the malaria and the reduced fertility would act strongly on the national character, would it not?

A perfect example both of the power and the impotence of such national capabilities, is offered in the history of the same people. After ages of the most exclusive, shy, unsociable, purely national existence, this strange people suddenly exhibited the most wonderful taste and capacity for all descriptions of commerce, gave themselves up to it, left even their holy land and holy city in order to profit by the great centres of exchange; until they became the leaders of all commercial enterprise, merchant princes, if ever there were such. This was certainly the ordinary Semitic bias; for the Carthaginians, Tyrians, and others had trod the same path before them. Only, why did it not exhibit itself, or at least, fully exhibit itself, until some four centuries before the beginning of our era? Whether it was because the national pride of the Jews and their hopes of earthly dominance had, then, only been sufficiently shaken; or whether it was that then only was there a proper opening for their peculiar talent; or whether, as seems most probable, both causes concurred towards the result; it is still undeniable that a national spirit, which had long lain latent in the Hebrews, suddenly, almost *per saltum*, became busy, living, and active; and sent forth the people into the world, in a new but seemingly equally permanent and national character.

That we should find the highest civilisation among ants, is by no means a matter for surprise; larger animals are stopped in their progress and entirely warped by man: dogs, for instance, have certainly progressed, but all their advance presupposes human civilisation, and whenever they are separated from this, they instantly fall back again to a very low level. Ants, however, are, we may say, entirely unconscious of man; and stand beyond his interference. If man overthrows an ant-hill, it is a cataclysm, a stroke of incomprehensible destiny; and no more disturbs the *mental basis of their development* than a shower of rain or a tempest of wind. They must feel themselves in precisely the same position of " superiority over the creatures " as man does; I doubt not that they think the world was made for them, and found theological arguments upon the supposition.

The statement that two and two are four is a mere definition of words, and cannot, I think, without error be regarded as an abstract proposition. It amounts simply to saying what we intend henceforward to designate by the symbol *four;* and hence, if any one calls the statement in question, he is simply using that symbol in another way—speaking a different language. It is startling how much of our science and philosophy can be reduced to a similar basis; it almost seems as if Adam's original task of naming the creatures was the only one to which his descendants can aspire. The first proposition of Euclid, for instance, is entirely similar to the " twice two is four "; or is a case of what I have already called the " juggle of x and z." You first make the sides equal; and then you remind the reader that you have so made them. When you come to such a proposition, however, as the forty-seventh, there is an appearance of something higher and more abstruse than this logical game of handy-dandy; but where the difference exactly lies and whether it is anything more than a mere appearance, I cannot at present see.

It may be more than a mere truism—I think it is—it has rather to me the appearance of being very significant—that " all human reasoning is simply declaratory." We are apt, I fancy, to think that we can rise into some higher mood than mere recognition of facts and statement of such facts as are recognised; but we cannot.

After all, what we claim as against current orthodoxy, is not simply the exclusion of free will. All that we ask is thoroughness of application: all that we aver is that our thought and lives are as completely governed by what appear to be laws, as is the course of a river or the direction of the wind. If you adhere to the old hypothesis about men, I must ask you likewise to hold as scientific truths that " the river wanders at its own sweet will " and that " the wind bloweth where it listeth." One thing still obstructs clear vision in the parallel; and that is, that while we can see only too well that men go astray and do not follow the best paths, we have a vague notion that everything in the physical world goes deftly and perfectly, like the play of an ideal machine. And yet think of all the wasted seed; think how often a dissipated wind destroys itself by getting into a wood or the court of some high building; think of the badly-rooted, precarious-looking trees that you have seen; think of the beautiful climates rendered useless by an ungrateful earth and the fertile soils that are lavished under ungrateful heavens.

———

The greater proportion of Milton's art is employed in finding violent coesmas. His favourite trick of leaving one word, especially a verb, isolated at the beginning of a new line, is a case in point; at the end of that wonderful passage on the fall of Mulciber, he seems to have felt the necessity for some exceptionally strong coesma—as it were, a dam after such a stream of sweetness—and he attained what he wanted by simply breaking off the metre with the unassimilable word " Again."

———

Consistency is the Latin name for dishonesty. I mean, of course, consistency, the personal virtue; not to be confounded with *congruity,* the objective fact. Two beliefs may happen to be congruous; but how a man is to maintain this so-called virtue, is to adhere to " quod dixi, dixi—quod credidi, credam," to keep himself deaf and blind to all the lessons and corrections that day by day are being thrust upon his notice—how he is to do all this, and yet be an honest man at the end of it, entirely passes my imagination. I find that the rule which applied for me last week, will not apply to-day; my right and wrong are variable and vacillating; and yet I must continue to follow the present impulse, the present apparent best; since I cannot anticipate the better wisdom of to-morrow, and dare not wilfully cling to what I now conceive was my error of yesterday. I can believe perhaps that in some singularly even and uneventful life, and with (if I may say it) some exceptionally stupid and unimpressionable man, right and wrong and truth and falsehood may retain something of congruity from one year's end to another. But in the ordinary whirl and variety of the world, only a god who has seen everything at once, or a fool who, from first to last, sees nothing at all, can live both honestly and consistently for three short weeks on end.

———

I cannot certainly return much thanks to preachers of vanity. It seems scarcely wise to embitter present life, on the chance of making death a little less alarming. If you were afraid that some fond husband would suffer surely if he were left a widower, would you proceed to blacken his wife's character and trouble the whole of his married existence? This seems like " taking from him that hath not, even that he hath."

———

(Ian John Stevenson). By the two farmer men, whose theosophy was refined by education and contact with the world, God was not introduced except on occasions of a certain importance and dignity, but now in our countryman's bald cosmology, we find him hauled in at every juncture and the whole world made to hand on a series of special divine intentions.

The purely personal standard—the measure of the stature of John Stevenson's interest—was unsparingly applied over the whole field of Providence. The growth of potatoes in his yard, the little chicanery of a country market, the renewal of his shoes if they were something old, and the sufferings of that one holy and perfect Church to which he belonged, as they were all equally matters of interest to John Stevenson, seemed all equally worthy occasions for the direct interference of an almighty God. In each and all of these affairs, he besought God's providential action; and in each and all of them, his prayers were answered by a direct and miraculous acquiescence, so that the field was made fruitful, the markets went ever after favourably, new boots were supplied by unexpected charity, and the Church was brought out of much tribulation into something of its old sovereign command on the bare representations of this humbly arrogant Augustine ploughman.

————

An age must be measured of its own standard; seventeenth century actions must not be tried by the moral notions of nineteenth-century enlightenment: the concrete, and the concrete only, can tell us anything that is worth the trouble of comprehension; and so if we would ever understand a bygone period in to the quick and recognise and rightly appreciate the notions that lay behind its outcome, whether for good or evil, we must judge it out of its own mouth, on its own intelligent and deliberate evidence. It is only out of memoirs written by violent and sincere partisans, that we can ever learn how deeds appeared to the actors themselves, what moral obliquities led them open-eyed into mistakes and crimes, and what sort of strength supplanted them through great, heroic undertakings; every self-deception, every dishonesty even, possesses for the critic a sort of hidden sincerity that throws as much light upon an age as the*   . He who makes a study of character seeks to learn the commonplaces of the period, the catch-words and shibboleths, the established decencies of thought and speech and conduct, in order that he may set them aside and see the man himself. The historian exactly reverses the process. For him, the man is of a very secondary importance; and his whole object is to abstract from all individual conditions, the salient characteristics of the period. Precisely what the one leaves, the other utilises. And hence, confessions and autobiographies are often more valuable to the critic of an age in their feints and disingenuousnesses than in those parts where the elemental face of the winter has thrust him out of the region of commonplace into that of statement and self-asserting individuality.

* Left blank by Stevenson.

It is only thus that we can see of the most differently circumstanced and widely divergent men, in how very little but all-important points, they hold together, of how very fine nerves and sentiment of thought a whole age is joined into one living organism.

It is very seldom that one can find a real point of change in the development of a nation; but such a critical period seems to me to have occurred in Scotland in 1688. Previous to that date there was but one Scotsman who could excite anything beyond a passing and purely local interest, and this one bleak and infertile corner of earth had produced a Hume, an Adam Smith, a Burns, and a Scott. After loving pruning and digging about the roots, this tree came suddenly into rich fructification. If we think of how few of those vast silences that lay before and behind the Roman eagle-bearer on the morrow of Agricola's victory, how there has gone forth wave after wave of shrewd and strenuous colonists, how sciences have been splendidly furthered, philosophies remodelled and a whole world of new and living literature has been produced for the delight of all mankind by this one scantly and little favoured race, we shall look surely with a more enlightened curiosity at the conditions that ushered in its period of productiveness and growth. Nor, I think, do these conditions want for a specific interest of their own. From the time that John Knox made a living, autonomous nation on what had been the mere tournament ground of unruly and unscrupulous nobles, the Scottish people had presented to the world an example of high, if narrow, enthusiasm. That people, as he left it, had already the consistency that comes of a strong common belief, and it was destined to be further welded into one by a long course of persecution and resistance. For years the history of Scotland was the history of an oppressed religious belief; suddenly, at the date of the Revolution, the pressure was moved, and the vigour, endurance, and self-denial that had been hitherto confined in this one channel, was suddenly enfranchised and now spread abroad in all directions as the larger spirit of a free period allowed each man to choose for himself and follow faithfully what he saw before him. The spirit, from the first, was serious and noble; it has remained serious and noble ever since.

The heart of the country has become so utterly divorced from nature by the influences of this terrifying dogma, that men fear even the caresses of their own children, lest they should make idols of them. I am not speaking without book. I know that one very devout and enlightened Scotsman, within the last decade or two, was filled upon his death with a keen and humiliating remorse because he had loved the wife who was watching over his sickbed and was so soon to become his widow. A woman of the lower classes was describing how terrified she had been during a thunderstorm. " Did you pray? " she was asked. " Na, na, the roof would fall in on me," she replied. In the midst of such terrible and widespread gloom, it is in vain for worthy clergymen to carry about the pretty pouncet-box of gospel hope: they have raised a spirit too potent for them to lay; all the rose-water theology in the world cannot quench the great fire of horror and terror that Christianity has kindled in the hearts of the Scottish people. I will not decide upon the comparative good and bad that such beliefs are capable of producing; on a soft, timorous race and in some airy and luxurious climate, nothing beyond a widespread depression and despair could have resulted; but the Scots were perhaps strong enough to bear this cruel medicine, and it is always at least a preparative for the grim reality that must be faced at last, of a thwarted and painful existence, haunted by vain aspiration after impossible good and fated, generation after generation, to settle down into mournful recognition of the inevitable evil. Calvinism is the religion of the strong; like the shrewd, hard climates of our northern coasts, it is fatal to the weakly but makes more manly and vigorous the selected few who can survive.

Therefore, I believe it will not be uninteresting to bring here together into a short space four pretty marked types of the Covenanting spirit.

Bossuet's *Histoire des variations des églises protestantes*.

Principal Cunningham's *Essays on the Reformers*. (Henley.)

At a delicate perfume, I am simply pained and troubled; the pleasure I feel dissatisfies me and I long to do I know not what with it, to turn it somehow to account. But I can remember a time when a beautiful landscape produced in me the same sensations.

John Knox and Women.

1st.

The moral character in Knox always good, the intellectual matter often feeble, often austere and condemnable. The preface.

Knox was always very conscious of his own position, heroic or otherwise, and spoke about it without concealment. This is not the greatest sort of man perhaps, but a very serviceable penetrating sort of man for all that, who makes everything serve.

The rhetoric of the title and conclusion are in Knox's best and most characteristic style. " Trumpet " was his favourite image; something male and warlike in the man's heart.

Goodman. *Aylmer's Harbarome. Le Reveil Matin des Francais & the other thing from Capefigue.*

2nd.

All the women of the period. Luther, Calvin, Montaigne, the women at Toulouse, etc.

3rd.

His own dependence upon women. A sort of dependence from above; such as God might feel (Xtian God) upon his creatures. Literary friendship.

In reality, this is the frame of mind of a Goethe;

the frame of mind that explains polygamy. It is, in fact, a spiritual polygamy. Knox's letter to his wife. Montaigne's " deux ou trois."

Scottish religion; ministers and women; here as everywhere else, Knox seems to epitomise and incarnate the after history of the Church he founded—the nation he founded.

1*st*. One can explain this book on two propositions. The narrow, practical head of Knox sought to explain anything that was wrong by some transgression of God's law. He saw Bloody Mary, Mary Stuart, Catherine de Medici: a practical difficulty and he found at once in the Old Testament and Paul the answer to the difficulty and developed it as a theory. Elizabeth's accession was a sore trouble to him; we shall see how he conducted himself then. Ever after, indeed, the sentiments of this hasty book hang about him like a log: he could not be logical, and he sought all manner of ways out of the impasse in which he found himself.

Sadler p. 535. M'Crie I. 288.

Coligny. The portrait gives one the idea, which is possibly the right one, of a man, conscientious, weak, and not so much ambitious as pursued by a vague desire to put things right, and a yet vaguer notion that somehow or other he could put them right, if only he were in power. In such heads, the ecstatic confidence engendered by a change of faith, is usually too strong a stimulus. They are eager to apply their yard-wand over the whole world of contentious and incompatible humanity; if the Admiral sees before him some hope that he may put down " the oaths and blasphemies too ordinary " in his age, and otherwise bend his fellow-men into some external conformity with his own opinions, he will always see the land of Beulah no great way before him.

For the Jno. Knox—About a man being a genius in a provincial sense.